Culture, Identities and Technology
in the *Star Wars* Films

Culture, Identities and Technology in the *Star Wars* Films

Essays on the Two Trilogies

EDITED BY CARL SILVIO AND
TONY M. VINCI

CRITICAL EXPLORATIONS IN
SCIENCE FICTION AND FANTASY, 3
Donald E. Palumbo *and* C.W. Sullivan III, *series editors*

McFarland & Company, Inc., Publishers
Jefferson, North Carolina, and London

CRITICAL EXPLORATIONS IN SCIENCE FICTION AND FANTASY
(a series edited by Donald E. Palumbo and C.W. Sullivan III)

1. *Worlds Apart? Dualism and Transgression in Contemporary Female Dystopias* (Dunja M. Mohr, 2005)
2. *Tolkien and Shakespeare: Essays on Shared Themes and Language* (edited by Janet Brennan Croft, forthcoming 2007)
3. *Culture, Identities and Technology in the* Star Wars *Films: Essays on the Two Trilogies* (edited by Carl Silvio and Tony M. Vinci, 2007)
4. *The Influence of* Star Trek *on Television, Film and Culture* (edited by Lincoln Geraghty, forthcoming 2007)
5. *Hugo Gernsback and the Century of Science Fiction* (Gary Westfahl, forthcoming 2007)

LIBRARY OF CONGRESS CATALOGUING-IN-PUBLICATION DATA

Culture, identities and technology in the Star wars films: essays on the two trilogies / edited by Carl Silvio and Tony M. Vinci.
    p. cm. — (Critical explorations in science fiction and fantasy ; 3)
    Includes bibliographical references and index.

    ISBN-13: 978-0-7864-2910-3
    (softcover : 50# alkaline paper) ∞

    1. Star Wars films—History and criticism.   I. Silvio, Carl.
II. Vinci, Tony M.
PN1995.9.S695S55   2007
791.43'75—dc22   2006038613

British Library cataloguing data are available

Cover image ©2007 Brand X Pictures

Manufactured in the United States of America

McFarland & Company, Inc., Publishers
 Box 611, Jefferson, North Carolina 28640
 www.mcfarlandpub.com

Table of Contents

v

Part III : Technology and the Public Imagination

Introduction

Moving Away from Myth:
Star Wars *as Cultural Artifact*

Few popular filmic narratives have so captivated the public's imagination and invited as much critical commentary as George Lucas's *Star Wars* series. First released in May of 1977, *Episode IV: A New Hope* (then, simply entitled *Star Wars*) quickly became the highest grossing film of all time as it redefined the cinematic use of special effects and ushered in a new era of the Hollywood blockbuster. With the release of each subsequent film in the franchise, the public's fascination with and affection for Lucas's creation grew in scope and depth. The films, numbering six at the time of this writing, now command a fan-base of millions worldwide and have generated scores of supplemental narratives in the form of novels, television shows, a holiday special, fan fiction, and more. The two *Star Wars* trilogies now stand as the "deep core" of an expanded universe that constantly evolves and changes with the addition of each new thread to its heterocosmic tapestry. This textual universe serves as one of our society's richest repositories of contemporary myth and social meaning, a galaxy where collective hopes and anxieties are both revealed and imaginarily resolved.

Since 1977, the majority of *Star Wars* criticism has focused on the films' use of mythic archetypes and trans-cultural, pan-human themes. In 1978, scarcely a year after the release of the first film, Andrew Gordon published his seminal essay, "*Star Wars*: A Myth for Our Time." In this text, Gordon attempted to account for the popularity of the film by explaining it in terms of the theories of Joseph Campbell and his extraordinarily influential idea of the monomyth. According to Gordon, Lucas translated certain universal mythic patterns, templates of human meaning, into the idiom of contemporary popular culture and, in so doing, provided viewers with a profound degree of emotional and philosophical

1

satisfaction that was presumably missing from their lives: "Lucas has constructed out of the usable past, out of bits of American pop culture, a new mythology which can satisfy the emotional needs of both children and adults" (324). Gordon defines myth as a story, or set of stories, that explains our place in the world and helps us to understand and express our relationship to a broader humanity. "Mythology," then, encourages an identification with patterns of meaning that transcend our immediate social context; mythology allows us to experience our individual existences as significant in a universal or trans-historical sense. Claiming that the films retell one of the central epic myths of Western culture—the story of a fall, a wandering, and an eventual return—David Wyatt expressed a similar idea in another early scholarly work on *Star Wars* (600). Accordingly, this mythic pattern imaginatively captures some common framework of (Western) human experience that is broader than our own individual experiences but within which our localized existences can be made to assume a deeper and more satisfactory meaning.

Lucas makes no secret of his interest in mythology or the fact that he drew heavily from such sources, the chief of which was Campbell, in producing his vision. Thus, interpretations of *Star Wars* like those of Gordon and Wyatt seem logical and appropriate in the approaches that they take to the films. In fact, such approaches worked so well that they shaped most of the subsequent scholarly work on this film series by establishing mythology and myth criticism as the explanatory modes best suited to understand the films' pervasive appeal to at least two generations of audiences and to elucidate the intricate semiotic patterns that Lucas has created. Jungian and Freudian approaches to the trilogies are also quite common, insofar as these schools of thought, like mythology, tend to posit shared, trans-cultural narrative explanations for human experience.[1] This sort of critical work has found eager audiences in non-academic circles as well. In 1997, the *Star Wars and the Magic of Myth* exhibit premiered at the Smithsonian Institution's National Air and Space Museum. This exhibit, along with its companion book of the same title by Mary Henderson, was phenomenally popular, so popular that the exhibit went on to tour the country after it closed in Washington in 1999. In the public's imagination, the terms "Myth" and "*Star Wars*" are very closely linked.

But in 1978, the same year that Gordon published his highly influential essay, Dan Rubey published another, less well known but by no means less significant, article on *Star Wars* that treated the film and its use of mythology very differently. In "*Star Wars*: Not So Long Ago, Not So Far Away," Rubey argued that "Lucas's picture of an unbroken tradition of adventure mythology stretching from Homer to John Ford ignores both the specific meanings these stories had for the societies which created them and the important differences between them. Myths and fantasies are not eternal; they are historical" (89). Rubey suggests that the term "mythology" can assume a much more culturally specific and political meaning than is usually assigned to it. If "mythology" describes a process by which we come to understand our relationship to the universe through narrative, then the term can equally describe the wide variety of discursive processes that render our relationships to our immediate social universe meaningful. "Mythology," in other words, also refers to a complex field of cultural production that both supports and can potentially contest the social production of belief.[2] As *Star Wars* scholar Kevin J. Wetmore observes,

> much myth criticism ignores the complicity of myth in establishing and maintaining social dominance and power structures. Many myths are created in order to explain why those in power are in power and why those who are oppressed or dominated are (and should be) oppressed and dominated [95].

To speak of popular mythology, then, is to speak of politics, economics, identity formation, and ideology to the extent that our relationships to these categories are thoroughly mediated by popular narratives.

In this sense, to analyze a film series like *Star Wars* as a modern mythological narrative is to explore the ways in which it represents the specific relationships of the contemporary subject to the current social order. Rubey in effect called for such ideological analysis shortly after the release of the original film, but the response to his call has been sporadic and unsustained. To be fair, there *is* a body of scholarly work on *Star Wars* that interprets it in an ideological context,[3] but this work has been overshadowed by the sheer amount of myth-oriented criticism that others have devoted to the trilogies. Generally speaking, then, we can imagine the history of *Star Wars* scholarship in terms of two basically separate if interrelated traditions, one myth-oriented, the other grounded in ideological analysis and identity politics. The former, more dominant, tradition has undoubtedly been highly influential and represents an extremely important volume of scholarly work. The latter, however, remains rich in unrealized potential and presents us with an irresistibly tempting subject for scholarship. Ironically, though it has almost become a cliché to proclaim the "cultural significance" of *Star Wars*, there have been regrettably few attempts to discuss the saga in light of scholarly advances in "cultural studies," however we may define that term. This is precisely the aim of this collection: to move away from myth-based criticism of *Star Wars* and adopt a cultural studies model that analyzes it as a culturally and historically specific phenomenon, that is, as a site of ideological investment that both reflects and shapes late twentieth and early twenty-first century global culture.

As the term is commonly understood, cultural studies refers to the critical mobilization of a variety of disciplinary perspectives that seeks to analyze how cultural phenomena intersect with social formations such as economics, technology, race, and gender. In keeping with this project, we have tried to apply as diverse an array of critical and theoretical viewpoints as possible to the *Star Wars* films in an effort to nudge the scholarly dialogue in what we hope will be new and even more intellectually fruitful directions. The essays in this book thus bring to bear an assortment of critical approaches upon the texts that comprise the *Star Wars* universe. These include a variety of political and economic analyses informed by feminism, contemporary race theory, Marxism, new media studies, and post-humanism. Moreover, we have tried to provide, not just a variety of critical approaches to this fictional universe, but to provide a range of opinion regarding its political orientation. In other words, some of the essays in this collection read *Star Wars* as complicit with contemporary hegemonic belief systems, while others interpret it as a critique of dominant ideology.

Given that *Star Wars* has exerted such an influential "force" on contemporary culture, this collection aims to read that force in new ways and to thus open it up to even more analytically productive possibilities. The first part of this book explores the connection between the *Star Wars* trilogies and our own cultural landscape. Since its emergence in the late seventies, critics have made connections between the *Star Wars* universe and contemporary culture; however, there have been very few serious studies that concentrate either on how the films comment on their cultural milieu or on how they produce ideology intertextually. "Part I: Cultural Contexts" responds to this void in criticism, offering three essays that deepen and extend previous cultural criticism by looking at the complex and often paradoxical ideologies inherent in the films.

Concerned with the relationship between the individual and the institution in the *Star Wars* trilogies, Tony M. Vinci claims that the prequel trilogy inadvertently subverts the original trilogy's innate anxiety regarding the institution and consequent valorization of the individual. In "The Fall of the Rebellion; or, Defiant and Obedient Heroes in a Galaxy Far, Far Away: Individualism and Intertextuality in the *Star Wars* Trilogies," Vinci contends that, while the prequel trilogy, especially *Revenge of the Sith*, attempts to align itself with the fervent individualism of the original trilogy by criticizing the anti-individualist actions of its political and spiritual heroes—specifically Amidala, Obi-Wan, and Yoda—it actually creates a narrative that encourages a disparaging apprehension regarding individualism and argues that only when one "follows the rules" and becomes a representative of the institution can individual action have social and political value. Vinci concludes that the trilogies' divergent ideologies result from the historic circumstances of each trilogy's creation, ultimately criticizing such radical conservatism in contemporary science fiction/fantasy film.

John Lyden's "Apocalyptic Determinism and *Star Wars*" explores the apocalyptic nature of the prequel trilogy by concentrating on the pessimistic feelings evoked by America's current political climate. Noting the public perception that government and politics are viewed as iniquitous, Lyden argues that the films' pre-known plot reflects a sense of unease endemic in contemporary Western culture that arises from feelings of powerlessness and disenfranchisement. Since the viewer knows Anakin's fall to the dark side is unavoidable, the films seem to suggest that individual agency is ultimately illusory and that dominant political systems control not only political destiny but personal destiny as well. Alluding to other cultural products, such as the *Left Behind* series, the *Matrix* trilogy, and the original *Star Wars* trilogy—all of which offer hopeful visions of a changeable, unfixed future—Lyden concludes that Episodes I–III of *Star Wars* create a deterministic narrative that obliterates hope of an improved political sphere, ultimately rendering politics as an impotent and ineffectual endeavor and leaving the search for salvation, if it is even possible, to the individual.

Carl Silvio's "The *Star Wars* Trilogies and Global Capitalism" also analyzes the films' seeming intentions—in this case, their implicit treatment of global capitalism. By comparing the two trilogies and treating them as cultural responses to specific moments in the history of late capitalism, Silvio suggests that the films work culturally as attempts to imaginarily resolve ideological conflicts inherent in our current regime of accumulation. By presenting and fetishizing large scale, advanced technology while simultaneously evoking nostalgia for older, pre-capitalist or entrepreneurial capitalist regimes, the original trilogy enables viewers to conceptually grasp the sheer unrepresentative nature of an emerging global system of production. Appearing two decades later, the prequel trilogy more overtly celebrates the idea of a benevolent global marketplace that benefits mankind. The films achieve this, in part, by displacing all the anxieties over the dehumanization inherent in late capitalism onto older, but less popular, versions of monopoly capitalism.

The three essays in "Part II: Identity Politics" address the often problematic issues of race and gender in the trilogies. Considering the radical popularity and influence of the *Star Wars* universe, its treatment of race and gender is of particular importance in understanding how the trilogies reflect and influence the formulation of individual and collective identities as well as participate in public discourse regarding such topics.

Christopher Deis attempts to refute the rather popular argument that the *Star Wars* trilogies have racist tendencies by indicating the extent of the films' "racial" diversity and the positive codification of those "races." In "May the Force (Not) Be With You: 'Race Critical' Readings and the *Star Wars* Universe," Deis asserts that the Empire in the original trilogy is coded as evil in part because of its intolerance of the other. Therefore, since a diversity of species fight against this Empire, those species, or "races," are ultimately coded as good. Responding specifically to critical race theorists that claim that the prequel trilogy presents a narrative that is both racist and xenophobic, Deis points to the diversity of species in the Jedi Order as well the racial inclusiveness of the Galactic Senate to argue the prequel trilogy's racial progressivism. Finally, he contends that the controversies over race in the *Star Wars* films obfuscate the more progressively political dimensions of the trilogies. Specifically, Deis does this by analyzing the Skywalker males and their relationship with Palpatine as a representation of how democratic ideals overcome political oppression.

Diana Dominguez's "Feminism and the Force: Empowerment and Disillusionment in a Galaxy Far, Far Away" explores the process by which young female audiences formulate an identity and become empowered through fictional narratives by questioning the seeming parallelism between the heroic nature of Leia and Amidala in the trilogies. While Leia presented viewing audiences of the late seventies and eighties with an independent, empowered female figure that endorsed Second Wave feminist ideals, Dominguez argues that Amidala might not have the same power to offer contemporary audiences, who are used to heroines such as Buffy and Xena, a role-model equal to that of her daughter. Focusing on the iconic significance of Leia and Amidala, Dominguez discusses whether or not a male-created female character can transcend stereotypical patriarchal ideals of feminism and become an authentic feminist sign.

In "Seduced by the Dark Side of the Force: Gender, Sexuality, and Moral Agency in George Lucas's *Star Wars* Universe," Veronica A. Wilson argues that Lucas aligns womanhood and femininity with the profoundly malevolent Dark Side of the Force, which has the influence to annihilate not only the spirit of the individual but the very ideal of representative democracy. Wilson considers this association through Anakin Skywalker's fall to the Dark Side. She reads Anakin's aggressively controlling fervor for his mother, Shmi, and his paramour, Padmé, along with the maneuverings of the sexually ambiguous Palpatine/Sidious, to be the primary reasons for his seduction to evil. By attributing Anakin's fall to his disconcerting relationship with femininity and comparing this with his son's lack of mother and spouse, Wilson posits that Luke is able to avoid the Emperor's seduction and redeem his father precisely because of his untainted, innocent masculinity, implying that the *Star Wars* trilogies are rooted firmly in misogyny and fear of female agency's ability to subjugate masculine moral action.

The final section, "Part III: Technology and the Public Imagination," explores the thematic implications of the trilogies' use and fetishization of technology as well as its relationship with the popular psyche. Dan North's "Kill Binks: Why the World Hated Its First Digital Actor" uses the public's decidedly negative response to the fully computer-generated Jar Jar Binks as a focal point to question the efficacy of the *Star Wars* trilogies' transition from older, more traditional modes of visual special effects production, such as animatronics and miniatures, to predominately state-of-the-art computer-generated effects as well as the films' transition from photochemical production processes to digital ones. These transitions frame North's discussion of how our perception and understanding of space and embodiment in the films have been altered. Concentrating on Jar Jar, North poses that Binks represents the potential of the virtual actor to make obsolete human performers, thus foregrounding concerns evoked by such digital embodiment. Transitioning away from the digital character, North then analyzes the digitally-created props and settings in the films and how these affect live actors. Ultimately, North examines the question: does Lucas's seeming obsession with altering his visions digitally—as he did in the 1997 re-release of the original trilogy—diminish the fantastical nature of the films by re-appropriating the imaginative processes of the audience?

Kevin J. Wetmore's "'Your Father's Lightsaber': The Fetishization of Objects Between the Trilogies" by Kevin J. Wetmore, Jr., positions the *Star Wars* trilogies as narrative advertisements which fetishize all material objects in the films and consequently prepare the consuming public to purchase real-world referents for each of those objects. Wetmore argues that, in light of the attention that the films' material objects receive, the narrative, linguistic, and thematic connections between the trilogies become secondary; the dominant links between the trilogies are objects, such as weapons, droids, and vehicles. By privileging fetishized objects over character, narrative, and theme, the *Star Wars* trilogies encourage the economic use of these fetishes not only to sell commodities that directly reference the films—action figures, toy vehicles, toy lightsabers—but unrelated products, such as breakfast cereals, toothpastes, and snack foods, ultimately fetishizing these tangentially-related products as well.

In the final essay of the collection, "The Emperor's New Clones; or, Digitization and Walter Benjamin in the *Star Wars* Universe," Graham Lyons and Janice Morris apply Walter Benjamin's notion of artistic aura to Lucas's revisions of the original trilogy in the release of the *Star Wars Special Edition* films and the preponderance of digitization in the prequel trilogy in an attempt to define the authenticity of the digitally-altered creations. Examining whether the digital nature of these revisions modify, improve, or damage the films' aura(s), Lyons and Morris contest Lucas's assertion that the digital "corrections" to Episodes IV-VI enhance the films by allowing him to fully realize the scope of his original vision. They posit that such digitization distorts drastically the uniqueness of the original versions of the films. Along with the addition of "extras" in the repackaged DVD release of the original trilogy that potentially revise audiences' experiences, the *Special Editions* of Episodes IV-VI jeopardize the films' aura of authenticity, denoting them as ineffectual reproductions of the original works of art.

The nine essays in this book attempt to reframe *Star Wars* criticism by offering a serious study of the cultural contexts of the *Star Wars* trilogies. While Campbell-based criticism provides a useful lens to see the "timeless" themes of the *Star Wars* films, it is decidedly limited in that it is unable to address the ever-evolving post-modern complexity of human affairs at the end of the twentieth and beginning of the twenty-first centuries. Therefore, this reframing is a necessary and progressive step toward exploring how *Star Wars* simultaneously codes and decodes a conflicting matrix of values, beliefs, and understandings that make up contemporary global culture.

Notes

1. See, for instance, Martin Miller and Robert Sprich's "The Appeal of *Star Wars*."
2. For an early recognition of this fact, see Ernest Cassirer's *The Myth of the State*.
3. See Anne Lancashire's "*Attack of the Clones* and the Politics of *Star Wars*"; and Kevin J. Wetmore's "The Tao of *Star Wars,* or, Cultural Appropriation in a Galaxy Far, Far Away" and *The Empire Triumphant: Race Religion and Rebellion in the* Star Wars *Films*.

Works Cited

Cassirer, Ernst. *The Myth of the State*. New Haven: Yale UP, 1961.
Lancashire, Anne. "*Attack of the Clones* and the Politics of *Star Wars*." *Dalhousie Review* 82 (2002): 235–53.
Miller, Martin, and Robert Sprich. "The Appeal of *Star Wars*." *American Imago* 38.2 (Summer 1981): 203–220.
Wetmore, Kevin J., Jr. *The Empire Triumphant: Race Religion and Rebellion in the* Star Wars *Films*. Jefferson, NC: McFarland, 2005.
_____. "The Tao of *Star Wars,* or, Cultural Appropriation in a Galaxy Far, Far Away." *Studies in Popular Culture* 23 (2000): 91–106.
Wyatt, David. "*Star Wars* and the Productions of Time." *Virginia Quarterly Review* 58.4 (1982): 600–15.

PART I

CULTURAL CONTEXTS

1

The Fall of the Rebellion; or, Defiant and Obedient Heroes in a Galaxy Far, Far Away

Individualism and Intertextuality in the Star Wars *Trilogies*

Tony M. Vinci

The final action sequence in *Star Wars Episode IV: A New Hope* is arguably one of the most significant and engaging in the *Star Wars* films: the survival of the entire Rebel Alliance is at risk; the morally ambiguous rogue, Han Solo, turns away from his seemingly overwhelming greed and is redeemed through his newly-found ethical sensibilities; for the first time, Luke Skywalker trusts his faith in the Force and wins the Rebel's initial substantial victory against the Empire; and perhaps most simply (and most significantly) none of the heroes in this scene are anonymous. Not only does each individual Rebel fighter pilot have a title—Red 5, Yellow Leader, etc.—they are given specific names—Wedge, Biggs, even what seems to be the tongue-in-cheek nickname, Porkins. This individualization of each otherwise anonymous protagonist privileges one of the original *Star Wars* trilogy's most noticeable thematic concerns: the power, significance, and valorization of the individual.

What punctuates this example that identifies the importance of the individual in *A New Hope* is that the narrative mirror of this scene in *The Phantom Menace*, the final space battle between the Naboo starfighter pilots and the Trade Federation's blockade, keeps every single protagonist fighter pilot, save one, anonymous. The only named pilot is the child-pilot-by-accident, Anakin Skywalker, who pointedly wins the battle not through his own expressive autonomy, like his son Luke does, but by pushing buttons randomly and destroying the Trade Federation's mothership accidentally, rendering the droid army on the surface useless. Ultimately, Anakin frees the entire planet of Naboo and defeats the Trade Federation and the Dark Lord of the Sith—all by mishap. Whereas in *A New Hope* the individual defeats the evil Galactic Empire through his own choices and gambles, it is through a parody of this autonomy that the individual triumphs in *The Phantom Menace*. Consequently, with the lack of personalization of individual fighter pilots and the robbing of power from the individual's autonomy, *The Phantom Menace*'s final battle sequence is not only much less engaging, but it points to a marked thematic difference between the original trilogy and the prequel trilogy.

Since the release of *Star Wars Episode I: The Phantom Menace*, critics and fans have struggled to define the nature of the relationship between the original trilogy and the prequel trilogy. While there are many discernible narrative and aesthetic similarities between them, perhaps the heart of this relationship lies in their treatment of the individual and his relationship to the institution. The original trilogy clearly valorizes the individual, privileging individual agency over institutional control; however, the prequel trilogy's handling of this relationship is more complicated.[1] This is seen most specifically in the two trilogies' handling of the Force, the Jedi Order, and politics.

In the original trilogy, The Force is defined as a universalized spiritual entity that has the potential to empower all individuals and unite all living things regardless of the individuals' place in a given culture; in the prequel trilogy, the Force is an institutionalized and elitist tool of cultural power used to train keepers of the peace and support the status quo. Likewise, highly-organized political structures in the original trilogy are coded as evil because they are destructive to the individual and are contested by the protagonists, while in the prequel trilogy they are coded as good and supported by the protagonists. What complicates the prequel trilogy's treatment of the individual is that it attempts to offer a critique of its protagonist's anti-individualist stance, seemingly aligning the prequel trilogy's handling of the individual with the original trilogy's; however, this critique is ultimately ineffectual and, in the end, the prequel trilogy undermines the original trilogies valorization of the individual.

The prequel trilogy's subversion of the original trilogy's pro-individualism through its treatment of the Force, the Jedi Order, and politics is perhaps best explored through the relationships between archetypal heroes in the original trilogy and, when appropriate, their narrative counterparts in the prequel trilogy—more specifically, the relationships between: Han Solo and Lando Calrissian, Princess Leia

Organna and Padmé Amidala, the depictions of Yoda and Obi-Wan Kenobi in each trilogy, and Luke and Anakin Skywalker. However, before these relationships are explained, the Empire's role in the original trilogy as an oppressive institution that attempts to assimilate and destroy the power of the individual must be explored in order to establish the original trilogy's individualist nature.

Obeying the Master: The Evil Galactic Empire and the Assimilation of the Individual

Even though the Emperor's fascist dictatorship can be situated as the ultimate expression of autonomy—this individual's every initiative and design become institutional dictates—it is, of course, the ultimate oppressive power in the *Star Wars* universe.[2] The two primary leading figures in the Empire, Darth Vader and the Emperor himself, through their actions and ideology, challenge clearly the individual. This is articulated most visibly in the Emperor and Vader's quest to assimilate Luke Skywalker into the Empire and to manipulate him to become an agent of the dark side of the Force.

This aspiration to subjugate Luke's values and code of conduct to those of the institution by way of mental manipulation and/or physical threat provides perhaps the most powerful example of the Empire's desire to annihilate the individual and therefore earns the Empire the position of antagonist in the original trilogy.[3] Much of Vader's and the Emperor's conversations about Luke's potential assimilation focuses on the power of collectivity and the danger individual autonomy presents to the institution. In *Return of the Jedi*, The Emperor tells Vader, "Only together can we turn [Skywalker]" to the dark side and make him "one of us." This phrase, "one of us," implies that Vader and the Emperor share an adherence to a pre-known system of values and behaviors, and, through their collective efforts, can not only transform Luke's self-culture but erase it and reprogram it with their own cultural system of principles and actions.

Even though we are told in *A New Hope* that "the Empire doesn't consider a small, one-man fighter to be a threat"—implying that, in its collective power, the Empire can only be destroyed by another collective with equal military or cultural power—by the time of *Return of the Jedi*'s final conflict, the Empire seems to be acutely aware that the autonomous individual who acts upon an intuitive moral edict is precisely the agent that has the influence to destroy it. The importance and value placed upon the successful assimilation of the individual is apparently so high that the Emperor tells Luke that if "[he]will not be turned, [he] will be destroyed." Of course, Luke is not turned and, through his individual agency, influences his father to also become an individual agent and ultimately destroy the Emperor.

This failed attempt to assimilate Luke is meant to be interpreted by the audience as evil. There are two reasons for this: first, the Empire is already coded as evil and therefore any action that they commit is also read as evil; second, by this point in the original trilogy's narrative arc, Luke is positioned as the metaphoric representation of the powerful individual who has developed from a powerless one to an authoritative and influential one who changes the nature of his cultural reality by adhering to his own intuitive sense of righteousness and expresses this self-culture through his actions. Any act that would attempt to subvert this ultimate expression of autonomy within the confines of this dictatorial system can only be identified as evil.

In addition to the Emperor's and Vader's attempt to assimilate Luke, the character of Vader himself becomes a principal symbol of the evil of assimilation in that, in the words of Obi-Wan Kenobi, Vader is "more machine than man, twisted and evil." The term "machine" here denotes a life that is not human or individualized in that it relies on an external system for survival. With this in mind, Vader's confession to Luke that he "must obey [his] master" can be read strictly as a literal necessity for survival; he is physically a part of a system, and to be unplugged from that system is to be destroyed. As Joseph Campbell states, Darth Vader is a "bureaucrat, living not in terms of himself but in terms of an imposed system" (144). Hence, Vader's appearance, which emphasizes his half-man/half-machine duality, becomes an ultimate cautionary image of the dangers of conformity and how the lack of pure individual agency can lead to a perilous dependency that quickly becomes necessary for survival.

While the Empire could represent or serve as an allegory for almost any institutional force in Western culture—big business, America as an oppressive world democracy, even a prophetic vision of the *Star Wars* film franchise empire itself and the era of blockbuster films that it ushered in—defining a specific cultural referent for the Empire to represent is unnecessary. What is significant is that the Empire is representational of a general cultural paradigm that assimilates and oppresses the expressive autonomy of the individual and that it is the dominant force that the highly-individualized protagonists of the original trilogy risk their lives to destroy, hence valorizing individualism and expressing a deep anxiety regarding the institution.

Rogues and Scoundrels: The Valorization of the Individual in the Original Star Wars Trilogy

Perhaps the two most conspicuous representatives of the power and value of expressive autonomy in the original trilogy are Han Solo and Lando Calrissian. These characters' roles as representative rogue individuals illustrate the differences between the trilogies in that the prequel trilogy does not have any narrative counterparts for them. The closest thing that the prequel trilogy has to a rogue agent protagonist is Qui Gon Jinn in his disobedience of the Jedi Council's edicts, and it would be difficult to equate a single Jedi who does not want to follow a couple of specific rules to two self-proclaimed scoundrels whose main preoccupations are to work outside of and openly against the law. (Qui-Gon's character will be considered in more depth later in this chapter.) What positions Han and Lando as heroes, even though they are morally ambiguous, is their fierce individualism.

Of course, it is Han Solo's name that initially marks his individualist ideology, but he asserts his autonomy vocally soon enough. During their escape attempt from the death star in *A New Hope*, Han states clearly his propensity and capacity to follow only his own directives. After she barks an order at him, he tells Leia, "I take orders from just one person: me." That Han uses the vocabulary of the institution—"take orders"— in his nonconformist declaration indicates the depth to which the cultural acceptance of codified law and its enforcement permeates the original trilogy. By positioning individual agency in its own hierarchal system wherein the individual is both governor and governed, Han parodies and subverts the Empire's quest for assimilation.

Leia echoes Han's declaration when she tells Luke that Han must "choose his own path." By choosing his own path, Han functions outside the typical moral and ethical edicts. As Lucas states in his directorial commentary in the 2004 DVD release of *A New Hope*, Han begins as a "cynical mercenary ... who only cares about himself." It is highly significant then, that when left to make his own moral decisions, Han not only makes an ethical choice but shows personal growth. Even though he leaves before the final battle against the death star in *A New Hope*, seemingly privileging his greed and selfishness over what would appear to be the ethical decision to act upon, he makes an autonomous decision to return and aide his comrades. He does not grow by following any social edicts; he is left alone to decide and reasons that, in this instance, it is appropriate for him to risk his safety and help the Rebels in their cause. The next time Han risks his life to help his friends, his actions are directly antithetical to the suggested actions of the Rebel Deck Officer. In *The Empire Strikes Back*, he risks Hoth's extreme environments for the very slim chance that he will actually be able to find and save Luke. This radical, illogical, and, it needs to be stated, successful expression of autonomy is precisely the reason why Han Solo is viewed as a hero in the context of the original trilogy; regardless of the situation, how his reputation will be affected, or even if he will live or die, Han Solo makes and follows his own rules.[4]

Lando Calrissian functions primarily as an alternate version of Han Solo. As Lucas states in his commentary of *The Empire Strikes Back*, Lando is "what Han was before he met Luke and Leia." A different day, a different decision, and Lando could have been in Mos Eisley, negotiating a fare for two refugees to travel to Alderaan. Where Lando differs from Han is primarily his position in the social order. While Han's positions in society are primarily as a smuggler and then an officer in the rebellion, Lando attempts to use his skill and expertise to become a "legitimate" member of the social order as an administrator of a somewhat self-reliant mining facility. This attempt, of course, fails, and this failure to function as a legitimate member of society indicates one of the principal dangers of living as a part of a mass culture that does not accept or nurture autonomy: the individual will be forced to sacrifice his autonomy and, in doing so, compromise his ethical integrity.

While Lando's intentions at Bespin seem to be altruistic, he is forced into an unethical situation by the Empire. In order to sustain rule over Bespin, he must forfeit the lives of his friends and his own code of ethics. As he tells Han and Leia directly before he hands them over to Vader, "Things have developed that will insure security. I've just made a deal that will keep the Empire out of here forever." He knows that his decision is unethical, but he believes that it is a unique situation, one that should not need to be repeated. As he tells Han, "I had no choice. They arrived right before you did. I'm sorry." As an audience, we do not question Lando's remorsefulness; however, his assertion that he did not have a choice but to betray Han becomes highly questionable. As John Lyden argues, "Immorality comes when we do not listen to our own inner voices and instead listen to others." Lando's selfish, let-me-make-the-best-deal-for-me-and-mine mentality is the result of the individual losing his autonomy in the midst of an institution. Additionally, this loss of autonomy can only be understood as the first step down a steep slope. After Vader alters their original arrangement, telling Lando that Leia and Chewbacca must never leave Bespin again and that Han will be turned over to Boba Fett, Lando recognizes the ethical difficulty of his situation and decides to leave the institution and once again become a rogue agent by helping Leia and the others escape. Of course, once he does this, he becomes a hero whose actions reveal a deep anxiety regarding the necessary change of the individual's ethics when involved with an institution.

Now that the evil of the Empire has been associated to its oppressively assimilating activities and the general valorization of the individual in the original trilogy has been explored through the rogue agents Han Solo and Lando Calrissian, who have no narrative counterparts in the prequel trilogy, an exploration of how the two trilogies differ in their treatment of the Force, the Jedi Order, and politics can begin.

The Princess and the Senator: The Value of Rebellion and the Dangers of Blind Democracy

The two primary political protagonists in the *Star Wars* films are undoubtedly Princess Leia Organna and her mother, Padmé Amidala. Both are political idealists, but while Leia proves herself to be a dissenter and a rebel, her mother Amidala puts her faith in the political institution of the Republic, diminishing the power of the individual.

Even though Leia begins *A New Hope* as a member of the Galactic Senate, this legitimate position in the ruling political organization of the galaxy is a front; her ultimate motivations are aligned with those of the Rebel Alliance as a revolutionary who endeavors to dispose of and destroy the Galactic Empire. Because of these motivations, it is obvious that she believes that the politics of the Senate are ultimately ineffectual and that in order for her to instigate change in the galaxy, she must first annihilate the institution wherein her expressive autonomy is rendered useless and work outside of that political system as a rebel. Therefore, Leia's heroism is rooted in her ability to function autonomously to subvert the institution. In this way, she functions as the "sophisticated, urbanized ruler" that Lucas says in his commentary to *A New Hope* he designed her to be.

Antithetical to her daughter's rebellious leanings, Amidala devotes her energies to being a legitimate leader in the Republic first as the elected queen of Naboo and next as the elected senator of Naboo. Even though she has many reasons to distrust the ethics and efficacy of the bureaucracy of the Republic Senate after it refuses to assist her planet's plight during the Trade Federation's occupation of Naboo, she ultimately does place her trust in the system of the Republic. This can be seen in the main thrust of *The Phantom Menace*'s plot. In order for Amidala to save her planet first from the Trade Federation's boycotting blockade and second from the Trade Federation's forceful occupancy of her planet and the potential destruction of Naboo's culture, she must find a way to the Republic's capital planet of Coruscant to "plead [her] case to the senate" and hope that they will save her. Instead of using her own autonomy and finding a way to retake her homeworld—which *is* ultimately what she is forced to do and succeeds at—she travels half way across the galaxy to go to a meeting and ask the institution in power for help.

It is at this point that the opportunity to reflect the valorization of the individual championed in the original trilogy arises. After the Senate is ultimately proven to be ineffectual, Amidala declares that the "Republic no longer functions," and she leaves Coruscant to return to Naboo. Through a brilliant plan of her own design, she is successful at freeing her people through her own autonomous action without any help or even support from the legitimate political organization of which she is a part. While this would seem to mirror the valorization of the individual typified by Leia's near apotheosis in the original trilogy, it must be remembered that, as noted at the beginning of this chapter, Naboo's victory is contingent upon Anakin's accidental destruction of the Trade Federation's mothership. This accident erases powerfully the potential valorization of individual agency because it implies that Naboo's freedom is won through luck, not the conscious actions of individuals.

What emphasizes this subversion of the original trilogy's positive attitude toward individual agency is Amidala's presence at the beginning of *Attack of the Clones* as a Senator for Naboo in the Republic Senate. Even though this political entity left her people to be destroyed and did nothing to help her in her plight, and she declared the Senate to be impotent and fraudulent, she nevertheless becomes its representative. What is worse, this shift is made without any narrative explanation. This baffling transition from a would-be revolutionary to a subordinate for the party in power enforces a type of mindless acceptance of the status quo and condones, even supports, the complete subjugation of the individual to a proved ineffectual system. Instead of using herself as a resource, Amidala continues to suppress herself and her people by working for and within a system that she has openly claimed to be corrupt.

Amidala's conversation with the new queen of Naboo demonstrates this further. When they discuss the fate of the Trade Federation in *Attack of the Clones* and the possibility that it might not have reduced its armies as it was instructed to do, the queen says that they "must keep [their] faith in the Republic." Instead of doing something themselves to find out the fate of their most potent enemy, they decide to trust a system they know does not work to help them even though it has refused to do so in the past. The queen continues with the platitude: "The day we stop believing democracy can work is the day we lose it." Considering that it has already been proven that this particular democracy has failed, this statement seems to be a type of propaganda popularizing the senseless acceptance of institutional order; this acceptance seems to be the dominant paradigm of the prequel trilogy.

It is surprising then that in *Revenge of the Sith*, Amidala offers a sharp critique of the political system that she has fought so fiercely to uphold. By questioning whether or not she is "on the wrong side" of the conflict between the Republic and the Seperatists, she implies that she and her fellow senators may be in part responsible for the fall of democracy by subjugating their autonomy to a system that provides the pretense of representative democracy but upholds none of its ideals. Once her feelings are proven correct and the Republic is renamed the First Galactic Empire, she states in horror: "So this is how liberty dies—with thunderous applause," indicating the dangers of her own complacency and lack of individual authority. However, this critique of anti-individualism is decidedly ineffectual; it carries little weight during the course of the film's narrative and functions more as a commentary on how Palpatine rises to power than on how the individuals of the Republic lose it. Ultimately, the prequel trilogy subverts the original trilogy's assertion that the efficacy of political idealism can be realized most powerfully when the individual is functioning as a rogue agent or a revolutionary and emphasizes its own agenda by claiming that a blind adherence to and support of the status quo is the individual's primary political responsibility. This subversion of the power of political individualism is mirrored and deepened by the prequel trilogy's treatment of the Force and the Jedi Order.

"A Disturbance in the Force": The Quantification of the Force and the Secularization of the Jedi Order

The disparities between the trilogies' treatment of the Force and the representation of the Jedi Order are perhaps the most obvious and striking way in which the prequel trilogy subverts the thematic concerns of the original trilogy. In the original trilogy, the Force is an unconscious spiritual energy that can potentially empower the individual, and the Jedi Order is a monkish group of individuals who each have a highly-personalized relationship with the Force. In the prequel trilogy, the Force is a highly-institutionalized tool of the cultural elite. We first see the Jedi in *The Phantom Menace* not as spiritual individuals but as political negotiators working to solve an economic problem for the political institution in charge. Not only are they not marginalized and solitary, as they are shown to be in the original trilogy, but they are working to solve purely secular issues that seem to be outside the Jedi's area of concern. Kevin Wetmore argues in *The Empire Triumphant: Race, Religion and Rebellion in the Star Wars Films* that, contrary to how the original trilogy's Obi-Wan describes the Jedi's role in the Old Republic—"the guardians of peace and justice"—"The purpose of the Jedi [in the prequel trilogy] ... is to preserve the status quo ... as administrators and diplomats ... The

Jedi may not be bureaucrats, but their sole purpose seems to be ... to keep the powerful (including themselves) in power and prevent any significant resistance to the domination of the Republic" (64).

In addition to the radical alteration of the Jedi's social duty and position, the Force can now be quantified (via an individual's Midi-chlorian count) and therefore understood and measured scientifically. The existence of the midi-chlorians intimates another significant shift in the definition of the Force and the place of the Jedi. Instead of having a *direct* connection to the Force, the individual needs to have a symbiotic relationship with another life-form to mediate between himself and the Force, thus degrading the significance of individual agency. In *The Phantom Menace*, Qui-Gon tells Anakin, "Without the midi-chlorians, life could not exist, and we would have no knowledge of the Force. They continually speak to you, telling you the will of the Force." The last part of Qui-Gon's message to Anakin is particularly important because not only can the Force be analyzed empirically in the prequel trilogy, but it is said to have a "will." Instead of being an "ally," the Force, through its own agency, becomes an oppressive energy equal to that of fate or predestination. This is directly antithetical to the Force of the original trilogy. In an article that likens the Force to the Eastern Tao, Wetmore asserts the utter un-authoritative nature of the Force in the original trilogy: "Unlike the Western notion of God, an authoritative, anthropomorphic patriarch, the Tao is both life giving and binding, yet does not actively control human beings or demand worship or authority" ("Tao" 94). However, in the prequel trilogy, the Force is utterly authoritative and has so much control over the individual that, through the midi-chlorians, it can conceive a life-form. Considering the potential controlling power of the Force and the significance of the individual, Qui-Gon's ominous pronouncement that, "Nothing happens by accident," takes on a decidedly oppressive feel. He tells the Jedi Council that, "Finding [Anakin] was the will of the Force." In this trilogy, the Force has a plan, and within the confines of this plan, there is little room for individual agency. In this way, the Force becomes every bit as oppressive as the Galactic Empire of the original trilogy.

While arguing the oppressive nature of the Empire, John Lyden states that, in the original trilogy, "The Dark forcemasters tend to speak of 'destiny' in a way that suggests free will is non-existent; but the good side always allows participants to choose their own destinies, granting that free choice can and does contribute to the direction of events." In the prequel trilogy, "destiny" is linked with the "will" of the Force which is in turn linked with "goodness," ultimately subverting the moral codification of the Force in the original trilogy. This subversion of the Force's original position in the *Star Wars* universe can be seen most clearly in the depictions of Yoda and Obi-Wan Kenobi in each trilogy and the thematic relationship between Luke Skywalker in the original trilogy and Darth Maul and Anakin Skywalker in the prequel trilogy.

The characters of Obi-Wan Kenobi and Yoda are both presented initially in the original trilogy as champions of individuality and as representations of the power of expressive autonomy. Their primary function in the original trilogy is to define the nature of the Force, which they do in two main scenes. The first, and it is the very first definition of the Force given in the *Star Wars* films, comes early in *A New Hope* when Obi-Wan tells Luke that the Force is an "energy field created by all living things." Here, as Andrew Gordon asserts, Obi-Wan functions as a type of "priest, last of ... a mystic religious order" who initiates the young Luke into a highly-individualized world (321). The second scene comes in *The Empire Strikes Back* during one of Yoda's didactic sessions with Luke; Yoda states, "my ally is the Force. And a powerful ally it is. Life creates it, makes it grow. Its energy surrounds us and binds us. Luminous beings are we, not this crude matter. You must feel the Force around you. Here, between you ... me ... the tree ... the rock ... everywhere!" These definitions denote the Force to be an unconscious energy that is not only connected to all individuals, but created by them. In this model, midichlorians have no place; the individual does not need them to survive or communicate with the Force, because the Force is *created* by the individual.

In addition to defining the Force in the original trilogy, Yoda and Obi-Wan represent cultural outsiders. Yoda's initial depiction as a non-cultural entity is strengthened through his connection to nature, as Dagobah shows no signs of technological advancement. Therefore, it is decidedly shocking when Yoda is introduced in *The Phantom Menace* on the city planet of Curoscant at the top of a circular tower and surrounded by vistas of technology and commerce.[5] Clearly, the Jedi have moved from being non-cultural entities to cultural ones; more specifically, they are defined in the prequel trilogy as "keepers of the peace." Their social positions have shifted from priests and teachers to police and military leaders.[6] This shift repositions the Jedi from being individual agents to defining them as obedient workers of the state. Not only do Yoda and Obi-Wan work by the Galactic Senate's political code, but they also subjugate themselves to a Jedi "code" and "the will of the Force."

Here, the Force shifts from a free-flowing, transcendental energy that enforces the valorization of the individual to a "will" that needs to be codified so that its edicts may be followed. By creating and adhering to a Jedi code, the intuitive nature of the individual's relationship to the Force is subverted. A disturbing paradox is created here. If a primary tenet of merging with the Force is to "let go your conscious self," as Obi-Wan tells Luke on the attack of the first death star in *A New Hope*, then one cannot follow a clearly-identified code. The Force of the original trilogy—intuitive and empowering—is opposed diametrically by the Force in the prequel trilogy, which is defined through a series of rules and is completely institutionalized. Hence, the ultimate source of individual power becomes an oppressive, political one. While Yoda's leadership role in the political institution of the Jedi Council and his subsequent role as military leader and strategist are disturbing, Obi-Wan's seemingly blind adherence to and fervor for the Jedi code is even more so.

As has been noted, Obi-Wan is introduced in the prequel trilogy as a political negotiator working to settle an economic dispute. From the beginning, he is defined not as a spiritual recluse, as he is in the original trilogy, but as a representative of the dominant political institution of the galaxy. Obi-Wan's institutionalization seems to have infiltrated all levels of his inner life as revealed in his conversation with Qui-Gon after his master disagrees with the Jedi council. Obi-Wan attempts to influence Qui-Gon to forfeit his autonomy and become as equally institutionalized as he is when he implores Qui-Gon to not "defy the council" and to "follow the code," but Qui-Gon refuses. Here, Qui-Gon is presented as an individualist who has repeatedly defied the orders of the Jedi Order and has even refused a seat of power on the Jedi Council by adhering to his own intuitive edicts. While Qui-Gon's defiance of the institution would seem to critique the anti-individualist stance of his fellow Jedi, it is coded as morally problematic and thus loses its legitimacy to critique. Both Yoda and Obi-Wan openly denounce Qui-Gon's individualist thinking, implying that the audience should do the same.

Obi-Wan's efforts to modify his master's mentality from one of self-reliance to one of senseless adherence to the political code of the Jedi seems tame in comparison to the edicts he delivers to his paduan, Anakin. Obi-Wan presents Anakin with a litany of pronouncements to obey in a seeming effort to annihilate any vestige of Anakin's autonomy. When discussing their role as Amidala's protectors in *Attack of the Clones*, he demands that he and Anakin do "exactly as the council has instructed." Later, when Anakin is preparing to embark with Amidala on their voyage to Naboo, he commands that Anakin not "do anything without first consulting either [himself] or the council." In relation to Obi-Wan's tutelage of Luke in the original trilogy, which focuses on inspiring Luke to trust his intuition and create a personal relationship with the Force, Obi-Wan's tutelage of Anakin is decidedly oppressive and creates open hostility towards Anakin's developing individualism.

It should be noted that Yoda and Obi-Wan are the only master Jedi characters in the original trilogy. Therefore, the transformation of the representations of Yoda and Obi-Wan from spiritual individuals to political tools further punctuates the subversion of the original trilogy's val-orization of the individual in that the characters that initially define and represent the Force and the Jedi—as well as what they stand for and how they function in the *Star Wars* universe—are shown in the prequel tril-ogy to act and believe antithetically to how they are originally shown. It is only in the character of Qui-Gon Jinn that the shade of individualism privileged in the original trilogy returns, and, while Qui-Gon's rebel-liousness might be meant to offer a critique of the position of the Jedi in the Republic, it is ultimately inadequate. The only other criticism of the Jedi that is offered comes from Palpatine in *Revenge of the Sith* when he declares that their point of view is "dogmatic" and "narrow" and that they are as power-hungry as the Sith. What limits the effectiveness of this critique is that it is presented only by the single most evil character in the *Star Wars* universe whose manipulative plotting is at the very heart of the prequel trilogy; it is never echoed by any of the Jedi in positions of authority.[7] Even though the criticism of the anti-individualist nature of the Jedi Order in the prequel trilogy exists, it is ultimately subjugated by the rule-bound, doctrinaire leanings of Yoda and Obi-Wan.

Father and Son: The Inversion of the Thematic Significance of Jedi Training

Luke Skywalker's spiritual training and practice and his develop-ment as a marginalized, anarchistic individual who becomes one of the most powerful in the *Star Wars* universe is a dominant focus of the orig-inal trilogy. Considering this narrative arc, Luke epitomoizes the definitive influence and social value of the individual, and this is coded in the films as morally and ethically good as well as spiritually ideal.

From the outset, Luke is defined as a marginalized individual who does not belong to his given culture.[8] Over the course of the original tril-ogy's narrative arc, Luke marginalizes himself further through his expres-sive autonomy. This continues to the point where he becomes the ultimate symbol for the power and necessity of individual agency both in spiritual and secular spheres. The first step toward this self-marginalization is when he finds his surrogate parents murdered by the Empire and decides to become a Jedi. By losing his family unit, Luke becomes orphaned again, and his first decision after this event is to fol-low a path that will emphasize his individuality and promote his exclu-sion from normative culture. As has been explored previously, the Jedi are almost mythical in the original trilogy; to become one is to be almost erased in the eyes of galactic culture.[9] Knowing the monkish, individu-alized nature of his endeavor, Luke's decision to "learn the ways of the

Force and become a Jedi like [his] father" defines the hero as an individual who lives his life without any thought of cultural acceptance; rather,
he pursues a sense of inner-peace and expressive autonomy. In fact, as
Gordon argues, Luke's responsibility is anarchistic in nature in that he
is to work toward the "destruction of the status quo in order to permit
renewal and restoration" (324).

Luke's training as a Jedi, and his observance of that training, helps
him to develop his expressive autonomy by nurturing his intuitive
processes and encourages him to "trust [his] feelings," especially when
making crucial decisions. When Luke approaches the exhaust port of the
death star in *A New Hope*, Obi-Wan instructs him to forgo the technological targeting aides aboard his X-Wing and "let go [his] conscious
self." After a few moments of deliberation, Luke decides to act upon his
intuition, turn off his targeting computer, close his eyes, and fire. This
action reveals Luke to be fundamentally different from the other pilots
he fights with, considering that, moments before this we see Red Leader
use his targeting computer to fire and miss the exhaust port. Even though
he is inside the machinery of his X-Wing, the moment is meant to be
taken as decidedly spiritual. By following his intuition, Luke transcends
his reliance upon technology and communes with the Force, which renders him a type of radical power that is asserted at both the spiritual and
experiential levels. Luke's attitude at this moment is clear: if he is going
to succeed or fail, he is going to do so on his own. As a representative
of powerful individualism, Luke's success in destroying the death star
accents the efficacy of any individual who acts upon his own intuition in
deference to a reliance on systems, technological or political.

As the trilogy progresses, Luke continues to enunciate the
significance of his individuality by training with Yoda. This training
moves Luke away from any cultural systems and deeper into his process
of individualization. He begins this by breaking away from the Rebel
fleet and traveling to an all-but-unoccupied planet based solely on a
dream vision and intuition. This fact alone emphasizes the significance
of individualism, but what compounds it is the films' visualization of
Dagobah. The technology-barren environment of the swamp-planet is
clearly not a host to human life, and boasts only one sentient being: Yoda.
While the importance of Yoda's solitary existence on this planet has
already been discussed, it needs to be developed here to emphasize the
significance of Luke's training on Dagobah. The planet itself becomes a
visual representation of the individual's relationship to the Force.
Dagobah, with all its verdant greenery and watery depths *is*, in part,
Yoda: natural, mysterious, and highly-individualized. For Luke, the
planet functions similarly in that he is able to descend physically into the
experiential manifestation of his subconscious: the cave. Here, Luke is

able to begin to deconstruct his socialized self and assemble a sense of self based solely on his own private sensibilities. Yoda furthers this process by telling Luke to, "unlearn what [he has] learned." This lesson inspires Luke to segregate himself even further from cultural teachings and behavioral norms by "unlearning" them, thus modeling Luke's cultural self-construction so that he may build a more individualized, authentic self.

Perhaps the most powerful assertion of expressive autonomy in the original trilogy is when Luke disobeys Yoda and travels to Bespin to assist Han and Leia. What makes this so significant is that Luke holds his own intuition to be even more significant than the rules of the two individuals that have taught him the most—Yoda and Obi-Wan. Paradoxically, Luke's disobedience is inspired by Obi-Wan's previous lesson to "trust [his] feelings." Not only is this faith in the self one of the most significant moments in the original trilogy, but it leads to one of the single most persuasive moments in any of the films that positions the individual as the ultimate heroic force. Moments after he severs Luke's hand, Vader tells his son that he "can destroy the Empire. The Emperor has foreseen it." This revelation, that it is the individual who has the power to destroy the ultimate oppressive institution in the galaxy, is punctuated by Luke's ultimate expression of autonomy: on two occasions, Luke chooses suicide over a partnership with what he considers to be evil—first when he lets himself fall into the bowels of Bespin, and second when he presents himself to the Emperor in *Return of the Jedi*, knowing that the Rebel fleet is on its way to destroy the space station he occupies.

Now that Luke's position as the ultimate hero because of his radical individuality has been established, his narrative counterparts and how they subvert the original trilogy's individualistic ideology can be explored. In the prequel trilogy, Luke Skywalker has two narrative counterparts: Darth Maul and Anakin Skywalker.

While it might seem initially disconcerting, Darth Maul has some striking narrative similarities to Luke Skywalker that bring into focus the de-valorization of the individual and show expressive autonomy to be dangerous and even evil. Like Luke, Darth Maul is culturally marginalized, and he is the last of his kind—the galaxy's only Sith apprentice. However, the most significant connection between the Jedi and the Sith is a pair of shots that cinematically position both Luke and Maul to be powerful individuals. The famous shot of Luke staring into Tatooine's twin sunrise, which invokes the Romantic artistic tradition of painting the individual from behind and in front of a vast landscape, is mimicked in *A Phantom Menace* by a similar shot of Maul staring off into Tatooine's horizon. While these connections are admittedly loose, they do intimate the notion that, through Maul, a character who functions similarly to

Luke, the prequel trilogy positions individual agency not as the path to heroism but as the path to evil.

The narrative and thematic relationships between Luke and his father Anakin provide a more stable basis for analysis of the two trilogies' treatment of the individual than the Luke/Darth Maul comparison; however, its thematic implications are similar and every bit as poignant. Anne Lancashire explores the Luke/Anakin relationship by arguing that, "Anakin Skywalker (eventual father of Luke) is this film's version of *A New Hope*'s Luke, going through narratively similar situations and experiences" (23).[10] If in the original trilogy Luke represents the ultimate power and social efficacy of the individual and this is coded as morally and ethically good as well as spiritually ideal, then Anakin Skywalker's affinity for autonomy and anarchy, which parallels his son's affinity to the same principles in many ways, is coded decidedly as evil, clearly subverting the valorization of the individual presented in the original trilogy.

In the prequel trilogy, Anakin Skywalker is shown as autonomous, egotistical, and anarchistic. This is first shown in his introduction on Tatooine. When Padmé identifies him as a slave in Watto's shop, he is quick to respond that he "is a person. And [his] name is Anakin." Since the title of "slave" indicates an obvious social position wherein the individual lacks all autonomy and is subjugated to a master, Anakin expresses forcefully and defensively his individualism. This forceful expression of individualism is further illustrated when, in a discussion of pod-racing, Anakin claims that he is "the only human who can do it." It needs to be emphasized here that as an audience, we are powerfully aware that the ten-year-old blond child Anakin Skywalker of *The Phantom Menace* will ultimately become Darth Vader—one of the most potent symbols of evil and oppression in the *Star Wars* universe. To introduce this character with an action of intense individual agency in a film that is almost erased of individualism, codes clearly individualism as morally questionable at best.

Like his son Luke to whom he is compared, Anakin's growing penchant for individualism is emphasized further in that he is shown to receive a significant amount of encouragement to be autonomous. When he is having doubts about leaving Tatooine and his mother, Shmi tells him that "the choice is [his] alone." Also, in a narrative reversal of Luke's pursuit to become a Jedi, Anakin's dream to become a Jedi is originally denied. However, given the position and preponderance of Jedi in the Republic, Anakin's exclusion from the Jedi Order has the same effect as Luke's inclusion in it: it marks him as a cultural outsider. After he is told that he will not be trained as a Jedi, Qui-Gon offers advice to Anakin that furthers this exclusion: "Your focus determines your reality." This comment is similar to Yoda's lesson to Luke's about unlearning, and its implication is also similar—

the individual should deflect cultural lessons and use one's self-culture to define his reality. What lends this advice to be autonomous an overtly iniquitous bent is that the future Emperor Palpatine provides Anakin with what is perhaps the most extreme advice for radical individualism when in *Attack of the Clones* he says to Anakin: "You don't need guidance." This implication that Anakin will be strongest as an individual and to listen to others will only diminish his efficacy is an echo of the original trilogy's valorization of individual agency. Of course, coming from Palpatine, this message is instantly subverted, and the individual is situated as evil.

That Anakin follows Palpatine's advice is indicated by his conversation about maturation with Amidala when he tells her that "sometimes we must let go of our pride and do what is requested of us." While Amidala accepts the statement as sincere and approves of it as a poignant sign of maturity, its preciseness of syntax—along with the fact that Anakin never seems to follow the content of the lesson—gives the expression of this edict a decidedly rehearsed feel, intimating that this is a rote lesson that Anakin has been told by his master again and again, and he reiterates it here solely to win favor with Amidala. This expression of autonomy is significant because it subverts pointedly the mindless adherence to illogical cultural institutions that Amidala represents so powerfully. Amidala's antidisestablishmentarianism is clearly adversarial to Anakin's antiestablishmentarian stance. Also, it is doubly significant that the substance of this lesson is analogous to the advice that Yoda and Obi-Wan tell Luke before he leaves his training prematurely on Dagobah. That both Luke and Anakin ultimately reject this lesson strengthens the narrative connection between them while simultaneously subverting the valorization of individual autonomy in the prequel trilogy by positioning Luke's decision as good and Anakin's as evil.

While Anakin commits many autonomous acts in the prequel trilogy—he pointedly oversteps the Council's mandate to only protect Amidala and ventures to discover her attacker to win favor with her, and he desires to reject the Jedi Council's edicts by pursuing a romantic relationship with Amidala—Anakin's most significant expression of autonomy and de-valorizing the individual comes in his political conversation with Amidala on Naboo in *Attack of the Clones*. Amidala tells Anakin of her history in public service, and he replies to her that he does not "think the system works." Even though this simplistic anarchistic proclamation would seem appropriate coming from any protagonist in the original trilogy—the plot of the entire original trilogy is driven by this type of antiestablishmentarian thinking—here it takes on a dark, foreboding feeling that aligns Anakin with the Emperor and classifies his individualism as evil.

Anakin's narrative trajectory—that he becomes Darth Vader—furthers this codification of individualism as evil, and by the end of *Attack of the Clones*, there can be no doubt as to the moral leanings of his character. After he slays the village of sand-people for capturing and torturing his mother, his anarchistic individualism becomes synonymous with power-hungry egotism. He tells Amidala that he "should be" all powerful and that "someday [he'll] be the most powerful Jedi ever." This individualism turned egotism is developed and complicated by Anakin's actions in *Revenge of the Sith*. At first, all of his individualism seems to be focused on helping others, an impulse that is decidedly at the very heart of Jedi dogma: he desires to save the clones who are being destroyed in the opening battle above Coruscant, he disobeys Obi-Wan's orders to leave him and save Chancellor Palpatine, he neglects Palpatine's order to leave General Grievous's ship without Obi-Wan, and, most significantly, he chooses to ally himself with Palpatine in order to save Padmé's life. Even though these actions would seem to align individual agency with moral goodness, they are eventually revealed to be selfish desires for more power that essentially feed Anakin's egotism by imaginarily positioning him as the definitive hero who can save everyone and ultimately conquer death.

Ultimately, it is the ability to choose that turns Anakin evil and offers the sharpest critique of individualism that the prequel trilogy offers. The Jedis' principal advice to Anakin is to be wary of his feelings and desires, to not trust that which the Jedi of the original trilogy considered to be most important. In the prequel trilogy the Jedi Council functions as a censor for Anakin, never allowing him to make decisions for himself. This limitation expresses an intense anxiety regarding the individual's ability to trust his intuition and make personal choices. Shmi and Palpatine are the only characters in the prequel trilogy that offer Anakin the opportunity to make these decisions. Shmi tells him that he must choose whether or not he should leave Tatooine and become a Jedi; Palpatine tells Anakin that he "must choose" either to allow Mace Windu to kill Palpatine, destroying any chance of saving Padmé from death during childbirth, or to save Palpatine and his wife by striking Windu down. It is significant that the second time Anakin is asked to make a choice, it results in both personal and political atrocity: the fall of the Republic, the rise of the Empire, the eradication of the Jedi Order, his own bodily corruption and imprisonment in a mechanized life-support system, the loss of his best friend, the death of his wife, and his estrangement from his children. Here the progressive themes of the original trilogy are conclusively over-simplified and subverted by positioning individual autonomy as the direct cause of the tragic events that both *Star Wars* trilogy's are founded on.

"I Have a Bad Feeling About This": How the Prequel Trilogy Killed the Rebellion

It must be noted that one could defend the prequel trilogy by arguing that Lucas intends for the films to be read intertextually. In this way, the prequel trilogy can be aligned with the original trilogy's individualist stance in that it offers exposition that justifies the need for the fierce individualism found in the original trilogy. Such a reading could argue that the ineffectual political system and institutionalized role of the Jedi in the prequel trilogy function primarily to set up the downfall of the Old Republic. Hence, the prequel trilogy's characters' faith in a failed democracy and the normative prescriptions of the status quo could be a result of arrogance and naivety and could therefore be the precise cause of the creation of the Empire and the destruction of the Jedi Order and the Old Republic. With this in mind, the original trilogy's individualist position could be viewed as a necessary response to the dangers of blind adherence to subsuming, normative values and behaviors, hence positioning the prequel trilogy's seeming anti-individualist stance in harmony with the themes and values of the original trilogy through narrative necessity.

However, there are too many obvious problems with this reading for it to be taken seriously. (1). A film, or series of films, especially if they have been as culture-changing as the *Star Wars* films, cannot be analyzed in a cultural vacuum. To observe the films without considering their historic moment would be to diminish their potential relevance and profundity. (2). A film should be able to stand on its own and express whatever themes are inherent within it as well as function intertextually to enhance, diverge away from, or revise thematic concerns of other related films. To rely on a series of films that are almost 30 years old to define another film's themes seems simply to highlight the poorly-crafted nature of the dependant work's narrative. (3). Ultimately, there is no reason that the prequel trilogy could not still function intertextually the same way—by setting up the reasons for such fierce individualism in the original trilogy—while expressing pro-individualist themes at the same time. Regardless of any intertextual connections, the dominant paradigms of the prequel trilogy are decidedly anti-individualistic. Therefore, while Episodes I-III may be meant as critiques of anti-individualism, they actually create a matrix of values that not only privileges systematic control over individual autonomy but demonizes the fervent individualism that the original trilogy works so hard to establish.

These thematic differences between the *Star Wars* trilogies can be explained through a fundamental difference between the cultures that engendered the films. The cultural climate when the original trilogy was created—the mid- to late- seventies—was one where individualism was valorized, especially anti-establishmentarianism. With the reverberations of Viet Nam and Watergate still echoing throughout the nation, individuals were suspect of large cultural institutions with the power to control the media in an attempt to manipulate cultural awareness and values. This connection between the original trilogy's interest in individualism and American culture in the 1970s is supported in an article written in 1982, before the release of *Return of the Jedi,* by David Wyatt in which he states, "the revolutionary bias of the movie seems particularly appropriate to our historical moment" (608). Conversely, at the turn of the century— when the prequel trilogy was created—it is the institution that lends the individual his power. In this time when everything in Western life can be commoditized, the cultural climate is decidedly conservative and accepting of the status quo.

This notion is illustrated clearly by Daniel Mackay in his "*Star Wars*: the Magic of Anti-Myth." Mackay champions the original trilogy's humanitarian themes by arguing that the wealth of myth criticism of *Star Wars* is misguided: "The *Star Wars* message is, in fact an anti-mythological message, precisely because its message about the human spirit is assembled from the remnants of the old mythologies—mythologies that no longer carry weight in the way we live our lives today—and runs perpendicular to the scientific capitalism mythology of our day" (74). Mackay's powerful argument that the original *Star Wars* trilogy is an anti-myth because it privileges spiritual and individualist themes is particularly poignant when applied to the prequel trilogy. Given his argument, that a contemporary myth would have to be rooted in scientific and capitalist themes, it could be argued that, unlike the original trilogy, the prequel trilogy *is* in fact a myth created from contemporary culture's dependency on scientific rhetoric and capitalism. This is quite sad in that, as Mackay argues, "Today, more than ever, we need to hear messages that challenge the rational strategizing and technocratic governing that threatens to overwhelm every aspect of our lives" (74).

It is surprising and disturbing in a post-Matrix/Lord of the Rings entertainment culture to find such radical conservatism in the world of Science Fiction/Fantasy film. It is even more disturbing that the film franchise that asserted so powerfully the value of fierce individualism has become so conservative. Perhaps what is most disturbing about the prequel trilogy's reversal of the original trilogy's individualist stance is that it casts an unalterable shadow on the original trilogy. As an audience, after we see the depth of corruption and ineffectualness of the Old Republic, it is nothing short of devastating to realize that this anti-individualist political system that led to the Empire's quest to subvert autonomy throughout the galaxy is precisely what the rebels are fighting to rebuild. In relation to the rebel's cause and its efficacy, Robin Wood notes that the original trilogy's tone is ultimately reassuringly conservative in that things change in the *Star Wars* universe only to reassert a set of comfortable and normative paradigms (162–65). He concludes that the rebels are ultimately only fighting to assert their own cultural and political power, which is similar to the power of the Empire. He asks, "What will the rebels against the Empire create if not another empire?" (170).[11] Thus, the prequel trilogy not only revises our understanding of the original trilogy's narrative, but it aligns that trilogy's fervent individualist ideology with the ideology of the corporate, institutional West, forever diminishing the cultural significance of the original *Star Wars* films that inspired so extraordinarily its viewers to an imaginary revolution.

Before the release of the prequel trilogy, the climax of *Return of the Jedi* heralded a bright new era of freedom and cultural significance for the individual in the *Star Wars* universe. With the defeat of the Galactic Empire, the Rebel Alliance is enabled to create a new, democratic political system based on the Old Republic: the New Republic. However, in light of the Old Republic's bureaucratic machinations and disempowerment of individual agency illuminated in the prequel trilogy, the Rebel's victory now implies the establishment of a form of government that is even more harmful to the individual than the Empire. Considering the revisionist effect of the prequel trilogy, the New Republic that the rebels will most likely create becomes a system that functions similarly to the computer program of the matrix in the eponymous film: it will offer the individual the illusory feeling of significance and autonomy while ultimately attempting to control him, subsuming him into a conservative, normative system of cultural values. The ultimate heroic moment for the Rebellion in the original trilogy now signifies the ultimate death of the individual, and the freedom that the Rebels fight for becomes nothing more than another system of control, subverting the ultimate valorization of autonomy and causing the fall of the rebellion.

Notes

1. In *The Empire Triumphant: Race, Religion and Rebellion in the* Star Wars *Films*, Kevin Wetmore references a review of *A New Hope* written by Dan Rubey for *Jump Cut* in 1978 in which Rubey argues that the film, in Wetmore's words, posits "the triumph of Western individualism over valuing the collective or the community" (61). To further support this interpretation that *A New Hope* privileges individualism, Wetmore quips that "The entire planet of Alderaan cannot stop the Death Star, but one blond-haired, blue-eyed young white man in a small ship can" (61). More seriously, he notes that even though leaders, spies, and soldiers were killed and tortured in their campaign to destroy the Death Star, "Luke and Han get the medals at the end.... it is the actions of individual heroes that really matter" (61).

2. The Empire is obviously coded as antithetical to the individual and, within the context of a narrative that focuses on liberation from tyrannical forces, evil: the storm troopers'

faceless visages are constant reminders of the Empire's assimilating power, as are their black and white uniforms; the other Imperial's uniforms invoke a Nazi-like obedience to institutional ideals; and the dominant geometric shape associated with the institution is the circle—the Death Star, the interrogation droid, the center of the tie fighter, the shape of the "board room" on the Death Star—denoting a redundant, implacable power.

3. As Wetmore states succinctly in *The Empire Triumphant*, "The original trilogy indicates a pro-Rebellion, anti-Empire perspective. The audience is intended to side with the Rebellion" (35).

4. The highly-customized Millennium Falcon functions as another powerful symbol of Han's individuality. Unlike the starships in the prequel trilogy, the Millennium Falcon has a unique title, privileging individualism. Also, the Falcon becomes a self-representation of Han.

5. The introduction of Yoda inside a circular room in a circular tower invokes powerfully the circles utilized by the Empire in the original trilogy, aligning the Jedi Order with the oppressiveness of the Empire.

6. The climactic battle of *Attack of the Clones* and much of *Revenge of the Sith*'s action positions the Jedi as the leaders of the clone armies.

7. It should be noted that in Mathew Stover's novelization of *Revenge of the Sith*, Yoda echoes Palpatine's view by admitting that the Jedi Order has failed in that it has been too dogmatic and outmoded.

8. While Tatooine is inhabited by humans, there is nothing to imply that human life is indigenous to the desert planet; in fact, given the variety of species displayed at Mos Eisley and the planet's extreme environments, the only two species that a viewer may determine to be indigenous to Tatooine are Sand People and Jawas. With this in mind, Luke's ethnic and cultural foundations are clearly not normative on the planet he has grown up on. This positioning of Luke as an outsider emphasizes powerfully his uniqueness. Also, Luke is an orphan, a social position that accentuates further his individuality by situating him as an inimitable other even within the confines of his own nuclear family unit. (The friction between Luke and Owen Lars works well to strengthen this position as outsider.)

9. It is difficult to remember that when Luke first converses with Obi-Wan in *A New Hope*, he has never even heard of the Force before. This enforces the Force's position as marginalized in the original trilogy.

10. Anne Lancashire develops the narrative comparisons between Luke and Anakin by saying, "Anakin, like Luke, is a young boy on the desert planet of Tatooine, from a "broken" family, who is suddenly given the opportunity to embark on an epic quest involving a beautiful, royal young woman in need of his help and a Jedi knight who becomes his mentor. Like Luke, Anakin accepts the opportunity and is flown through space with his mentor to face a test (for Luke, the Death Star rescue of Leia; for Anakin, a literal test before the Jedi Council). Like *A New Hope*, the film then ends with the boy's special powers (including his capacity for friendship and love) permitting him to save his friends from annihilation by destroying an enemy battle station. Details of the narrative also correspond from one film to the other: the Jedi mentor's advice to the protagonist to rely on his feelings, the death of the mentor in a light-saber duel, the association of allies with ancient sacred ruins" (23).

11. For a more detailed argument that aligns the political and cultural perspectives of the Rebellion with the Empire, see Chapter One of Wetmore's *The Empire Triumphant*.

Works Cited

Campbell, Joseph, and Bill Moyers. *The Power of Myth*. New York: Doubleday, 1988.

Gordon, Andrew. "*Star Wars*: A Myth for Our Time." *Literature and Film Quarterly* 6 (1978): 314–26.

Lancashire, Anne. "*The Phantom Menace*: Repetition, Variation, Integration." *Film Criticism* 24.3 (2000): 23.

Lyden, John. "The Apocalyptic Cosmology of *Star Wars*." *Journal of Religion and Film* 4.1 (April 2000). 28 Feb. 2006. <www.unomaha.edu/~wwwjrf/LydenStWars.htm>.

Mackay, Daniel. "*Star Wars*: The Magic of the Anti-Myth." *Foundation* 76 (1999): 63–75.
Star Wars Episode I: The Phantom Menace. Dir. George Lucas. Screenplay by George Lucas. Twentieth Century Fox, 1999.
Star Wars Episode II: Attack of the Clones. Dir. George Lucas. Screenplay by George Lucas and Jonathan Hales. Twentieth Century Fox, 2002.
Star Wars Episode III: Revenge of the Sith. Dir. George Lucas. Screenplay by George Lucas. Twentieth Century Fox, 2005.
Star Wars Episode IV: A New Hope. Dir. George Lucas. Screenplay by George Lucas. Twentieth Century Fox, 1977.
Star Wars Episode V: The Empire Strikes Back. Dir. Irvin Kershner. Screenplay by Leigh Brackett and Lawrence Kasdan. Story by George Lucas. Twentieth Century Fox, 1980.
Star Wars Episode VI: Return of the Jedi. Dir. Richard Marquand. Screenplay by Lawrence Kasdan and George Lucas. Story by George Lucas. Twentieth Century Fox, 1983.
Stover, Mathew. *Revenge of the Sith*. New York: Lucas Books, 2005.
Wetmore, Kevin J., Jr. *The Empire Triumphant: Race, Religion and Rebellion in the* Star Wars *Films*. Jefferson: McFarland, 2005.
_____. "The Tao of *Star Wars*, Or, Cultural Appropriation in a Galaxy Far, Far Away." *Studies in Popular Culture* (2000): 91-eoa.
Wood, Robin. *Hollywood from Vietnam to Regan*. New York: Columbia University Press, 1986.
Wyatt, David. "*Star Wars* and the Productions of Time." *Virginia Quarterly Review* 58.4 (1982): 600–15.

2

Apocalyptic Determinism and *Star Wars*

JOHN LYDEN

It is clear that apocalyptic ideas have been present in western culture for at least two thousand years, beginning with early Christian ideas about an imminent return of Christ, followed by a final judgment and eschatological kingdom. Judaism had developed similar apocalyptic ideas earlier, but only with their adaptation into gentile culture via Christianity did these ideas have the opportunity to influence multiple nations and cultures, especially after the conversion of the Roman Empire to Christianity in the fourth century. Apocalyptic—a way of thinking that predicts an imminent judgment on and end to the current world—is therefore central to western culture, in as much as Christianity is central to western culture.

However, apocalyptic has always rested somewhat uneasily within western culture, and even within Christianity, due to its world-annihilating qualities that seem to make much of life in this world irrelevant. If the world is going to cease to exist in the near future, there isn't much point in getting married and raising a family, founding a government, or even trying to reform existing societies. If judgment is soon and unavoidable, there follows a tendency to make individual contributions to society almost meaningless, for all that individuals can really do is make their own peace with the judgment, deciding to live well enough to escape the cataclysm when it comes. Thus apocalyptic has often been on the fringe of societies, expressing fundamental frustrations or dissatisfactions of disaffected groups, but it has largely been avoided by the policy makers and the successful.

All this makes it seem odd that apocalyptic is perhaps at an all-time high in western culture and in the United States in particular. This country is powerful, affluent, well-educated, and is the undisputed world power militarily, politically, economically, and perhaps even culturally. Those who are drawn to apocalyptic in our time clearly have different reasons for this attraction that transcend its ability to comfort the politically downtrodden in the face of oppression. Still, apocalyptic continues to appeal to and gain new converts to its way of thinking, even in this affluent country, and its proponents view themselves as oppressed underdogs even though they are often very financially successful and politically influential. But a besieged mentality seems to be part of the form of apocalypticism, so that even the successful feel constrained to view themselves as without power. Perhaps the more basic question is why ever-increasing numbers are drawn to apocalyptic and what its appeal is for them.

This essay cannot attempt anything like a full answer to that question, but we can gain some sense of apocalyptic's appeal by looking to its success in the realm of popular culture. Series like *Left Behind* sell millions of books, which aid the popularity of apocalyptic, but this is also an indication that Americans are already predisposed to accept this belief system. There is something in apocalyptic that appeals to Americans, especially today, and it is in popular culture products that cater to this apocalyptic longing that we see this fundamental desire reaching well beyond the religious realm per se into secular culture. Of course, if so-called "secular" popular culture can function as religiously as recognized "religions" (as I have argued in *Film as Religion*), then it is just as worthwhile to study its religious form and effects as it is to study traditional religions. Indeed, it is arguable that the influence of secular media over the religious ideas of Americans is greater than that of traditional religion.

If one is going to look for the influence of media culture, there is no better place to start than *Star Wars*. These six films comprise the most successful movie series of all time[1] and have created generations of devoted fans as well as massive income not only from the films but also the associated commercial by-products (e.g., toys and tie-ins). It is clear that *Star Wars* struck a chord for many Americans in a way that could not have been predicted by market analysts, so that its success cannot be attributed just to "hype." Many a film has been sold as hard as *Star Wars* that has not done nearly as well. And while the more recently made films (Episodes I–III) are clearly inferior to the earlier films (Episodes IV–VI), the success of the later films is also an index of how successful the original trilogy was, as many fans went to the later films mainly because they loved the original films so much. *Star Wars* also contains many of the ideas one finds in apocalyptic[2] and these elements seem to be heightened in the more recent films. Comparing the two trilogies, then, is one way to index the ways that apocalyptic ideas have been portrayed and have appealed in two different decades of American history.

The differences that are found suggest some evolution of apocalyptic ideas in popular culture, in particular, an increasing acceptance of the determinism and fatalism of apocalyptic.

Before turning to *Star Wars*, I will define what elements comprise apocalyptic, and briefly examine the role of apocalyptic ideas in American history, attempting to indicate some reasons for their central role. I will then examine how popular culture has processed apocalyptic in recent years, in both biblical and non-biblical forms, especially since Sept. 11, 2001. Lastly, I will compare the two *Star Wars* trilogies to see what the differences may suggest to us about changing American attitudes about destiny and freedom as seen through the lens of apocalyptic.

Elements and History of American Apocalyptic

The word "apocalyptic" comes from the Greek word meaning to unveil or reveal hidden things. It is almost always associated today with a revealing of a plan for the end of the world, largely because the final book of the New Testament, which deals with such matters, purports to be a revelation of such a future plan to John of Patmos. For my purposes, I will define apocalyptic as involving five basic elements. This definition is necessarily a simplification and will not accurately reflect everything that has been classified as apocalyptic. However, it describes in broad strokes the main features of it that I will focus upon in my analysis.

Disaster

First, apocalyptic predicts a radical change in the present state of things, a disaster to come that will eliminate the normal world we know, and in this way, it is associated with judgment and destruction. Supernatural intervention in history brings this judgment, which may take bizarre and unforeseen forms. Blood falls from the sky, the stars fail to follow their courses, violence erupts everywhere, and the earth itself becomes dead, all as evidence of the judgment of God on the world (Lohse 57). Apocalyptic seems to revel in the fact that the unbelievers are unprepared for this judgment, whereas believers have had plenty of time to prepare to relish the destruction of their enemies.

Dualism

Second, apocalyptic has a dualistic attitude, positing a clear and absolute difference between good and evil; in the final battle, there is no ambiguity as to which is which, and the moral qualities of those who fight for one side or the other are defined by how they are thus aligned. Absolute battles do not allow one to be wishy-washy, nor do they allow for otherwise good people who might, for various reasons beyond their control, find themselves fighting for an immoral side. As President George W. Bush has famously stated in regards to the war on terrorism, "if you are not with us, you are against us," indicating that one can only be good or evil, not in between, and this sentiment clearly resonates with apocalyptic's oversimplification of moral complexities and the subsequent judgments resulting from this.

Determinism

Third, apocalyptic has a deterministic character to it, suggesting that the plan revealed for the future is set and no one can change it. God is sovereign over history and has absolute power, so there can be no lack of knowledge on God's part of what will happen. Although the Almighty may not choose to share all the details with the faithful, what is shared through scripture is taken as fixed, for to declare otherwise would be to admit God can make an error (or at least that the writers of the texts could). Beliefs in predestination are often linked to this determinism, but it is not only the predestination of individual souls that is decided—rather all the details of world history are fixed as described in the apocalyptic text.

Decision

Fourth, and this stands to a certain extent in contradiction with the deterministic character of apocalyptic, there is an emphasis on the need for individuals to decide for or against God, to decide whose side they are on. Up to a point, there is free will, and this is essential in order for the appeal to evangelism to work. Most modern American apocalyptic suggests that individuals have this free choice until the events of the apocalypse enter a certain phase, a point-of-no-return after which individual freedom ceases to exist. This very fact, of course, is to encourage one to make the right choice while there is yet time and the freedom to do so.

Deliverance

Fifth, at the end of all the cataclysmic destruction and judgment, there is a final salvation for the faithful who manage to persist through all this. Hope is held out at the end of the line, for without a happy ending, there would be no point in believing any of this. The faithful are exonerated and rewarded, and the wicked are punished everlastingly, as God's unquestionable judgments take hold.

These five elements can certainly be seen in most forms of apocalypticism present in American culture. The reasons for the success of apocalypticism in the United States are complex and resist analysis, but a few ideas suggest themselves. First, the United States was populated in its early days by some religious groups that were too extreme for Europe, thus bringing here precisely those disaffected elements that did not fit into European society. As oppressed sectarians, these were the groups to whom apocalyptic ideas most appealed. The promise of religious freedom in America first brought the Puritans, who were full of apocalyptic ideas that they linked to the new world; other groups followed (Boyer 68–79). But the apocalypticism of the Puritans often took a this-worldly form, looking to America as the fulfillment of ancient promises God made to Israel about a future world of peace and justice governed by the "chosen people"—who became the Americans rather than Israelites (Boyer 84–86). In the years of the founding of the Republic, scenarios of total disaster and judgment for worldly governments would hardly have fit the spirit of the times, and this more optimistic form of utopianism was more popular.

As the 19th century wore on, however, apocalyptic prospered in America, with the rise of movements that tapped into the need some felt for a detailed plan for the apocalypse, complete with dates. Their ideas did not suggest that the world could be saved by Christians so much as that Christians could be saved from the world. The individualism of American culture gave fertile soil to this kind of apocalyptic, as the destiny of individuals became more important than the general direction of society. At the same time, conservative Christians who did not want to reform society still wanted to evangelize and so desired to have some impact on society, at least by gaining converts to their own form of Christianity.

The pessimistic form of apocalyptic that eschewed hopes for social reform and embraced scenarios of disaster for the future began to gain strength in the United States with Millerism, a form of prophecy belief founded by William Miller in the early 19th century. He originally predicted that the Second Coming of Jesus would occur in 1843, although this date obviously had to be revised. His movement, however, was significant in making apocalyptic prediction seem rational and scientific as well democratically open to all, not only the "experts" (Boyer 83–84). This democratic and rationalistic form of apocalyptic was expanded upon by John Darby (1800–1882) in a movement that came to be known as Dispensationalism, which described history through a series of ages or "dispensations." These stages would culminate soon in the "Rapture," when the faithful would be removed from the Earth prior to Antichrist's conquest of it and the subsequent "Tribulation" of suffering and catastrophe. After seven years, a final battle with evil ("Armageddon") will lead to the defeat of Antichrist by the genuine Christ and result in the ensuing thousand year reign of the latter (the "Millennium"). This would be followed by a final effort by Satan to take control as well as the resurrection and final judgment of the living and the dead (Boyer 86–88).

Darby influenced Christians well beyond his own denomination, the Plymouth Brethren, as his ideas were picked up by Presbyterian minister James H. Brookes (1830–1897) and by the popular evangelist Dwight L. Moody (1837–1899). Cyrus Scofield (1843–1921) published the Scofield Reference Bible in 1909 which included annotations reinforcing the Dispensationalist view of the Bible, and this proved enormously successful. (Ahlstrom 809–810.) Darby's theories still form the basis for much contemporary apocalyptic, including that of the *Left Behind* series. These books describe through fictional characters a set of events set in the near future, which begin with the mysterious disappearance of Christians (the rapture) and continue as the Antichrist comes to world power, and a small "Tribulation Force" of new Christians battles his forces until Judgment Day. It is remarkable how few Christians seem to realize how much of this dispensationalist view is not biblical and the extent to which it is the invention of a relatively recent movement (Rossing 19–46). What is perhaps more remarkable is the extent of its influence, as premillenial "rapture" proponents have multiplied, especially in recent times. In fact, such beliefs have been popular with a certain sort of Christian since their inception, as each succeeding generation has located the end-times in their own times, duly identifying key events in their own history with the allegedly foretold events of apocalyptic. It is easy to see how people might find evidence of the coming apocalyptic catastrophe in war, from the American Civil War to World Wars I and II, but to suggest that apocalyptic was successful mainly as a way to explain the admittedly horrific violence of modern warfare misses the fact that apocalyptic also prospered in the many decades of peace time. In addition, apocalyptic beliefs were not limited to the poor and disenfranchised, so a straightforward Marxist analysis that would suggest these beliefs were simply compensatory fantasies for worldly failure also misses the point; believers in apocalyptic were often among the most wealthy (Boyer 100). Instead, apocalyptic seems to have its lasting appeal due to its ability to provide a sense of identity for conservative evangelical Christians, so that they can define themselves against the godless, against the world, and against the encroaching forces of modernity that threatened their identity. As Fundamentalism appeared at the beginning of the twentieth century as a reaction against modern science (in particular Darwins's theories on human evolution), biblical criticism, and a perceived dissolution of Christian values in American culture (perhaps occasioned by urbanization, secularization, and an

increasing ethnic and religious pluralism), so apocalyptic beliefs appealed
to the same set of people for the same reasons. It reassured them that
they were the chosen, that they would be vindicated even though tough
times lay ahead and that their efforts to remain faithful to God would be
rewarded, so that even though the confusion of modern times made it
difficult to have confidence, it was worth it to persevere.[3]

As apocalyptic beliefs have developed over the past century and a
half, so have the concerns of their adherents. There has been a great
amount of fear of sexual liberation, related to increased power for women,
access to birth control, abortion, and homosexual rights; there have also
been significant efforts to bring religion into the public realm, whether
in school prayer, town hall Christmas displays, or biblically-based "creation science" education. The identification of the Antichrist also changes
with the times, usually being identified with the leader or leaders of America's foe of the moment—candidates have included Kaiser Wilhelm, Mus-
solini, Hitler, all the Soviet leaders, and most recently Saddam Hussein.
But what remains consistent in all eras of apocalyptic belief is the effort
to view the age in which one lives as the final age. This was probably
easy during World War II due to the large scale of the conflict, and also
the Cold War offered its own reasons for fear of final catastrophe in the
possibility of total world destruction (even though peace remained the
norm).

Our own time also offers apocalyptic possibilities in the perceived
threat of a militant and politicized global Islam that has challenged the
West through terrorism (most notably on September 11, 2001), and that
has inspired large-scale military action by the United States against
Afghanistan and Iraq. I use the word "perceived" deliberately, as it is far
from certain that there is a unified entity we should call global Islam—
although it is clear that terrorists who consider themselves Muslim have
been very effective, and our reaction to them has gone a long way towards
creating an Islam unified in its opposition to the United States and its
actions. But I would reiterate that apocalyptic fantasies are not created
by war, though they may be fueled by it and contribute to the dualistic
worldviews that are usually popular in wartime. We would do well to
remember that *Left Behind* was already a popular series prior to 2001,
and other prophecy literature was popular well before that, e.g., Hal
Lindsey's best-selling books of the 1970's. The persistence of apocalyptic beliefs through times of both peace and war is evidence that it deals
with issues that transcend international politics and that deal more with
identity politics; conservative Christians define themselves as such by
certain issues (e.g., pro-war, anti-abortion, anti-gay) which vary with
the times but which always serve the purpose of identifying how they
differ from the "secular" society.

Apocalyptic and Popular Culture

Apocalyptic has remained consistent as a part of American culture, despite variations in form, in its ability to provide conservative Christians with an identity defined against the dominant secular culture. What seems to be new is the fact that the dominant, largely secular culture itself is increasingly making use of apocalyptic themes in literature and film. This may be due to the prominence of evangelical culture itself as a part of American culture and the fact that its influence is being increasingly felt beyond the narrower confines of the evangelical community. But it also indicates that apocalyptic is undergoing some transformations as its form is adopted into secular media that cater to non-evangelicals and that do not specifically subscribe to a literal prediction of the end-times. Even those people who do not have a formal belief system that involves the end-times are drawn to the form of apocalyptic and see its appeal. This is particularly true in a "post–911" world, as even non–Christians feel the tenuousness of existence more keenly, giving them a "palpable sense of apocalypse," as Glenn Shuck puts it (21).

One might point out, of course, that even during the Cold War, end-of-the-world scenarios were common in popular films as Hollywood contemplated the threat of nuclear annihilation. But films that depicted the possibility of nuclear catastrophe like *Fail-Safe* (1964) and *Dr. Strangelove, or: How I Learned to Stop Worrying and Love the Bomb* (1964) as well as films that depicted the aftermath of nuclear holocaust, like *Planet of the Apes* (1968) and *The Omega Man* (1971), do not really exhibit the features of apocalyptic I have defined. There is no need to decide for or against an inexorable evil in the face of a cosmic, dualistic battle; there is only the threatened possibility that humans may destroy themselves. Admittedly, this is an apocalyptic motif, but it does not share all the features of religious apocalyptic as it functions mainly as moral and political exhortation.

It is also true that films like *The Omen* (1976) and its two sequels (*Damien—Omen II* (1978) and *The Final Conflict* (1981)) dealt explicitly with the coming of Antichrist according to Christian apocalyptic beliefs. This may itself be the product of religious syncretism and a "New Age" tendency to combine religious ideas from various sources into new polyglot stories. Be that as it may, films like the *Matrix* and *Terminator* trilogies, as well as *Star Wars*, have utilized apocalyptic for their basic structure. In addition, we have continued to see the popularity of Christian apocalyptic themes in products such as Mel Gibson's *The Passion of the Christ* and in the *Left Behind* series. A brief examination of these will give a basis for comparing how the two *Star Wars* trilogies also echo the themes of apocalyptic in popular form.

The *Left Behind* books (more so than the films based on them) are obviously the most significant effort to date to bring explicitly Christian apocalyptic ideas into contemporary popular culture, having sold over 62 million copies at this time (*JerryJenkins.com*). Of particular interest here is how the series has processed the tension between free will and determinism that is present in all apocalyptic.

The series clearly has all five of the key aspects of apocalyptic I have enumerated above; however, there is a significant tension between its fatalism and its effort to emphasize free choice. American evangelicals have traditionally embraced the idea that everyone has a choice in regards to Christ, and none are predestined to refuse him apart from their own free decision. This dates to the success of John Wesley's Arminian theology over his colleague George Whitefield's stricter Calvinist determinism in early 18th century America (Ahlstrom 326–327). Evangelicals still prefer to believe in the freedom of the will in this regard, in spite of the fact that major Protestant theologians like Luther and Calvin embraced predestination; Luther even intimated that it was the major difference between his own view of reliance on God's grace alone and the Roman Catholic view that there is a spark of free will we must exercise to be saved (Luther 166–203). But apocalyptic embraces determinism in a different way by insisting on a fixed blueprint for the end-times that the mainline reformers never supported. In this way, apocalyptic believers hold to both a more deterministic, and at the same time, more free view of salvation than mainline Christianity.[4]

In *Left Behind*, this tension between determinism and free will takes shape in the narrative around the "Mark of the Beast." Apocalyptic believers have long held that, once this mark is voluntarily accepted by someone, that soul is damned and he or she cannot do anything to change that (Revelation 14:9–11). Free will exists up until that choice is made, but after that, all is fixed. The *Left Behind* books, however, question this. Believers bear a Mark of Christ that distinguishes them from those who bear the Mark of the Beast, but there is one individual who manages to hold both, a teenage computer whiz named Chang Wong. He takes the Mark of the Beast rather than accept martyrdom, but he then claims he is still a Christian who can now spy on the enemy more effectively (Shuck 154–155). Chang's liminal status allows him the ambiguity the Tribulation Force needs to gain intelligence about the enemy, even though they may not approve of his methods (Shuck 178). In the end, Chang's Mark of the Beast is miraculously removed through the prayers of his fellow Christians so that he can be saved (Shuck 187). But if this would seem to relativize the importance of taking the Mark, the authors make it clear that for all others who have taken it, damnation is inescapable, even if they repent and confess faith (Shuck 189)! This contradiction in the narrative goes unacknowledged, but clearly demonstrates the fix in which apocalyptic believers find themselves, wanting to embrace both the fairness of God's judgments (based as they must be on choices individuals make) as well as their inexorability.

Even Mel Gibson's *Passion of the Christ* (2004) has apocalyptic references that echo this tension between free will and destiny. Satan expects Christ to fail in his mission to redeem the world and tempts him to give it up in the Garden of Gethsemane; Jesus rejects the temptation, stamping on his snake-like form (in a clear attempt to show the fulfillment of the prophesy in Genesis 3:15, "He shall bruise your head"). But Satan continues to appear in the film, as if to show that he still expects Jesus to reject the path of suffering and so fail in his effort to save the world. Satan even appears with his own child, the Antichrist, during the scourging of Jesus, to taunt him with his own powers and to give a foretaste of the apocalyptic disaster that he will bring. In this latter, most violent scene of the movie, Jesus clearly chooses that the beating continue longer than it might have; he has collapsed, and the torturers have ceased, but when he glimpses his mother his will is strengthened, and he picks himself up in order to expose himself to even more brutality. This suggests that even the Son of God, whose role in this is certainly predestined, has free will in regards to his acceptance of his mission as he can even choose supererogatory suffering that may be more than is needed but which exemplifies his own willingness to embrace his horrific task for the sake of others. When Jesus dies, we see Satan scream with frustration, as he realizes he has lost due to the persistence of the Christ. This film frames the atonement as part of an apocalyptic struggle between good and evil that is foreordained, and the roles of the characters (e.g., Jesus, Judas, Caiaphas, Mary, etc.) seem fixed as well as in the medieval passion plays it imitates—and yet, their choices remain paradoxically free, for they could not be held culpable or rewarded for their roles otherwise.

Moving to non-biblically based apocalyptic films, the *Matrix* trilogy of films sets up a world in which the fact that humans have been enslaved by machines is concealed from them through an elaborate virtual reality construct. A final battle with the machines is forecast, and a Messiah-like figure ("The One") is prophesied to come and aid in this effort. The first film, *The Matrix* (1999), traces how Neo is enlisted by the resistance, and it appears he is the One, as he has the ability to manipulate the programming of the matrix and so alter the virtual reality to his advantage; he also undergoes an almost miraculous rescue from death (courtesy of the fairy-tale like kiss of his true love, Trinity). In the second film, *The Matrix Reloaded* (2003), the resistance seeks a way to bring down the machines and follows a trail of clues that turns out to be merely a trap laid by the Architect of the Matrix. He explains that all has been foreordained and that free will is only an illusion allowed by the machines to increase the compliance of humans. Even the existence of Neo and the resistance to the machines are necessary to create the illusion that humans can fight back, but they are destined to fail as they have through many similar cycles before. Neo, however, refuses to accept this lack of freedom and defies the Architect by continuing the fight. In the third film, *The Matrix Revolutions* (2003), we learn that not everything is predestined after all, as the machines failed to predict the appearance of a virus in the form of a renegade computer program, Agent Smith, who is now copying himself onto everything and so threatens to crash the system. The machines make a deal with Neo, that they will not destroy the resistance if he will destroy Agent Smith. Smith cannot understand why Neo fights him, and when he asks, Neo only answers, "because I choose to." This is an existential religion, one that cannot guarantee success but that can offer individuals the opportunity to make their own destiny through their choices, even though they cannot control the outcome of them. When Neo is apparently killed by Smith, the latter is unexpectedly destroyed as well, perhaps because he cannot exist without his doppelganger—Smith having been inadvertently created by Neo and being in many respects Neo's mirror image, as he himself realizes. Neo has then sacrificed himself to forestall the apocalypse, once again indicating that individual choice survives even in an apparently deterministic universe, although its effects are limited to what the script of the overall plan will allow.

Another popular science fiction trilogy of films that used apocalyptic motifs is the *Terminator* series. Once more, machines are the enemy of humanity, and both are locked in a struggle for final survival. There is also ambiguity about the extent to which the future is fixed and the extent to which individual choices can affect it. In the first film, *The Terminator* (1984), Sarah Connor learns that she is targeted for death by a robot executioner from the future because she will give birth to the leader of the resistance, John Connor (note the messianic initials). A human from the future, Kyle Reese, saves her and destroys the terminator, along the way managing to impregnate her with the child who will destroy the machines. In the second film, *Terminator 2: Judgment Day* (1991), Sarah has ended up in an insane asylum after attempting to destroy the factory she believes will invent the malevolent machines. She is unwilling to blithely accept the apocalypse and all the death that will come with it, instead seeking a way to avoid the "judgment day" for humanity by preventing the rise of the machines. Her opportunity is presented when another terminator from the future comes back in time to attempt to kill her son, who is now a child, and a terminator reprogrammed to help the resistance is also sent back to save John. This "good" terminator is convinced to help them forestall the apocalypse by destroying the factory and all records of the research that will lead to the terminators. After destroying the other terminator, he destroys himself as well in a gesture of self-sacrifice that also echoes Christian themes. In the first film, Kyle Reese had given Sarah a message from her adult son in the future that is referred to again in this film and that sums up its message: "The future is not set, there's no fate but what we make." The characters have shown this is true by altering future history and the timeline for the apocalypse. The film presents a hopeful message that humans are not destined to create weapons that will result in their own self-destruction, that instead they can choose life rather than death. As Sarah, reflecting on the sacrifice of the benevolent terminator, says at the close of the film, "if a machine can learn the value of human life, maybe we can too."

Had the saga ended there, it would have had an open-ended and optimistic quality that suggests we are not predestined for destruction. The apocalyptic warning in this case functions to change behavior and so to prevent disaster, as Ebenezer Scrooge's visions change his life in *A Christmas Carol* so that the future he has foreseen never takes place.[5] But in *Terminator 3: The Rise of the Machines* (2003), the deterministic character of apocalyptic asserts itself, as we learn that catastrophe has not been avoided but only postponed. Once again, there is a bad terminator trying to kill John Connor and a good one trying to save him, but the larger plot involves the machines becoming self-aware and taking over through an unstopable computer virus that spreads everywhere. John meets his future wife, Kate Brewster, which we are also told was "destined," as it turns out they had originally met when they were both children, just before the coming of the second wave of terminators. But if John and Kate are destined to end up together to found the resistance, the machines are also destined to kill billions of people, as no one can change these facts and survival for humanity can only come at the other end of the apocalypse. There is little free will here, and no chance anymore of avoiding the apocalypse as it seemed there was in the previous film.

This last of the *Terminator* films invites comparisons with *Left Behind* both in its downbeat fatalism about total destruction and its tendency to subvert individual action by a predestined plan. One wonders why the series took this direction at this time; it might have something to do with the fact that James Cameron, who made the first two films, had much less to do with the third, but it also suggests that popular films are increasingly catering to apocalyptic fatalism and decreasing the role of individual freedom in such narratives. Just as Neo's victory over the machines in the *Matrix* films seems to have less to do with his decisions than with the destiny laid out for him, and the accidental fact that he creates and then is able to destroy Agent Smith becomes his bargaining chip with the machines, so John Connor has no real choice about his role in the final battle which has proven unavoidable.

Perhaps viewers are oddly comforted by knowing that there is a destiny planned for all, even if this undercuts free will and suggests that individuals cannot change large-scale events, because this fits with a fatalism they have already accepted. But this sense of fatalism has markedly increased since Sept. 11, 2001, and it is worth noting that the films made after this date express an increasingly apocalyptic worldview, particularly in their pessimistic determinism. This shift can also be seen by comparing the two *Star Wars* trilogies, which were the product of two very different decades in American history.

Star Wars *and Apocalyptic Fatalism*

An examination of the two *Star Wars* trilogies may give some clues to how apocalyptic themes have played out in this most popular of all movie series, as apocalyptic themes run through both. In Episodes IV-VI (1977–1983), the original trilogy, the battle is already raging between good and evil, and the rebels are clearly the underdogs. But, as the title of Episode IV indicates, there is *A New Hope* as Luke Skywalker joins the resistance. Much seems to be result of chance in this film—but not entirely. The plans for the Death Star just happen to walk onto Luke's farm (in the form of R2-D2), which results in the death of his Aunt and Uncle and his own decision to join the resistance, but this also occurred because Princess Leia is trying to get the plans to Obi Wan Kenobi, who is looking after Luke on Tatooine. Luke meets Obi Wan for the first time and is introduced to the Force, not realizing his own close link to the central personalities of the war, especially the fact that Darth Vader is his own father and Leia is his twin sister.

Still, there is apparently plenty of room for free will and chance in Episode IV. Even though Obi Wan can say, "in my experience, there's no such thing as luck," it seems to be good luck that allows Obi Wan to recruit Han Solo as a pilot, as he helps them recapture the Death Star plans and rescue Leia. Even more importantly, Han saves Luke at the end of the film when he is about to be shot down by Darth Vader, thus allowing Luke to destroy the Death Star. Without the presence of this renegade mercenary who does not even believe in the Force, it is hard to see how the resistance could have survived. One can suggest, in the manner of a true believer, that even Han is being used by the Force to accomplish good, as an "anonymous Jedi," but there is no evidence of coercion. The Force seems to allow individuals the free will to decide for or against good or evil. There is also quite a lot of room for free will regarding faith in Episode IV, as the power of the Force is seldom present in such a way as to compel belief. Obi Wan can use mind tricks on stormtroopers, and Luke can fight blindfolded as well as make a pinpoint hit on the Death Star without a targeting computer; but these do seem to be more a matter of luck than products of supernatural forces. Even when Luke hears Obi Wan's voice after his death, it is not clear to him whether he is imagining it or not.

In *Episode V: The Empire Strikes Back* (1980), however, we have more evidence of the Force's power, as Luke is able to communicate with Obi Wan more easily and from Yoda learns both telekinesis and precognition. But the emphasis on free will persists as Yoda instructs Luke that the future is not set ("always in motion is the future"), and that Luke must make his own decision about whether or not to leave his Jedi training to attempt the rescue of his friends and so expose himself to danger. Darth Vader, on the other hand, tries to convince Luke that he has no free will, as it is "useless to resist" the Dark Side for it is "his destiny" to join it. Those who follow the Dark Side, which operates on the basis of coercion, will not admit that individuals have free will in regards to it, while those who follow the Good Side insist there is always freedom and indeterminacy. Luke still believes he has a choice, but his worldview is altered by the revelation that Darth Vader is his father, as it suggests that one may make the wrong choice or lose the ability to freely choose the good. He may even fear that that his fate may be the same as his father's.

In *Episode VI: Return of the Jedi* (1983), Luke decides to go against the advice of both Obi Wan and Yoda and attempt to convert his father back to the good side. The Emperor and Darth Vader are confident that he has played into their hands and that they will easily win him over. When they fail, they are surprised. The Emperor, who has smugly been saying that everything has been going as he had foreseen it, did not foresee this failure. He reacts with rage, and his subsequent torture of Luke is the trigger that results in Darth Vader breaking free of the Emperor's grip and destroying him. It seems that not "destiny" but rather the free choices of Luke and Vader are the reason why the Empire is defeated. There is also some luck involved in bringing down the shield generator for the Death Star on the planet below, related to the unexpected strength of the Ewok attack on the stormtroopers as well as a clever ruse created by Han and Chewbacca. In this way, a number of important things prove to be unforeseen.

The first trilogy, then, sends the message that in this apocalyptic battle between good and evil all is not predestined, as the decisions of individuals to love and care for others can overcome the hatred and greed of the Dark Side. This is a considerably more upbeat message than most apocalyptic, which suggests individuals can make little difference except regarding their own lives and that there is little hope of worldly success in regards to evil. In 1978, Andrew Gordon commented on the hopefulness of *Star Wars* in relation to the times:

> We are in a period in which the heroes have been cast down through such national catastrophes as Vietnam and Watergate, when the lines between good and evil grow cloudy, and when sexual identities have been redefined by the women's movement. Meanwhile, we have created a machine world for ourselves, a world that seems drained of spiritual values, a world in which we feel impotent and alien. We desperately need a renewal of faith in ourselves as Americans, as good guys on the world scene, as men and women, as human beings who count, and so we return to the simpler patterns of the past [82].

This passage seems almost prophetic now in predicting not only the success of Ronald Reagan's presidency, appealing as he did to precisely those traditional values in an era that longed to evade the cynicism of the 1970's, but also the rise of the Christian Right (courted by Reagan), Fundamentalism, and apocalyptic. Conservative Americans choose a simplistic and dualistic worldview and react against the ambiguities of modern sexuality and secularity, viewing the world as easily divided into good and evil, democracy and terrorism. The original *Star Wars* films were not completely apocalyptic in their attention to individual freedom and values, but their triumphalist optimism and easy dualism found a receptive audience at a time when Americans desired the simplicity of mythology and its clearly delineated options. This Reaganesque optimism still finds expression in the naïve "domino theory" of democracy which drives George W. Bush's foreign policy, in his expressed hope that mideastern dictatorships will topple as people happily accept western ideology and values.[6]

But if the original *Star Wars* films resonated with Americans precisely in ways which were *not* apocalyptic in their individualism and optimism, it is worth noting that the more recent films in the series are decidedly more apocalyptic and fatalistic. Perhaps the optimism of the 1980's has left most Americans in the wake of 9/11 and an increasingly conservative America is being drawn to the determinism of apocalyptic.

At the outset, of course, one has to admit that Episodes I–III (1999–2005) are bound to seem more apocalyptic, as there are many things that are necessarily "predestined" simply because the later episodes have already been made. We already know that Obi Wan will train Anakin Skywalker and that Anakin will turn on him and join the Emperor in destroying the Jedi; that Anakin Skywalker will become Darth Vader; and that he will have two children who grow up to become Luke and Leia. But Episodes I–III bear the same gloomy fatalism we have seen in other popular apocalyptic not only because we know the ending but due to the way the story is told. For instance, Anakin's birth seems predestined, as he appears to be "the chosen one" who has been prophesied to come due to his virgin birth and high level of "Midi-Chlorians." The latter are first identified in *Episode I: The Phantom Menace* (1999) as a microscopic life form that dwells in those who can access the power of the Force. This indicates a scientific reduction of something that was understood more mystically in the original trilogy, but it also fits with modern apocalyptic's attempt to rationalistically explain everything that happens, giving it greater certainty and solidity. It is suggested that the Midi-Chlorians have "chosen" to create Anakin in this way as the one who will "bring balance to the Force," i.e., in the conflict between good and evil, Jedi and Sith lords.

Palpatine also seems to control almost everything that happens in Episodes I–III, practically erasing the importance of individual decisions. It is he, in the form of the Sith Lord Darth Sidious, who backs the Trade Federation in its bid for power but cares nothing for its success as it is only a tool to his own power. By creating enemies of the Republic, such as the Trade Federation, Palpatine can make an effective bid for power in the Senate of the Republic to the point that he is given the powers of a dictator and democracy ceases to exist. He also arranges for the creation of a clone army which Yoda and the other Jedi unwittingly accept as allies, not realizing that the army is faithful to Palpatine alone, and that they have been programmed to kill the Jedi when given "order 66" (note the resemblance to the number of the Beast in the Book of Revelation, 666).[7] Palpatine also creates and as easily disposes of apprentices to the Dark Side, such as when he arranges for Anakin to kill Count Dooku, in order to replace the latter with the former and also to increase Anakin's anger and hatred. Anakin realizes he should have taken Dooku prisoner but wantonly kills him with the encouragement of Palpatine, showing the same un-jedi-like hatred he did when he murdered the sand people who killed his mother (an act Palpatine applauds as "only natural"). Palpatine also uses Anakin's love for Padmé Amidala against him when Anakin's precognition tells him Padmé will die in childbirth and Palpatine promises to teach Anakin a way to prevent her death, utilizing the Dark Side of the Force. This proves to be Anakin's undoing when he intervenes in a battle between Palpatine and Jedi leader Mace Windu. Concerned that Palpatine will be killed and take with him the knowledge of how to save Padmé, Anakin disarms Windu, allowing Palpatine to kill the latter. At this point Anakin seems to accept that he cannot turn back; he accepts Palpatine's will, takes the name Darth Vader, and goes to execute his orders to kill the Jedi children and then the Separatist leaders. Anakin is briefly reunited with Padmé, who realizes he has turned to the

Dark Side and rejects him; Anakin's anger at this is turned towards Obi Wan, and their battle finally leaves Anakin legless and half-dead in hot lava. Palpatine saves him by constructing the robot body of Darth Vader and tells Vader untruthfully that Vader's own anger has destroyed Padmé, when in fact she has died of grief after giving birth to her twins.

Palpatine's manipulation of Anakin is so complete through all this that we can hardly blame Anakin for turning to the Dark Side. This serves the story to the extent that we can still believe that "there is still good in him," as Luke will later tell him, and as proves to be true, in the end. Anakin's seduction has to be unavoidable to the extent that it makes us feel he could not help himself; it has a tragic dimension, especially in that it is precisely Anakin's desire to avoid Padmé's death that inevitably causes it. But it also falls short of genuine tragedy in the fact that Anakin's free will is so circumscribed that it seems he could not have done otherwise at any point. He is a pawn of events rather than a tragic hero who freely chooses the destiny that destroys him. Could he have chosen not to love Padmé? Not to trust Palpatine, who acts towards him like the father he never had? Not to be angered at being separated from his mother? He was found by the Jedi late and was born with such great power that he becomes willful, disobedient and disdainful towards those with less power, such as the members of the Jedi Council. It is hard to see how he could have been different.

All this seems to contrast with the emphasis on freedom in Episodes IV–VI, which allows for Luke's decision to save his father and Vader's decision to kill Palpatine and save his son. The clever plans of the emperor, which seem inexorable in Episodes I–III, are frustrated in Episodes IV-VI by a turn none of the characters expected or could have predicted. And yet from the vantage point of the first three episodes, one could even understand Darth Vader's final rejection of the Emperor as part of the plans made by the predestinating Midi-Chlorians when they decided to create Anakin. After Anakin becomes Darth Vader in Episode III, the Jedi are amazed that the "chosen one" could turn to evil, as he was to "bring balance to the Force." But Yoda has already suggested to them, not that the prophecy may have been *wrong*, but that it may have been *misread*. This indicates that it is possible that Anakin will yet bring balance to the Force in a way that none of them can foresee, which is exactly what happens by the end of Episode VI with Anakin/Vader's destruction of the Sith. The apparently unpredictable and free character of events in the later episodes can be re-read as part of a predestined plan, set in the context of the first three episodes.

And this is how prophecy works, re-writing free will into a larger plan to erase the need for individual decision or to understand God's will to underlie the illusion of human free will. The question remains, what is the appeal of this predestinarian apocalyptic thinking today? It may be that, in an age of apparently dualistic conflict such as the post–911 world, Americans are comforted by the idea that there is a plan that has anticipated everything and that each of us has a place in that plan which is foreordained—just like Anakin and Luke Skywalker. In an age of uncertainty, the idea that we have free will and are indeterminate is not as reassuring as the hope that God has every event planned. Although the notion of divine sovereignty has always been part of Christianity, in our current culture it has been feverishly embraced as part of an apocalyptic worldview that is more popular now than ever. Products of popular culture like the *Star Wars* films did not create apocalyptic thinking, but they do further it; they also express both the fears of total destruction and the longing for a meaning that transcends this world of confused uncertainty.

The threat is that this dualistic fatalism will eclipse a belief that humans are free and that societies can change for the better, which has always been part of American thinking. The hopefulness of the original *Star Wars*, which may have served a conservative agenda at the time, today represents the sort of optimism we may need to escape an onslaught of pessimism and passivity. Although President George W. Bush speaks optimistically rather than deterministically most of the time, many of the conservative Christians who support him are drawn to a darker vision, and the larger society has begun to echo this pessimism in increasing political apathy and indifference. Popular culture is not to blame for this transition, but it is an index to the extent to which our society is increasingly accepting a fatalism in which individuals have limited influence, and most hope is deferred to the next world.

Notes

1. Episodes I–IV are on the list of the highest grossing 25 films of all time; when adjusted for inflation, Episodes I and IV-VI are still in the top twenty ("List"). This only takes account of box office revenue.

2. I dealt with apocalyptic in relation to Episodes IV-VI, primarily, in John Lyden, "The Apocalyptic Cosmology of *Star Wars*."

3. Glenn Shuck, in *Marks of the Beast*, suggested that the *Left Behind* novels in many ways function more as "adjustment narratives" than as "escape narratives" in helping conservative Christians cope with life in this world rather than prepare for another (197).

4. In what follows, I am indebted to the discussion of free will and determinism in John Stroup and Glenn W. Shuck and, in particular, their chapter provisionally entitled, "Perhaps Today: The Dialectic of Despair and Activism in Popular Evangelical Literature." The authors find the basically Arminian beliefs of American Evangelicals to be formally upheld by Dispensationalists but also that a strong determinist counterbalance exists.

5. Barbara Rossing suggests that apocalyptic is meant to function like Scrooge's dream, not as a prediction of what will be, but as an image of what could be if no changes are made (82–85).

6. For an astute analysis of how *Star Wars* reflects Reagan era values, see Michael Ryan and Douglas Kellner (228–236). I have previously criticized their analysis for reduc-

ing the films to merely conservative political ideology (see John Lyden, "To Commend or to Critique? The Question of Religion and Film Studies.") While I stand by my critique of their political reductionism, I have come to appreciate better their analysis of how popular films can express conservative political values, especially as the United States turns towards the political and religious right.

7. A host of details about Palpatine's plans are explained in fan websites such as *SuperShadow.com*.

Works Cited

Ahlstrom, Sidney E. *A Religious History of the American People*. New Haven: Yale University Press, 1972.

Boyer, Paul S. *When Time Shall Be No More: Prophecy Belief in Modern American Culture*. Cambridge: Harvard University Press, 1992.

Gordon, Andrew. "*Star Wars*: A Myth for Our Times." *Screening the Sacred: Religion, Myth, and Ideology in Popular American Film*. Eds. Joel W. Martin and Conrad E. Ostwalt, Jr. Boulder: Westview, 1995. 73–82.

JerryJenkins.com. 2005. 28 Aug. 2005. <http://www.jerryjenkins.com/>.

"List of Highest-Grossing Films." *Answers.com*. 8 Aug, 2005. <http://www.answers.com>.

Lohse, Eduard. *The New Testament Environment*. Trans. John E. Steely. Nashville: Abingdon, 1976.

Luther, Martin. "The Bondage of the Will." *Martin Luther: Selections from His Writings*. Ed. John Dillenberger. New York: Anchor, 1961. 166–203.

Lyden, John. "The Apocalyptic Cosmology of *Star Wars*." *Journal of Religion and Film* 4:1 (April 2000). <www.unomaha.edu/~wwwjrf/LydenStWars.htm>.

_____. *Film as Religion: Myths, Morals, and Rituals*. New York: NYU Press, 2003.

_____. "To Commend or to Critique? The Question of Religion and Film Studies." *Journal of Religion and Film* 2:1 (April 1998). <www.unomaha.edu/~wwwjrf/tocommend.htm>.

The Matrix Revolutions. Dir. Andy Wachowski and Larry Wachowski. 2003. DVD. Warner Home Video.

New Oxford Annotated Bible with the Apocrypha, Revised Standard Version. Eds. Herbert G. May and Bruce M. Metzger. New York: Oxford University Press, 1977.

Rossing, Barbara. *The Rapture Exposed: The Message of Hope in the Book of Revelation*. Boulder, CO: Westview, 2004.

Ryan, Michael, and Douglas Kellner. *Camera Politica: The Politics and Ideology of Contemporary Hollywood Film*. Bloomington: Indiana University Press, 1988.

Shuck, Glenn. *Marks of the Beast: The Left Behind Novels and the Search for Evangelical Identity*. New York: New York University Press, 2005.

Star Wars Episode I: The Phantom Menace. Dir. George Lucas. Screenplay by George Lucas. Twentieth Century Fox, 1999.

Star Wars Episode II: Attack of the Clones. Dir. George Lucas. Screenplay by George Lucas and Jonathan Hales. Twentieth Century Fox, 2002.

Star Wars Episode III: Revenge of the Sith. Dir. George Lucas. Screenplay by George Lucas. Twentieth Century Fox, 2005.

Star Wars Episode IV: A New Hope. Dir. George Lucas. Screenplay by George Lucas. Twentieth Century Fox, 1977.

Star Wars Episode V: The Empire Strikes Back. Dir. Irvin Kershner. Screenplay by Leigh Brackett and Lawrence Kasdan. Story by George Lucas. Twentieth Century Fox, 1980.

Star Wars Episode VI: Return of the Jedi. Dir. Richard Marquand. Screenplay by Lawrence Kasdan and George Lucas. Story by George Lucas. Twentieth Century Fox, 1983.

Stroup, John, and Glenn Shuck. *Escape into the Future*. Waco: Baylor University Press, 2007 (forthcoming).

SuperShadow.com. 2005. 28 Aug. 2005 <http://www.supershadow.com/ starwars/jedi_sith. html>.

Terminator 2: Judgment Day. Dir. James Cameron. 1991. DVD. Artisan, 1997.

3

The *Star Wars* Trilogies and Global Capitalism

CARL SILVIO

Introduction

Given the enormous popularity and commercial success of George Lucas's *Star Wars* trilogies, it is not surprising that the franchise has attracted a great deal of scholarly attention. But while many critical examinations of the *Star Wars* trilogies have described their subject in terms of the mythic trans-cultural patterns that films embody and reproduce, surprisingly few have attempted to understand these films in terms of the specific cultural context that produced them. Surely, the films' popularity indicates that they resonate with audiences on a variety of levels in addition to the mythic, and yet the history of scholarship on them reveals a dearth of criticism that accounts for their popularity in terms of how they emerge from and respond to specific social formations and trends.[1] In an attempt to do so, this essay analyzes the relationship between the two *Star Wars* trilogies and the emergence and consolidation of what is today often referred to as global capitalism. Specifically, it will examine how the two trilogies that comprise this saga both express and diffuse latent cultural anxieties about the emergence of late capitalism while naturalizing the fundamental logic and assumptions that underpin this system. The films enable viewers to imaginarily grasp their relationship to this emergent economic regime of production in a way that imaginarily resolves its inherent contradictions and makes its basic structure seem normal and correct. Because each trilogy was produced at a specific point in time that corresponds to a specific stage in the development of late capitalism, they each perform this ideological work differently. A comparison of the trilogies can thus reveal a great deal about the social attitudes, beliefs, and anxieties about late capitalism that existed at the time each trilogy was produced.

The original *Star Wars* trilogy appeared at a time of transition between an older Fordist regime of production and a newer global one, a time of economic turmoil and epistemological crisis. We will see how this trilogy metaphorically represents this developing economic system through its construction of a high-tech "globalized" galaxy filled with sublime objects of technology that function as conceptual analogues for our experience of the information age. Simultaneously, the films render this representation less threatening by effacing all evidence of the mode of production that makes such wonders possible and substitutes in its place romanticized versions of earlier modes of economic production, particularly pre-capitalism and maverick entrepreneurialism. The films thus lessen the crisis evoked by the shift to late capitalism by presenting a nostalgic vision of the past in conjunction with its visual metaphors of the future. The second, or prequel, trilogy appeared during the late 1990s at a time when the existence of a new global economy had been accepted and largely celebrated by the public. The crisis evoked by this period in late capitalism's development is not the failure of people to understand its mode of operation, but rather the failure to resolve the contradictions inherent in a "benevolent" system that supposedly benefits humanity, while it simultaneously reduces the quality of human life by subsuming all aspects of it to the logic of capital. The prequel trilogy helps to alleviate these anxieties by presenting the "good" aspects of global capital as the core values of a vast galactic republic while displacing the negative aspects of this system onto older outdated modes of production such as heavily industrialized forms of monopoly capitalism.

The Original Trilogy

During the late 1960s and early 1970s, the Fordist regime of accumulation that had dominated American economy since the end of World War II was in a state of crisis. Capital's inability to respond to foreign competition, fixed, long-term investments in large scale manufacturing, and a general trend toward overproduction all contributed to this situation. Rising inflation, the west's inability to respond to OPEC's decision to raise oil prices and the subsequent energy crisis, waves of labor unrest, the sharp recession of 1973, and New York City's declaration of bankruptcy in 1975 were just a few representative examples marking this period (Harvey 141–50). But, as it has done in the past, capital responded to this crisis by reorganizing itself. From our current historical vantage point, we can more easily see that the decade of the 1970s marked the beginning of just such a process of reorganization as capital shifted from an older mode of production to what David Harvey has described as a new regime of "flexible accumulation" (Harvey 141–50). This latest epoch goes by other names as well including "late," "third stage," "post-industrial," "multinational," or as it is more popularly known, "global" capitalism.[2] This new stage of capitalist development is obviously quite complex and cannot be thoroughly detailed here, but we can characterize it by several of its most salient features: (1) a shift from a predominantly manufacturing based, goods producing economy to an economy organized around the production and exchange of services and information, (2) the radical decentralization of production forces and financial services across the globe in ways that allow them to transcend older political boundaries, (3) the subsumption of most, if not all, aspects of human culture to the logic of capital, and (4) the proliferation of increasingly complex technologies, particularly communications technologies, that drive and enable these changes (Dyer-Witherford 17–18).

Mainstream economists often promoted, positively valorized, and theoretically justified the shift to this new capitalist regime by arguing that the trend marked the beginning of a new and advanced stage of human development that would create more equality in society and perhaps even render the entire notion of class obsolete.[3] Such ideas, often grouped together under the general heading of "neoliberal economics," would serve in large part as the ideological rationale of Reaganomics. Eventually these positive interpretations of the new mode of production began to trickle down (excuse the pun) into the general public consciousness in the form of buzz words like "information age" or "post industrial society." As the decade of the 1970s drew to a close, an overall feeling of change for the better characterized the time, a feeling that finds its most overt expression in the eventual election of Ronald Reagan as president in 1979.

But this readjustment of capital, which continues to accelerate throughout the Reagan era, also provokes a sense of crisis in a few key ways. First, and most obviously, it invokes a fear of unemployment as traditional manufacturing jobs begin to vanish in the face of a boom in lower paying service oriented and clerical work. But the shift also initiates a much more subtle crisis in the way individuals perceive, or more accurately, fail to perceive their individual relationship to the newly emerging global economic system. As the networks of power and capital that structure our lives become more decentralized and diffuse, they become less "visible," less able to be cognitively grasped and, because of this, more powerful. Global capitalism thus initiates a sense of epistemological crisis as individuals struggle understand their relationship to a network of control that is swiftly becoming the organizational foundation for all aspects of our social existence. Frederic Jameson, who equates the rise of late capitalism with the emergence of the social and cultural formation of postmodernism, describes our confrontation with this "enormous and threatening, yet only dimly perceivable, other reality of economic and social intuitions" as an encounter with the "postmodern sublime" (38). This postmodern, or what we can by extension term a "late capitalist," sublime involves the sensation of unease, uncertainty, and perhaps sometimes terror when we as individuals feel dwarfed by the vast networks of capital that not only completely structure our existence but exceed our very ability to even imagine how they function.

Thus, during the late 1970s and 1980s, a palpable contradiction comes to haunt the cultural experience of global capitalism. On the one hand, we find a general belief in society's progression into new and better period of history while, on the other, we see the suggestion of an overall sense of epistemological uncertainty in the face of the late capitalist sublime. It is precisely at this point in history that *Star Wars*, the most wildly successful film to date, bursts upon the scene. I suggest that the staggering popularity of the original film and its sequels derives in part from their capacity to tap into, express and, to some extent resolve, collective feelings and anxieties about this major economic and cultural shift. In other words, when considered in relation to its overall social context, the original *Star Wars* trilogy appears as both an expression of, and an attempt to imaginarily resolve, the contradictions evoked by this time of historical transition. At the very least, the films work exceptionally well as conceptual analogues or metaphors that precisely capture some of the most salient aspects of our experience of global capitalism.

It is really not terribly difficult to see how the *Star Wars* galaxy can function as a metaphor for a global economy. In it, Lucas presents us with a panoply of different alien races and cultures, all of which are knitted together in complex networks of trade relations. We find the clearest articulation of this sort of "global" sensibility in the Mos Eisley spaceport, located on Tatooine. Though situated in a remote corner of this fictional heterocosm, this spaceport is home to the famous cantina whose diverse clientele of various alien species metonymically represents the heteroglossic nature of the entire galaxy. Technological advancements under late capitalism have facilitated the creation and expansion of a diverse array of new markets, allowing commodities, services, fashions, and life-styles (now also functioning commodities), once available only locally, to be distributed around the globe. This dispersal, combined with the ways in which dramatic and accelerating changes in telecommunications technology have altered our experience of space, creates the sense that our world has been geographical compressed. Observers frequently cite this sensation of the local being annihilated by the global as one of the most characteristic features of late capitalism. Hence, this economic and social formation is often described in terms of collage, fragmentation, dispersal and the recombination of cultural elements all of which reflect the conditions of flexible accumulation (Harvey 302). Not only does the intensely mixed cultural flavor of the *Star Wars* galaxy metaphorically represent this aspect of late capitalist culture, but its dominant mode of travel, flight through hyperspace, similarly reflects our experience of space compression. What could possibly serve as a better analog for the ever shrinking "global village" than the way a hyperdrive engine collapses the unimaginable distances of interplanetary space into a human scale?

But the most significant parallel between the *Star Wars* universe and our own experience of global capitalism must certainly be the prevalence and fetishization of advanced and fantastic technology in the films. The importance of spectacular and highly aestheticized technologies to these films becomes apparent after just an initial, cursory viewing. Lucas and the production staff of this franchise have spent an unbelievable amount of time and energy making the starships, droids, weapons and overall technological environment of this galaxy as visually stunning as possible. Dan Rubey, writing shortly after the original release of Episode IV, recognizes the centrality of the representation of imaginary technology to the film's aesthetic: "The visual aesthetic of *Star Wars* is a machine aesthetic, one that invests machine surfaces with the life and interest denied human forms" (83). The real visual pleasure of *Star Wars* then involves the pleasure of looking at the gadgetry, but why should such an aesthetic gain such traction in the public's imagination at this particular historical juncture?

I suggest that, while breakthrough advancements in special effects wizardry contribute to the films' overall appeal by simply creating a "really cool" visual surface, the proliferation of high-tech and fantastic machines also works as a powerful metaphor for conflicting cultural attitudes toward global capital. Jameson argues that cultural representations of advanced technologies often serve as metaphors, or conceptual approximations, of our attempts to understand the elusive complexities of the global networks of power and control that structure our world. According to him, the fascination with technology in late capitalist culture grows directly out of our experience of this postmodern sublime. Such technology "is therefore mesmerizing and fascinating not so much in its own right but because it seems to offer some representational shorthand for grasping a network of power and control even more difficult for our minds and imaginations to grasp: the whole new decentered global network of the third [late] stage of capital itself" (37–38). The unbelievable technologies of *Star Wars* work in a similar way, as expressions, that is, of the sense of wonder and fear that we feel when confronting global capitalism.

Moreover, they represent our attempts to imaginatively represent that which is unrepresentable, namely the scope of capital which has expanded beyond a human scale of perception. Joseph Tabbi's excellent research on the postmodern sublime corroborates this idea. He argues that the representation of "[s]uch transcendental technology has its economic correlative ... in a culture where technological advances come to represent advances in consciousness even though such technological processes need not be grasped, and often could not ever *be* grasped by any one human mind" (9). This capacity of technology to represent abstract economic relations and allow us to visualize social relations may explain the appeal and the power of Episode IV's opening shot. Who can forget the thrill of seeing the impossible and terrifying immensity of the Darth Vader's Imperial Star Destroyer for the first time, so huge that its dimensions easily exceeded the frame's capacity to contain it, as it bears down upon Princess Leia's Rebel Blockade Runner. This shot captivated audiences to such an extent that it inaugurated a tradition in *Star Wars* films, which have subsequently all opened with a shot of a spacecraft gleaming against the backdrop of space. The opening scene of *A New Hope* enthralls us, in part, because it invites us to invest it with both our fascination and fears of late capitalist techno culture. I believe this investment explains audiences' overall preoccupation with the technologies of the *Star Wars* universe which often, though not always, appear to be, like global capital itself, so much vaster than the sentient beings who supposedly control it. Consider the planet sized immensity of the Death Star or the enormity of the cloud city on Bespin in *Episode V: The Empire Strikes Back*. What could serve as a more apt metaphor for a world subsumed by the logic of capital than the Death Star, a world that actually is entirely manufactured and therefore a commodity, or at least an enormous assemblage of commodities, in its own right? Or take for example Luke Skywalker's famous duel with Vader on Bespin in *The Empire Strikes Back*. At one critical point in this light saber battle, Skywalker finds himself dangling above the seemingly bottomless hollow core of Bespin's Cloud City, a gigantic expanse of cold and inhuman industrial landscape looming behind and beneath him. The camera shoots him from above, highlighting the unfathomable nature of the depths that yawn beneath him. This shot emphasizes the vulnerability of his human form by juxtaposing it with this monstrous engine of capitalism that threatens to devour it. Cloud City is, after all, a commercial mining facility.

The original trilogy abounds with such instances in which technology practically cries out for interpretation as metaphor for our experience of late capitalism and, at times, the parallels seem obvious. Consider for instance Han Solo's freezing in the carbonite chamber on Bespin in *Empire Strikes Back*. In this scene, Darth Vader has Solo turned into a kind of living, hibernating statue in order to trade him to Boba Fett in payment for Fett's help in tracking the rebels to Bespin. Fett, in turn, intends to sell Solo to the Smuggler chief, Jabba the Hutt in order to collect a bounty. Solo has thus been literally turned into a commodity and his humanity reduced to a physical object that can be bought, sold, and exchanged on the market. This sequence of events of events can be read as a perfect literalization of Marx's argument concerning "real subsumption," that capital will eventually subsume all facets of human life to its logic. Marx, of course, argued that as capitalism evolves, all aspects of human life—science, art, leisure time, family life, etc—become increasingly understood in terms of their relation to the world of commerce (1026–40). Many contemporary theorists and cultural analysts locate the ultimate culmination of this trend in our own contemporary moment, in which it is almost impossible to imagine a single instance of our existences that cannot be understood somehow as an expression of exchange value and therefore sold on the market.[4] One of the best contemporary examples of real subsumption can be found in the famous MasterCard television commercials that present us with a list of commodities and their respective prices, followed by the revelation of some "special" moment of human interaction that transcends the logic of exchange value and is thus priceless. Of course, the commercials imply that it is the purchasing of the various commodities that actually enables the experiencing of this moment, thus in effect, nullifying its priceless status. In our current phase of late capitalism, even supposedly "priceless," formerly nonexchangist, moments of human experience can be realized as a expressions of exchange value, a cultural development represented in *The Empire Strikes Back* by the image of Solo's life literally frozen in a block of carbonite and sold like a thing on the market.

It could be argued, of course, that the original *Star Wars* trilogy works as an overt critique of capital based on the fact that most of these examples of the technological sublime are associated with the Empire. Lucas's attempts to draw parallels between the Empire and capitalism lead Kevin J. Wetmore, for instance, to use the term "capitalistic" to define the Empire's relentlessly imperialistic nature (99). Based on such an observation, we might be tempted to read the trilogy as a critique of capitalism. But while I agree that the original trilogy *does* narratively couple its representations of advanced capitalism to the Empire's blatantly evil policies, we should not assume that this necessarily translates into a straightforward condemnation of capitalism. To do so would be to ignore the incredibly heightened, scopophilic[5] pleasure and fascination that we feel when we gaze upon the images of technological sublimity that pack these films. In other words, while the films may link these images of technology to the idea of evil at the level of plot, the audience does not necessarily experience them as entirely repellant. Though impossible to measure, whatever moral abhorrence we may have for these images is probably exceeded by the sheer visual pleasure that they provide us with. Rubey recognizes this fact when he observes that "[i]n *Star Wars* the special effects—the speed, lasers explosions, the jump into hyperspace, the noise—excite and satisfy the audience almost apart from any connection to the narrative line" (85). Anyone who doubts this need only ask a hard-core *Star Wars* fan if knowing that the Imperial AT-AT Walkers in the Battle of Hoth serve the forces of evil makes them any less cool to look at. I argue that this scopophilic pleasure, aptly described by Rubey, reflects how the technology of the *Star Wars* universe works as a visual approximation for an array of cultural attitudes toward the rise of global capitalism. These attitudes range from fascination, to fear, to awe, to the struggle and failure to comprehend it in its awesome global totality.

Yet, while these films certainly capture and reflect our collectively anxieties concerning this crisis in the knowable, they also contain elements that seem to deflect them as well. In other words, the original *Star Wars* trilogy not only expresses society's contradictory feelings about the rise of late capitalism in the mid to late 1970s, but also helps to naturalize this emergent system of economic organization by making it seem normal, correct and inevitable. Such naturalization takes place largely through a process of familiarization in which elements that seem comforting and recognizable are deployed in conjunction with those that evoke the sublime. In a superficial sense, the films accomplish this by making their representations of technology look as realistic and believable as possible. Lucas went to great lengths to insure that the technology in the films looked worn, used, and lived in to increase its sense of realism. Furthermore, chief sound engineer Ben Burtt delights in explaining how almost of all the sounds made by the technology of *Star Wars* were originally recorded from real world sources, a technique that helps to bolster the reality effect that they produce (Lucas, "Commentary" *Star Wars: Episode IV*). This juxtaposition of the credible and the incredible can be read not only as an additional metaphor for our attempts to grasp the experience of sublimity coincident with the advent of global capitalism but also as an attempt to normalize it. This is part of the ideological work performed by these films; they represent our experience of late capitalism and naturalize that experience by articulating that representation as somewhat familiar.

Of course, the conflation of the alien and the familiar is by no means something that Lucas invented. We find this practice at work as a hallmark and goal of most, if not all, science fiction films ever made (Sobchack 88). One might argue that one of the chief pleasures for a science fiction audience arises from the sensation of paradox engendered by the cinematic conjunction of the fantastically alien presented in a form that renders it oddly familiar. *Star Wars*, however, accomplishes this objective to a degree not even approached by earlier films. It succeeds because of the incredible conceptual "distance" that Lucas manages to create for us between the fantastic and the believable in his imaginary technological creations. Never before had a science fiction film made the utterly fantastic appear *so* believable (or alternately, the familiar seem so utterly fantastic). Obviously, technological developments in the field of special effects, combined with the Lucas' brilliant visual imagination, enabled the first *Star Wars* trilogy to take an inherent feature of all science fiction film to such an entirely new plane. But while this advancement should certainly interest us for its significance as part of the history of film, in this context it reveals something especially significant about the production of ideology that accompanied the emergence of global capitalism.[6]

This process of familiarization, in which conceptual stand-ins for late capitalist advances are rendered less threatening, also works on another less obvious level. The original S*tar Wars* trilogy also makes its elaborate metaphor for global capitalism seem more familiar by completely eliding any representation of a means of production or economic system that could make such a universe possible. In other words, we see little evidence of how these fascinating technologies could actually be produced by this fictional universe. I am not talking here about the representation of factories and such, though the original trilogy offers few examples of this sort. Rather, I refer to the fact that the culture of the *Star Wars* universe, or what we see of it on screen, seems to in no way correspond to our "real-world" expectations of the social and economic conditions necessary to produce such technology. In place of such a "realistic" social context, the trilogy offers its audience a nostalgic vision of earlier capitalist or pre-capitalist modes of production as a substitution for the late capitalist one that frustrates our powers to understand it.

This substitution is responsible for much of this fictional heterocosm's "feel" and "flavor" and may also explain the incredible feeling of originality that it provoked in early audiences. I believe that a significant part of what makes the *Star Wars* universe seem so distinct and so compelling to main stream audiences arises from its conflation of highly technology with elements suggesting early capitalism and feudalism.[7] For instance, the first planet we see in the series is Tatooine, whose inhabitants often ride on domesticated animals, use beasts of burden, and participate in a low scale economy of barter and trade that seems to be the planet's main economic base. Such elements appear strangely incongruous alongside of the planet's equally prevalent starships and repulsorlift powered land-speeders. Early in *A New Hope*, we are introduced to the

Jawas, desert scavengers who essentially engage in the junk trade. When we see Luke's Uncle Owen haggling over the price of a scavenged C-3PO with a Jawa trader, we could be witnessing an example of how business was commonly done a century ago, if not earlier. All of Tatooine's inhabitants seem to conduct business in this way, in a face to face manner as they haggle over the exchange of concrete, tangible goods. Such market relations in no way reflect the sort of economic base that a civilization would need to produce an interstellar starship. Bear in mind that these early scenes on Tatooine immediately follow the opening sequence that prominently features the looming technological grandeur of an Imperial Star Destroyer, thereby heightening the disjunctive effect arising from the conflation of the new and the nostalgic.

I realize, of course, that Star Destroyers are not produced on Tatooine and that the desert planet lies on the fringes of "civilization" in the *Star Wars* galaxy; the empire manufactures such monstrosities elsewhere. It also seems fairly clear that Lucas has self-consciously placed certain motifs in opposition with one another as part of his mythic vision: high versus low tech, impenetrable bureaucracy versus face to face human interaction, the center versus the margin, etc. Moreover, I realize that he has mapped the overarching theme of good versus evil onto to these oppositions in a move that may entice some to read the trilogy as critique of advanced capitalism. But I am not as concerned with how the films' plots are driven by the conflicts arising from these thematic oppositions as I am by how they function together as signifiers that help us understand and experience the entire *Star Wars* universe as a credible fictional place. These elements which represent both high and low technology operate synecdochally; from these small pieces of a larger whole we must imaginatively project an entire fictional ontology. But as signifiers, these elements semiotically participate in and reference systems of meaning that exist in the real world outside the film and can thus connote ideas and cultural attitudes concerning social formations like economic systems. In order to construct a coherent fictional ontology from these signifiers, we must imagine a late capitalist galaxy that coexists with a nostalgic version of older modes of economic production. In other words, we must imagine a logical relationship between two somewhat antithetical systems, one familiar and one alienating. This process of imaginarily reconciling these systems so that they form a coherent whole helps to normalize our experience of late capitalism. It is beside the point then that we can ultimately create a plausible justification for this conjunction of early and advanced modes of capitalism in the *Star Wars* galaxy. More to the point is that a fantastically popular blockbuster film like this invites us to perform such an imaginative operation at this particular moment of historical and economic transition.

By analyzing the films in this way, I am, in effect, privileging the "form" of the *Star Wars* universe over its narrative "content." As Slavoj Žižek stresses, when conducting an ideological analysis of a textual phenomenon, we should not be seduced into thinking that an analysis of the text's content yields more fruitful results than an analysis of its form. He claims that both Freud and Marx, perhaps the two most influential pioneers in modern ideological and textual analysis, emphasize the importance of *form* over content; for Freud it was the form of the dream that was most important in dream analysis, for Marx the form of the commodity. This crucial homology serves as a key link between their respective theories. Žižek argues that "In both cases [Freud and Marx] the point is to avoid the properly fetishistic fascination of the 'content' supposedly hidden behind the form: the 'secret' to be unveiled through analysis is not the content hidden by the form (the form of commodities, the form of dreams) but, on the contrary, *the 'secret' of the form itself*" (11). While it is never easy to accurately or definitively separate form from content, and while the comments of Žižek, Freud, or Marx on this subject are certainly up for debate and interpretation, I propose that the entire filmic heterocosm—the diegetic space—within which these stories take place can arguably function, in this context, as the "form" of the original trilogy.[8] The stories themselves, that is, the specific plots of the *Star Wars* films similarly stand as its narrative content.

If we confine our analysis exclusively to an examination of how Lucas has narratively pitted signs associated with late capitalism against those that evoke earlier epochs, then the original trilogy certainly can look like a critique of advanced capitalism.[9] But if we look more closely into the "secret," to use Žižek's term, that underlies the construction of this universe and avoid fetishizing the films' narrative content, the situation becomes more complex. The form of the *Star Wars* universe is characterized by the intersection of two systems of signs, each of which is semiotically associated alternate versions of capitalism. Though, in the audience's reality, these registers often signify contradiction, they work logically together within the films as key components of a credible and ontologically coherent imaginary universe. By thus providing, or asking us to provide, an imaginary resolution to the contradiction implied by these registers, the original trilogy helps us to imaginarily resolve the dilemma posed by late capitalism. In other words, it helps us to imagine our relationship to the real conditions of our social and economic reality in a way that seems less alienating. Through the simultaneity of its deployment of images associated with both early and late capitalism, the films help us to imagine a comforting and representationally stable version of our own contemporary moment.

Throughout the original trilogy, Lucas inserts an assortment of nostalgic references to early stages of capital's development within his high-tech "global" galaxy. We find two obvious ones in the characters of Han Solo and Lando Calrissian, swashbuckling businessmen with hearts of gold who represent the maverick spirit that we associate with entrepreneurial capitalism. By pursuing their individual desires to make profit they ultimately achieve success. Note that, in these characters, we always find the mercenary drive to make money counterbalanced with a genuine respect and concern for the welfare of others. One moment that illustrates such a tendency occurs when Calrissian expresses concern over the Empire's threat to the mining facility that he owns on Bespin. Rather than being anxious about the obviously looming profit loss, his first concern is to his workers. He says "I don't want anything to happen to all that we've built here." While this sentiment certainly makes the character appealing, Calrissian, with his "people before profits" attitude does not really seem credible as somebody running a gigantic production facility like the one we see on Bespin. In our world, such operations inevitably require intricate and, correspondingly alienating, bureaucratic systems in order to function, systems that often seem more dehumanizing than empowering. Yet, in the case of the *Star Wars* universe, we must imagine that this vast commercial enterprise is run by Calrissian, a single charismatic entrepreneur, an owner/manager with moxy, charm, and a healthy does of compassion. This image of the capitalist entrepreneur who cares just, if not more, about his team of employees and his community than he does his profits is frequently invoked and used today by multinational corporations who seek to associate its "feel good" connotations with their own public image. They do so even as real wages sink from year to year and more and more core jobs within such organizations are outsourced. The original *Star Wars* trilogy performs a similar association by consistently juxtaposing this non–threatening entrepreneurial image with metaphors for the technological sublime that evoke global capital.

Even the entrepreneurs who *are* threatening, in the films, still help to counterbalance the epistemological threat posed by late capitalism. Take for instance, Jabba the Hut. Even though Jabba sits at the center of and controls an enormous galactic smuggling network, he seems awfully small scale. Within his fortress, surrounded by a score or two of thugs, Jabba seems more like a local gang leader than the nerve center of a system whose power presumably stretches across the galaxy. In this sense, he represents our desires to imagine that such networks of power actually *have* centers. The networks of finance and power in our late capitalist world evoke anxiety because we cannot even begin to understand them. After all, how can we resist or challenge what we cannot even imaginatively grasp. Jabba thus comforts us as an enemy who we know, at least in theory, how to deal with. Thus, even though on one level the plot inscribes Jabba as thoroughly evil, there may be something paradoxically reassuring about him in so far as he expresses our need to believe that we can ultimately find something tangible and concrete at the heart of contemporary systems of corporate power. The Hutt's massive corpulent bulk, his sheer material excess, and the fact that we never see him move in the original trilogy make him an ideal vehicle to embody our desires for such epistemological solidity. At the very least, whether the original trilogy's entrepreneurs fight for good or evil, they are all characterized by an abundance of *personality* that "humanizes" them (even Jabba) and lends a sense of conceptual familiarity to the business that they conduct. This, in turn, counterbalances the uncertainty evoked by the metaphors of the sublime that we encounter elsewhere in this universe.

In addition to providing us with nostalgic images of entrepreneurial capitalism, the films also show pre-capitalist, pre-industrial societies interacting and competing on a somewhat equal footing with the universe's advanced capitalist inhabitants. Here, I primarily refer to the Ewoks, those loveable stone-age creatures from *Episode VI: Return of the Jedi* who manage to defeat, or at least crucially hold off, the Imperial garrison on Endor that guards the shield generators protecting the Emperor's new Death Star. Through its representation of this military feat, the film implies that late capitalism may be vulnerable to a threat from outside itself. At the very least, we might be tempted to argue that the film imagines an equivalence between the heretofore inconceivable power of capital and that of earlier modes of social organization. But again, we must be careful to avoid such a surface level reading. I would argue instead that, on the basis of its portrayal of the Ewoks, we can rightly include *Return of the Jedi* in that category of art commonly known as "primitivism." This type of art is usually characterized by its representations of and fascination with so-called "primitive" cultures. A primitivist art work typically presents the primitive as an imaginary Other that supposedly inverts the values or ideological assumptions of its own historical moment. Marianna Torgovnick, in her landmark study of primitivism, argues that representations of the primitive "usually begin by defining it as different from (usually opposite to) the present. After that, reactions to the present take over. Is the present too materialistic? Primitive life is not—it is a precapitalist utopia in which only use value, never exchange value prevails" (8). It is important to realize, however, that such utopian versions of the primitive are always constructions, fictions, and imaginary alternatives to the contemporary moment.[10]

By drawing upon and mobilizing a complex set of cultural images and clichés that signify the primitive in our own cultural imagination—

stone headed spears, loin cloths, teeth necklaces, quaint "witch doc-
tors"—*Return of the Jedi* replicates this very process. It appeals to our
fantasies that the global power of capital—the system—can be overthrown
by those who otherwise seem to be completely dominated by it. It thus
asks us to imagine a utopian alternative to the world that the empire
metaphorically represents. But even this imagined alternative to late capitalism should not be interpreted as any real meaningful critique. The
culture of the Ewoks, after all, works much like other forms of utopian
nostalgia; it represents our longing for an inaccessible past that never was
and which thus offers no meaningful solution. Moreover, this representation actually provokes within us an awareness of the *inaccessibility* of
this past and, in so doing, highlights the very absence of our object of
desire. Uses of the primitive that seem to critique capitalism may actually reinforce it by providing ideological "safety valves" that imaginarily
satisfy our wishes concerning the vulnerability of late capitalism, while
simultaneously figuring this vulnerability as completely outside our lived
reality.[11] Though, in one sense, we may take pleasure in watching the
Ewoks destroy a great deal of Imperial hardware, in another and I suggest more crucial one, we really take pleasure in imagining a universe in
which such a conflict is even possible. But in doing so, we must inevitably
recognize that this act of resistance can *only* take place within the realm
of fantasy. In this way, the film helps to make our relationship to late capitalism more livable; it allows us to imagine the theoretical *possibility* of
resistance while simultaneously realizing that the conditions that would
enable it remain palpably absent from our world.

The Prequels

In the previous section, I argued that the original *Star Wars* can be
read as both a reflection of and an attempt to imaginarily resolve the contradictions inherent in the experience of late capitalism during the late
1970s and early 1980s. In short, a profound sense of epistemological uncertainty contradicted the promise associated with this cultural shift. By the
time of the *Star Wars* prequel trilogy's release in 1999, late capitalism
could no longer really be experienced as a "new" cultural phenomenon.
During the intervening years separating the two trilogies, the Soviet
Union collapsed and Francis Fukuyama, in *The End of History and the
Last Man*, infamously declared that we had arrived at the end of history.
Strongly influenced by Hegel, he argued that the lengthy series of strug-
gles, conflicts and revolutions that make up human history represent a tele-
ological progression toward increasingly free and equitable human society.
For Fukuyama, the ultimate culmination of this progression realizes itself

in the form of our current late, capitalist, information society. While he may not have been widely read by the general public, I believe his ideas express a kind of general zeitgeist of the time, an attitude reinforced by the explosion of the internet, the increasing popularity of the stock market and securities trading, and the expansion of capital into more and more sectors of our daily lives. In short, by the late 1990s, global capitalism had become a virtually unquestioned, unexamined reality for most Americans; it was "of course" the most natural and obviously correct way for a society (or planet) to be organized.

This is not to say that global capital does not still provoke feelings of anxiety given its sheer scale and the way it continues to resist conceptual representation. But we have lived with this feeling of sublimity for several decades now and, consequently, find its existence has been somewhat normalized. Despite this, the logic of any capitalist system still remains marked by internal contradictions, contradictions that the products of the mass media and culture industry often attempt to resolve. I suggest that the chief contradiction of this later period lies in the dissonance that many Americans feel between the supposedly benevolent and progressive nature of our new global economy and the way that this economy does not always appear to benefit the middle or working classes of the country. Over the course of the 1980s and 1990s, wages for working Americans consistently fell in relation to the cost of living, a trend offset in most cases by employees working longer and longer hours. Between 1989 and 1997, the earnings of a median American worker fell 3.1 percent, the income of a median American family declined by 2.1 percent, while the amount of time that such a family spent at work increased by six weeks per year. This steady erosion of middle and working class wealth occurred while the general productive capacity of the economy grew by eight percent and the average salary of CEOs more than doubled (Mishel). And yet we find ourselves constantly bombarded with hype about how the new information age, systems thinking, and globalization are revolutionizing our world for the better. For instance, in spite of what these economic trends seem to indicate for the future of the working and middle classes of America, Edward Simon president of Herman Miller, can actually argue that "[b]usiness is the only institution that has a chance, as far as I can see, to fundamentally improve the injustice that exists in the world" (qtd. in Senge 5).

The *Star Wars* prequel trilogy both reflects and offers an imaginary resolution to the contradiction implied by this statement and hundreds like it. It does so through its deployment of visual metaphors which express and help to contain our attitudes toward these economic realities and global capital itself. The most salient of these metaphors is the Galactic Republic's capital city of Coruscant. We would be hard pressed

to imagine a more visually stunning and conceptually perfect metaphor
for the supposedly positive aspects of global capital than what Lucas has
provided us with in this city.[12] Given that the image of the urban sky-
scraper has become synonymous with the idea of corporate power in late
capitalist America, we cannot look at its infinite skyline and not think of
the world of commerce. This connection between the image of the contemporary urban skyline and the power of global capitalism is made
explicit by Robert Goldamn of *The Landscapes of Global Capital* web
project:

> a standard image in the construction of urban landscapes is [the] cor-
> porate skyline shot. This scene features an imposing phalanx of cor-
> porate towers that looks rather like a postcard shot—panoramic,
> inspiring, professionally framed. As a symbol for corporate capital,
> this imagery makes sense insofar as scenes like this represent an enor-
> mous concentration of corporate capital and condensation of space.

The visual construction of Coruscant as an endless, abstract, Manhattan-
esque skyline, interlaced with seemingly infinite streams of starship traffic,
serves this exact symbolic function by semiotically linking the city to
popular ideas surrounding capitalism and commerce. Moreover, the city
of Coruscant suggests the *totality* of global capital by virtue of the fact
that it encompasses the entire planet for which it is named. The importance of this urban splendor to the overall mood of the prequel trilogy
becomes especially apparent in *Episode II: Attack of the Clones* and *Episode
III: Revenge of the Sith*. In these films, Lucas seems to shoot as many
scenes as possible "against" the technologically saturated background of
Coruscant's cityscape. Often revealed by gigantic picture windows, the
planet-city's endless streams of starship traffic and excruciatingly intricate architecture serve as the visual backdrop of many scenes, often over-
shadowing the actor's who perform before them. In *Episode III*, more than
half of the interior scenes that take place on Coruscant are shot in this
way. Even when Lucas excludes the urban skyline from the mise-en-
scene, he more often than not uses it for an establishing shot that sets
up the interior scene that follows. The ubiquity of these richly digitized,
corporate backgrounds calls to mind the continuous networks of commerce and finance that knit our own globe together and remind us of
how they similarly form an invisible backdrop to our daily lives.

As such a globalized world, Coruscant embodies and cinematically
literalizes the experience of space in late capitalism as explained by Henri
Lefebvre in his classic study on the subject. He claims:

> Capitalism and neo-capitalism have produced an abstract space that
> is a reflection of the world of business on both a national and inter-
> national level, as well as the power of money and the 'politique' of

the state. This abstract space depends on vast networks of banks, businesses, and great centres of production. There is also the spatial intervention of highways, airports, and information networks. In this space, the cradle of accumulation, the place of richness, the subject of history, the centre of historical space, in other words, the city, has exploded.

In his presentation of the incredibly arresting vistas of Coruscant, I believe that Lucas has precisely captured the "exploded" quality that Lefebvre describes. Coruscant, as a metaphor for the late capitalist city, and like late capitalism itself, overwhelms us with its density of meaning and information and assumes a scale that lies beyond our powers of comprehension. But whereas the original trilogy narratively linked its metaphors for global capital to evil, here such conceptual stand-ins for the sublime are overtly figured as "good." Coruscant is after all the center of a benevolent (if somewhat ineffectual) galactic republic, the very thing that Palpatine eventually supplants with his evil empire. Few people would want to live on the Death Star, but many might want to be a resident of Coruscant.

But if Coruscant functions as a positive metaphor for globalization and late capitalism, then how do we account for the evil entities that the films array against the Galactic Republic like the Trade Federation, the droid foundries of Geonosis, the Techno Union, or the Banking Clan? Because so many of the prequel trilogy's villains assume the form of commercial institutions, *Episodes I-III* may upon first examination appear to explicitly reject, or at least call into question, the values currently associated with capital. This is how Anne Lancashire reads *Attack of the Clones*. She argues that the film's use of overtly capitalistic institutions as its villains "provides a scathing indictment of the toxic combination of greed and political ambition that ... has brought America, over the past year or so, the corporate scandals of all of Enron, Arthur Andersen, Tyco World Com and more" (236). For Lancashire, the use of commercial institutions as the film's villains reflects the public's growing concern with the ethics of global capital. While I agree with her connection of the film to the economic climate of the late 1990s, I disagree with her over the assessment its ideological effects.

I argue instead that the casting of the Trade Federation (and organizations like it) as evil in the prequel trilogy does not so much represent a critique of capitalism as it does a *displacement* of the negative effects of late capitalism onto older and outmoded forms of monopoly capitalism. In other words, while the Trade Federation certainly serves as a metaphor for capitalism, it is less likely to evoke the current epoch of capital than the "bad," old style of capitalism that global capital has supposedly liberated us from. A perfect illustration of this effect occurs in *Attack of the*

Clones when Anakin Skywalker's hand is severed on the Geonosian assembly line only to be replaced by a mechanical one. This scene reproduces a motif that recurs throughout the entire *Star Wars* epic, the transformation of the human into the mechanical and the threat to an overall sense of human value that this suggests. Clearly, in this case, the transformation can be read as a powerful linkage between capitalism, symbolized by the droid factory, and it's potentially dehumanizing effects. By showing Anakin literally going down an assembly line, which not-so coincidentally produces mechanical beings, Lucas tries to explicitly connect the theme of dehumanization to the idea of mass production and heavy industry. But, by evoking an earlier epic of capital in order to make this linkage, the film undercuts its intended critique.

In other words, throughout the prequel trilogy, the capitalistic villains are portrayed in terms of images and ideas that semiotically evoke and reference the "dark ages" of fixed capital and heavy industry: assembly lines, the desire to monopolize trade, the bosses (Neimoidians) who oversee the entire operation from a lofty position of hierarchical superiority, etc. But this regime of production and accumulation has largely been devalued in our world. While managerial and manufacturing processes associated with fixed capital certainly still exist in our society, modern corporations no longer tend to reference them for advertising purposes or as part of their promotional rhetoric designed to celebrate globalization. Thus, in the prequel trilogy, all that we fear about global capital, namely its dehumanizing effects, is displaced onto a metaphoric substitute for an economic system and philosophy more reminiscent of older and now unfashionable versions of capitalism associated with fixed accumulation, Fordism, and the philosophies of F. W. Taylor.

Thus, while the prequel trilogy does launch a critique of the dehumanizing effects of capital, it harmlessly directs its opposition against a form of capitalism that no longer exists for the most part. This displacement of counter hegemonic energy really works then as a form of containment that jettisons the dehumanizing aspects of global capital and attaches them to the scapegoat of monopoly capitalism, thereby allowing the supposedly "good" aspects of capital to remain conceptually "uncontaminated." Critics who read the prequel trilogy as an anti-capitalist critique fail to realize that all the scenes of Coruscant, whose urban landscape looks like a spectacularly "exploded" composite of all the world's financial centers, metaphorically represent capitalism just as much as the droid foundries or the Trade Federations mass produced workers. The difference is that we are supposed to *like* the version of capitalism projected by Coruscant. More exactly, the film causes us to misrecognize this city as a metaphor for capitalism at all, and to perceive it instead as simply part of the lived reality, or the *form*, of the *Star Wars* universe.

By comparing certain key features of the two *Star Wars* trilogies to each other and to the cultural moments that produced them, we can discern several interesting parallels between the films and the emergence of global capital. I do not wish to suggest that analyzing these films in terms of economics and other related social forces provides the only possible, or even the best, way to account for their popularity. But I do believe that certain matters of plot and form in the *Star Wars* saga reveal a great deal about the variety of ways in which an enormously popular narrative like this participates in the overall production of social meaning and serves as a crucial site of ideological investment. Of course, to read the films in this way goes against the grain of most political criticism on *Star Wars* that wants to see them as politically progressive. As I have noted, the trilogies contain several narrative and thematic elements that definitely support such interpretations when considered from certain vantage points. Such elements undoubtedly exist because Lucas has put them there as part of an attempt to make films that critique the status quo and contemporary American hegemony as much as they entertain. But the fact that Lucas apparently intends *Star Wars* as a critique of dominant ideology does not invalidate my argument as much as it simply indicates the complexity and contradictory nature of ideology itself. I read *Star Wars* as an intricate and subtle response to global capital that simultaneously critiques and ideologically naturalizes it. The saga, as an expression of late twentieth and early twenty first century culture, is thus decidedly overdetermined; it represents and embodies a convergence of multiple and often contradictory societal beliefs, attitudes, and desires. *Star Wars*, like global capital itself, resists attempts to intellectually grasp it. But in so doing, the trilogies show us just how ambiguous our relationship to ideology can be.

Notes

1. There are of course some noteworthy exceptions to this trend. See, for instance, Dan Rubey's "*Star Wars* 'Not So Long Ago, Not So Far Away'"; Anne Lancashire's "*Attack of the Clones* and the Politics of *Star Wars*"; Kevin J. Wetmore, Jr.'s *The Empire Triumphant" Race Religion and Rebellion in the* Star Wars *Films*; and Tom Carson's "Jedi Uber Alles."
2. This concept was first described and theorized in 1975 by Ernest Mandel in his influential work *Late Capitalism*.
3. The most famous of these arguments is made by Daniel Bell in *The Coming of Post-Industrial Society*.
4. See, for instance, Michael Hardt and Antonio Negri's *Empire*.
5. In using this term, I am specifically thinking of how it was first used by Christian Metz in his classic essay, "History/Discourse: Note of Two Voyeurisms." Therein, he argues that this pleasure in looking derives from the spectator's unconscious experience of the screen images as projections of his or her own fantasy (24).
6. To be sure, it is not so much this particular advancement in film making itself, but the *historical context* surrounding its invention, that resonates so strongly as an ideological

response to late capitalism. In other words, these films do not invite us to ideologically link them to the emergence of late capitalism because of any sense of breakout originality they may have. Rather, we are encouraged to make this linkage by the fact that they invent new and more realistic cinematic for juxtaposing the familiar and the strange at *this* particular historical moment.

7. This is of course not particularly new in and of itself. Frank Herbert's *Dune* performed a similar conflation as did many "Saturday matinee" style space operas upon which *Star Wars* was based. Lucas, however, used advances in special effects technology to realize this type futuristic medieval universe in a way that had never been done before. *Star Wars* thus struck audiences as extremely novel.

8. "Form," in this context, should not be entirely equated with "setting." The form of the *Star Wars* universe, as I define it, certainly includes the immediate setting of Lucas's stories, but also includes the overall imaginary cultural context of that universe, its values, ideologies, and basic underlying assumptions. These characteristics may be *implied* by the films as well as directly represented on screen.

9. For a seminal discussion of how nostalgia can serve a conservative agenda that may ultimately reinforce the logic of capital, even when purporting to resist it, see Raymond Williams's *The Country and the City*.

10. For a related discussion of how the Ewoks can be read as part of this history of primitivism in Western art see Wetmore's *The Empire Triumphant* (174–76).

11. In a way, the Ewoks serve this purpose in a double sense in that, as a race that never existed, they are a fictionalized version of a cultural cliché that is itself always a fiction. They are thus doubly removed from reality.

12. For quite some time, critics have interpreted and analyzed fictional representations of the urban environments as expressions of cultural attitudes towards modern society and capitalism. See, for instance, Leonard Sharpe and William Wallock's *Visions of the Modern City* as well as Mark Shiel and Tony Fitzmaurice's *Screening the City*.

Works Cited

Althusser, Louis. "Ideology and Ideological State Apparatuses." *Lenin and Philosophy and Other Essays*. Trans. Ben Brewster. London: New Left, 1972. 123–73.

Bell, Daniel. *The Coming of Post-Industrial Society*. New York: Basic, 1973.

Carson, Tom. "Jedi Uber Alles." *A Galaxy Not So Far Away: Writers and Artists on Twenty Five Years of* Star Wars. Ed. Genn Kenny. New York: Henry Holt, 2002. 160–71.

Cassirer, Ernst. *The Myth of the State*. New Haven: Yale University Press, 1946.

Fukuyama, Francis. *The End of History and the Last Man*. New York: Macmilllan, 1992.

Goldman, Robert; Stephen Papson; and Noah Kersey. *Landscapes of Capital*. 14 Feb. 2005. <http://it.stlawu.edu/~global/>.

Gordon, Andrew. "*Star Wars*: A Myth for Our Time." *Literature/Film Quarterly* 6 (1978): 314–26.

Hardt, Michael, and Antonio Negri. *Empire*. Cambridge: Harvard University Press, 2001.

Harvey, David. *The Condition of Postmodernity*. Cambridge: Blackwell, 1989.

Herbert, Frank. *Dune*. 1965. New York: Ace, 1990.

Jameson, Fredric. *Postmodernism or, the Cultural Logic of Late Capitalism*. Durham: Duke University Press, 1991.

Lancashire, Anne. "*Attack of the Clones* and the Politics of *Star Wars*." *Dalhousie Review* 82 (2002): 235–53.

Lefebvre, Henri. *The Production of Space*. Trans. Donald Nicholson-Smith. New York: Blackwell, 1991.

Mandel, Ernest. *Late Capitalism*. Trans. Joris De Bres. London: New Left, 1975.

Marx, Karl, and Ernest Mandel. *Capital: A Critique of Political Economy. Volume One*. Trans. Ben Fowkes. New York: Vintage, 1977.

Metz, Christian. "History/Discourse: Note on Two Voyeurisms." *Edinburgh 76 Magazine* (1976): 21–25.

Mishel, Lawerence, Jared Bernstein, and John Schmitt. *The State of Working America, 1989–99.* Ithaca: Cornell University Press, 1999.

Rubey, Dan. "*Star Wars* 'Not So Long Ago, Not So Far Away.'" *Jump Cut.* Ed. Peter Steven. New York: Praeger, 1985. 83–105.

Senge, Peter M. *The Fifth Discipline: The Art and Practice of the Learning Organization.* New York: Doubleday, 1990.

Sharpe, William, and Leonard Wallock, eds. *Visions of the Modern City: Essays in History, Art, and Literature.* Baltimore: Johns Hopkins University Press, 1987.

Shiel, Mark, and Tony Fitzmaurice, eds. *Screening the City.* London: Verso, 2003.

Star Wars Episode I: The Phantom Menace. Dir. George Lucas. Screenplay by George Lucas. Twentieth Century Fox, 1999.

Star Wars Episode II: Attack of the Clones. Dir. George Lucas. Screenplay by George Lucas and Jonathan Hales. Twentieth Century Fox, 2002.

Star Wars Episode III: Revenge of the Sith. Dir. George Lucas. Screenplay by George Lucas. Twentieth Century Fox, 2005.

Star Wars Episode IV: A New Hope. 1977. Dir. George Lucas. Screenplay by George Lucas. Twentieth Century Fox. 1981.

Star Wars Episode V: The Empire Strikes Back. Dir. Irvin Kershner. Screenplay by Leigh Brackett and Lawrence Kasdan. Story by George Lucas. Twentieth Century Fox, 1980.

Star Wars Episode VI: Return of the Jedi. Dir. Richard Marquand. Screenplay by Lawrence Kasdan and George Lucas. Story by George Lucas. Twentieth Century Fox, 1983.

Tabbi, Joseph. *Postmodern Sublime: Technology and American Writing from Mailer to Cyberpunk.* Ithaca: Cornell University Press, 1995.

Torgovnick, Marianna. *Gone Primitive: Savage Intellects, Modern Lives.* Chicago: University of Chicago Press, 1990.

Wetmore, Kevin J., Jr. *The Empire Triumphant: Race, Religion and Rebellion in the* Star Wars *Films.* Jefferson: McFarland 2005.

_____. "The Tao of *Star Wars*, or, Cultural Appropriation in a Galaxy Far, Far Away." *Studies in Popular Culture* 23 (2000): 91–106.

Williams, Raymond. *The Country and the City.* New York: Oxford University Press, 1973.

Wyatt, David. "*Star Wars* and the Production of Time." *Virginia Quarterly Review* 58 (1982): 600–615.

Žižek, Slavoj. *The Sublime Object of Ideology.* London: Verso, 1989.

PART II

IDENTITY POLITICS

4

May the Force (Not) Be with You

"Race Critical" Readings and the Star Wars Universe

CHRISTOPHER DEIS

Introduction

Star Wars: A New Hope (1977) and its subsequent chapters, *The Empire Strikes Back* (1980) and *Return of the Jedi* (1983), have been embraced by viewing publics and occupy a privileged location within American, as well as global, popular culture. The original trilogy resonated with the public imagination because of its groundbreaking special effects, rich imaginary rooted in classic mythology, moral clarity, exciting action sequences, and endearing characters. As a result, the original trilogy has received a great deal of critical attention from scholars across a variety of disciplines.[1] However, (and excluding a few notable exceptions), there is a lack of sustained scholarship that examines questions surrounding race and difference within the *Star Wars* universe.[2]

In this chapter, I look to this void in the critical literature and suggest that while the original trilogy enjoys great popularity because of Lucas's masterful integration of universal themes with the genre of space fantasy, its popularity can also be understood to be a function of the ways in which the *Star Wars* films can be read as being a tolerant and inclusive film imaginary. And although not unproblematic in regards to, nor consistently overt, in their reproduction of a progressive narrative, the original trilogy can be read as a text in which a diverse group of heroes (consisting of aliens, droids, and humans) do battle with an "evil empire" that is constituted as both a racial and totalitarian imperial state.[3]

In contrast to an understanding of the original trilogy as racially inclusive, some have interpreted the *Star Wars* prequels (*The Phantom Menace*
[1999]; *Attack of the Clones* [2002]; and *Revenge of the Sith* [2005]) as narratives that are both xenophobic and racist.[4] In this chapter, I take this tension as an animating force and ask: how have the *Star Wars* prequels
encouraged a (re)imagining of race and difference within the *Star Wars*
universe? What are the consequences of this (re)imagining for an understanding of Lucas's films as hopeful, diverse, and inclusive? Hinting at the
conclusion of this chapter, I argue that this "race critical," oppositional
reading[5] of the *Star Wars* prequels, and by extension the *Star Wars* meta-
narrative, as being dominated by racism and fear of the Other has contributed to an oversight where the many progressive themes that are present
in the *Star Wars* imaginary (e.g. anti-militarism, a diverse Jedi Order, an
inclusive Galactic Senate, and a cautionary critique of how fear can work
to undermine democratic ideals) are marginalized and made peripheral to
other systems of meaning which have been constructed around the films.

This piece is organized in the following fashion. First, I turn to the
original trilogy and explore the ways in which these chapters can be
interpreted as advancing themes of inclusivity and tolerance. In the following section, I problematize this interpretation by reconciling readings
of the original trilogy, which express concern over the lack of racial diversity among the human characters in these films, with what I assert to be
the surprising and counter-intuitive centrality of *A New Hope*, *The Empire
Strikes Back*, and *Return of the Jedi* within the black popular imagination.
I then move forward to accusations by "race critical" scholars that The
Star Wars prequels depict a set of problematic values and work through
how these readings force a reinterpretation of the *Star Wars* meta-
narrative. I conclude this chapter with an examination of the politically
progressive themes that are at work in the *Star Wars* saga by centering
my discussion around the triad of Luke Skywalker, Darth Vader/Anakin
Skywalker, and Darth Sidious/Emperor Palpatine, where I take their relationship to be a metaphor for the merits of democracy and the triumph
of freedom and cooperation over terror, fear, and totalitarian rule.

This chapter has the following limitations and delimitations. Primarily, while the focus of this chapter is on questions surrounding how
race and identity are encoded in the *Star Wars* saga, its aims are more
robust. A focus on race provides a framework for, and imparts critical
energy to, a project that seeks to question other constructions of identity within the *Star Wars* universe. In addition, an exploration of these
oppositional readings helps us to look broadly as we situate these critiques within a larger constellation of interpretation, emotion, and reaction to the latest chapters in Lucas's film series.

As a complement to the above, this chapter's engagement with critical and oppositional readings of the *Star Wars* saga *is not one of arbitration*. While acknowledging that some readings of a given text are more persuasive than others, this chapter does not divert from what has become a dominant framework for film and cultural studies: a postmodern, audience-centered, interpretive lens through which to view popular culture which privileges the construction of multiple meanings around, as well as the varied receptivities of, a given object of popular culture among audiences.[6] Alternatively stated, I am less interested in exploring *why* one understanding of the *Star Wars* text is "more accurate" than another and more interested in exploring *how* alternative readings impact our understandings of the ways in which questions of tolerance, inclusion, and race are animated within the *Star Wars* saga.[7, 8]

The Imperial March: The Galactic Empire as a Racial State

The observation that there is something "political" at work in the imagery, metaphor, symbols, text, and meta-narrative of the *Star Wars* saga has become a truism which persists across varied analyses of the films.[9] These interpretations are not surprising given Lucas's aim to create a film that was a response to the conservative, post-Vietnam moment; the socio-political lethargy which afflicted the United States following Nixon's resignation; the "stagflation" and oil embargo of the 1970s; and what some would described as an "end of innocence," or a "new maturity," that was represented by the gravity of the commercial film genre in the 1970s.[10] However, while a reading of the *Star Wars* saga as being somehow political is not rare, we see few interpretations that link the Galactic Empire's constitution as a totalitarian, military state to its relationship with those that it has "raced" as being "the Other." This oversight is problematic because the Galactic Empire's relationship to racialized and marginalized Others is central to any effort to read race into *Star Wars* for two primary reasons.

First, the Galactic Empire is the only identifiable State authority in original trilogy. Consequently, the ways in which the Galactic Empire constructs meaning around notions of difference enhances our understanding of the saga's racial encoding(s) and is foundational for this chapter's claim that the *Star Wars* imaginary is one which is tolerant and inclusive.[11] Second, the narrative and thematic structure of the *Star Wars* films emphasizes binary relationships (Henderson 4–120). As an extension of this style of story-telling, the Rebel Alliance is an opposite of the Galactic Empire. The latter is a large, juggernaut-like bureaucracy, which uses fear, terror, and raw power to advance its aims. The former is a small, "ragtag" group of rebels, relying on dexterity, quick wit, faith in the Force, and a belief in their own moral superiority to overcome a vastly more powerful foe (Meyer 106). This repeated use of binaries also extends to this chapter's excavation of the *Star Wars* saga's themes of tolerance and inclusion and an examination of the policies of the Galactic Empire helps us to gain additional understanding of the Rebel Alliance's position in the *Star Wars* imaginary.

The argument advanced in this section rests upon the assertion that the Galactic Empire is constituted as a racial state, a concept detailed by the political theorist Theodore Golberg in his foundational text, *The Racial State*:

> It must be insisted relatedly that the racial state is racial not merely or reductively because of the racial composition of its personnel or the racial implications of its policies—though clearly both play a part. States are racial more deeply because of the structural position they occupy in producing and reproducing, constituting and effecting racially shaped spaces and places, groups and events, life worlds and possibilities, accesses and restrictions, inclusions and exclusions, conceptions and modes of representation [104].

Adding texture to this claim is the discourse within the scholarship on race and social theory regarding the particular "work" that racial difference does in a given society. As described by this (admittedly) simplistic and functional model, the concept of race and the value placed around out-group and in-group membership by those in power grants privileges to some, at the expense of others, and helps to determine "who gets what, where, when, and why?"[12] In liberal-democratic polities, there is a tension between claims of tolerance, inclusivity, and fairness for all members of society and the underlying reality of historical and contemporary racial discrimination. Race is real, but rhetoric(s) of tolerance and an inclusive notion of people-hood often dominate the national mythos as both elites, as well as many segments of the public, reproduce and embrace these hegemony-reproducing narratives. In totalitarian and colonial/imperial states, by contrast, these narratives of peoplehood and of race, applied here as meaning both phenotypical difference and a sense of nationhood, are naked and transparent. Race and a sense of difference from whatever group is defined by elites, and understood by the public at large, to be the Other is the social glue that helps give legitimacy to these States (Goldberg 34, 109–112, 271).

The ways in which Racial States behave towards the Other, and the policies that are formulated to marginalize the racially marked, are historically, politically, and socially contingent (e.g. Colonialism; Imperialism; and Benign or Modern Racism). And while the modern racism of "good culture" vs. "bad culture" and its rhetoric of "color blindness" does not manifest itself as genocide, the core ethic, that those whom are not members of the racial in-group are subject to discrimination and therefore due fewer rights within the public sphere and the polity, is a consistent one. The *Star Wars* films provide both symbolic and narrative evidence for these formulations.

Looking to the former, Lucas employs color to both capture broader thematic elements and to signal narrative and character development to the audience. During the progression from *The Phantom Menace* to *The Return of the Jedi* color does symbolic work as a barometer for *The* Republic's collapse and the rise of *The* Galactic Empire. In *The Phantom Menace,* for example, bright, primary colors are metaphors for life and hope. The lush grasslands and classic architecture of Naboo, the Gungan's underwater kingdom, the dress of the characters, Coruscant's skyline, and the interiors of key buildings are painted in a healthy glow that symbolizes political innocence. As the *Star Wars* prequels progress to *A New Hope,* there is a desaturation of color in which grays, blacks, and reds supplant healthy and vibrant tones. The warm, primary colors that typified democracy are increasingly replaced by colors that are symbolic of the rise of a Nazi-like, militaristic, fascist State. Accordingly, as the narrative advances from a time of peace to one of perpetual war and conflict, the color palate of the chancellor's office begins to feature the color red—a color that symbolizes violence and bloodshed—with the blue Senatorial Guards that were fixtures of *The* Republic being replaced in *Attack of the Clones* by the Emperor's iconic, red Imperial Guards.[13]

Color also works in a more literal fashion to represent themes of diversity and inclusion within the *Star Wars* prequels specifically and the *Star Wars* saga more generally. The bright and earthy colors that are closely associated with the *Star Wars* prequels correlate with the diversity of peoples that populate the Republic. As the narrative progresses, and the democratic institutions of the Republic decay and eventually collapse, we see the beginnings of an increasingly homogenous universe. Here, as color literally disappears from the film, the diversity of peoples and aliens literally disappear as well. Turning to the prequels, the worlds depicted by the films are populated by a myriad of sentient beings. For example, the streets of Coruscant and Tatooine are alive with activity and feature multitudes of non-anthropocentric humanity. The Galactic Senate, the heart of the Republic's democracy, features familiar alien races such as Wookies, Gungans, Twi'leks, Rodians, and Ithorians. The Jedi Order, the spiritual center of the Republic, is equally diverse as both the Jedi Knights and the Jedi Council represent a wide array of alien and human types.

As the color palate becomes more restrained, and the Galactic Empire begins its slow yet inevitable rise, we see a marked decline in human and alien diversity. The conclusion of *Revenge of the Sith* in which

Darth Vader, Emperor Palpatine, and Admiral Tarkin oversee the beginning stages of the Death Star's construction is of particular symbolic weight because here the warmth and vibrancy of The Republic is supplanted by the cold, industrial, and functional designs of the newly created Galactic Empire.

This scene is critical for two reasons. First, the end of *Revenge of the Sith* is important for its role in the *Star Wars* story arc because it bridges the original trilogy with the *Star Wars* prequels by introducing familiar elements, such as the Imperial Star Destroyer and the Death Star, to the audience. Second, this concluding scene exemplifies color usage as a symbol of diversity and tolerance, because it portends a "colorless" future where the multicultural vibrancy and multi-species society that was the Republic is replaced by a human-centric State that is far less tolerant of inter-species difference and political dissent. The Galactic Empire's future policies are further foreshadowed by the racial and gender homogeneity of the Imperial officers on the Star Destroyer's bridge (they are all white, male, and human) and the transformation in uniform and regalia from the earth tones of the Republic to the familiar and Nazi-like color schemes of the Imperial officers (Henderson 144–7; Ryan 228–236).

Both the *Star Wars* film texts and *The Star Wars Expanded Universe* (the novels, role-playing games, comics, and information from Lucas Films's *Star Wars* databank) provide additional evidence to advance the claim that the Galactic Empire is constituted as a Racial and totalitarian State where fear and exclusion of the Other does important political work. In the broadest example, (which is discussed in greater detail later in this chapter), Senator Palpatine's political machinations and his rise to power as Emperor involve the skillful use of fear and terror to undermine democratic institutions. While this may be an obvious plot point, what is less transparent are the particular ways in which Palpatine's political schemes take on new meaning when contextualized within the larger *Star Wars* narrative and examined with an eye towards exploring how the emergent Empire comes to view the Other.

In the *Star Wars* prequels, there is a centralization of governmental power that is fueled by the creation of new political enemies. In these films, Senator Palpatine/Darth Sidious manipulates the Trade Federation into occupying the planet Naboo and, through that action, into providing the spark that (eventually) begins the Clone Wars. The Trade Federation is led by the Neimoidians whom come to be key members of the Confederacy of Independent Systems that opposes the Republic. While a multitude of aliens populates both the Republic and the Confederacy of Independent Systems, the leadership of the respective groups is quite different. Humans lead the Republic. In contrast, while humans are present (most notably in the character of Count Dooku/Darth Tyranus), the Trade Federation and the Confederacy of Independent Systems, as depicted in *Attack of The Clones*, are dominated by "exotic" alien species.

This divergence represents deeper tensions within the *Star Wars* narrative. While the language of "us" vs. "them" is never explicit within the films, the sentiment it evokes is undeniable as human clonetroopers and the more familiar aliens (e.g. Wookies) that serve the Republic under Palpatine's leadership do battle with an unfamiliar menace, which seeks independence and, by *Revenge of the Sith*, threatens the core worlds of human civilization. Count Dooku, the ostensible leader of the Confederacy of Independent Systems and ally of Darth Sidious, alludes to his desire to create a human-centric society in the novelization of *Revenge of the Sith*, where Dooku's feelings towards aliens are described:

> The new government ... This had been their star of destiny for lo, these many years. A government clean, pure, direct: none of the messy scramble for the favor of ignorant rabble and subhuman creatures that made up the Republic he so despised. The government he would serve would be Authority personified. *Human* authority. It was no accident that the primary powers of the Confederacy of Independent Systems were Neimoidian, Skakoan, Quarren and Aqualish, Muun and Gossam, Sy Myrthian and Koorivar and Geonosian. At war's end the aliens would be crushed, stripped of all they possessed, and their systems and their wealth would be given into the hands of the only beings who could be trusted with them. Human beings. Dooku would serve an Empire of Man [Stover 51].

Following the fall of the Republic, the Galactic Empire inaugurates "The New Order," a set of policy initiatives in which the vestiges of democracy are swept away by totalitarian rule.[14] Because the Republic was a State prefaced on the cooperation of many worlds and species under rule of democratic law, the Galactic Empire, as a function of its desire to remake political society, moves away from this model of cooperation and transforms what was formerly a multicultural and multispecies society into one where humans and human culture are privileged. As a corollary to The New Order, the Galactic Empire eliminates enemies both from within and from without. Pursuant to these policies, aliens are marginalized as anti-slavery laws are repealed, non-humans are prohibited from enlisting in the Imperial military, and guarantees of fairness and equality under the law are eliminated.[15]

The films echo these events. For example, during *A New Hope*, it is on the Outer Rim planet of Tatooine where the audience first encounters a diversity of alien species in the iconic Mos Eisley cantina scene. In comparison to the sterile, homogeneous, and "white" spaces that begin

A New Hope, Tatooine and its cantina are teaming with a diversity of human and non-human characters. By *A New Hope*, the alien Other has been removed from the center of galactic civilization and literally, as well as symbolically, "ghettoized" to the hinterlands of the Galactic Empire.

This concept of center and periphery lies at the heart of the Galactic Empire's imperial and colonial policies. The Galactic Empire serves as a metaphor for colonial and imperial era Europe during which its nation states dominated Asia, Africa, and The Americas. The British accents of the Imperial naval officers, the emphasis on the galactic fleet, and the harsh Outer Rim territories where the imperial military confronts the Rebel Alliance evoke the maintenance of a far-flung regime that is struggling to police its borders and to suppress "insurgent" and "rebel" activity. Kevin J. Wetmore Jr. buttresses this formulation with his observation that

> Yet, from the four current films, the construction of a colonial discourse is apparent ... Governor Tarkin uses the Death Star as the colonial powers in Africa and Asia used their military might to keep the locals "in line." *Star Wars* places the theories of post-colonial political analyst Franz Fanon in outer space: colonialism is "violence in its natural state," and "it will only yield when confronted with greater violence," that is, armed rebellion ... In fact, Lucas's use of direct articles and capital letters (The Rebellion, The Empire) in the *Star Wars* trilogy seemingly suggests an archetypal colonial structure and struggle. *The Wretched of the Earth* becomes "The Wretched of the Galaxy" ["Tao"].

The maintenance of European empires involved, reflected, and necessitated the creation of norms of difference which marked out territory geographically but that also involved the creation of racial hierarchies. These understandings of racial difference legitimated the exploitive systems that European nations depended upon for their economic and military expansion. As political theorist Charles Mills details, these ideologies divided the world into "the exploited" and "the exploitable":

> Correspondingly, various moral and legal doctrines were propounded which can be seen as specific manifestations and instantiations, appropriately adjusted to circumstances, of the overarching Racial Contract. These specific subsidiary contracts designed for different modes of exploiting the resources and people of the world for Europe: the expropriation contract, the slavery contract, the colonial contract ... It would be a fundamental error, then—a point to which I will return—to see racism as anomalous, a mysterious deviation from European Enlightenment humanism. Rather, it needs to be realized that, in keeping with the Roman precedent, *European humanism meant only that Europeans were human* ... By the nineteenth century, conventional white opinion casually assumed the uncontroversial validity of a hierarchy of "higher" and "lower," "master" and "subject" races, for whom, it is obvious, different rules must apply [23–4, 26–7].

The idea of subject and object races in which some humans, (and in *Star Wars*, where aliens serve as a proxy for the Other), are expendable and therefore necessarily due less respect and dignity than others, is the bedrock of imperial and colonial systems. For example, In *A New Hope*, Han Solo, Luke Skywalker, and Chewbacca attempt to infiltrate the cell block where Princess Leia is awaiting execution. In this scene, the rebels manipulate the Imperials' anti-alien prejudice and their assumption that Chewbacca is a prisoner (and perhaps a runaway slave) in order to free Princess Leia. The rebels succeed because of their quick thinking but also because the Imperials were blinded by their overconfidence that Chewbacca, "this thing," would know its place as a member of a subject race and that he could not escape nor do the Imperial guards any harm.

In the *Star Wars* prequels, the aliens of the Confederacy of Independent Systems are an external Other which the Republic rallies against. As Palpatine moves inward in his consolidation of power, the next target becomes the Jedi Order, and they are subsequently marked as traitors which Emperor Palpatine famously declares to be "enemies of the Republic." The Jedi are certainly a dire threat to Palpatine as both a Sith Lord and as an emerging dictator. A surface reading would look to this conflict as "merely" one of good and evil, where the Jedi must be eliminated because they oppose Palpatine and the Galactic Empire. This reading is correct in the most basic, narrative sense. However, a deeper reading reveals the possibility that the Jedi are also constructed as a new category of racial Other—an Other that replaces the outward threat posed by the Confederacy of Independent Systems and the Trade Federation.

The *Star Wars* prequels have provided viewers with new information regarding the Jedi that helps to buttress this claim. Originally, the Force was depicted in *A New Hope* as an energy field that all could use if they possessed sufficient faith. In *The Phantom Menace*, we learn that the ability to become a Jedi is determined by an individual's "midichlorian" count: sympathetic life forms that give those hosts privileged enough to have them in sufficient number the potential to become a Jedi. While this "mystical energy field binds us, penetrates us, and holds the galaxy together," all people are not able to access or control it. With the addition of this new information, the Jedi remain mystical warrior-monks that are distinguished by their dress, temperament, and belief in a strict code of behavior. However, while the Jedi do not share a common phenotype (as the species diversity in the Jedi Order demonstrates), the Jedi are certainly marked as different by both the role they play as guardians of the Republic and because of the biological distinction of their high midi-chlorian counts.

By leveraging the concept of the Galactic Empire as a Racial State, we can also read the exclusion of the Jedi as one in which they are racially marked, or "raced," by the Galactic Empire. Centering this understanding of the Jedi in our readings of the *Star Wars* saga grants additional meaning to Palpatine's agenda. In *Revenge of The Sith*, Emperor Palpatine issues "Order 66"—the code that signals his Stormtroopers to purge the Jedi Knights. The Jedi Knights are brutally murdered not simply because they are enemies of the Galactic Empire but because of whom and what they are (and in keeping with the theme of the alien as Other, all the characters that are killed during Revenge of The Sith's montage of the Jedi purge are non-human). If we accept that the Jedi are a people, the Emperor's edict is not merely an order to eliminate one's political enemies, but a genocidal act against a group that are marked as being outside of some constructed norm of political and social community.

To this point, I have suggested that the Galactic Empire is a Racial State typified by its external and internal policies of xenophobia, discrimination, ghettoization, and in the most extreme cases, genocide, towards the alien and Jedi Other. As noted earlier, the *Star Wars* narrative utilizes binaries and opposites as storytelling devices. If the Galactic Empire is a Racial State, how then do we read the Rebel Alliance and its relationship with the Other? And how is a reading of the original trilogy, (and the *Star Wars* imaginary more generally), as one that advances themes of tolerance and inclusion complicated by the paucity of non-white, human characters in these films?

"You Know of the Rebellion Against the Empire?": Luke Skywalker, the Rebel Alliance, and Tatooine

In *A New Hope*, Luke Skywalker describes his home planet of Tatooine: "if there is a bright center to the universe, you are on the planet that it's farther from." This quip hints at the mythological structure of *Star Wars* and its relationship to the literal, as well as metaphorical, journeys that Luke Skywalker will experience in the original trilogy. For example, as has been frequently documented by scholars of myth and folklore, Luke Skywalker will literally make a journey of distance from his humble beginnings on Tatooine to fulfill his destiny as a Jedi Knight. As the mythic hero, Luke will journey a metaphorical distance in his "first steps into a broader universe" and gain a second sight and special skills not accessible to most as he learns the ways of the Force. Skywalker's guide, Obi-Wan Kenobi, gives Luke his father's lightsaber which serves both as a symbolic link to his rightful place as a "sky walker" and as a magical talisman that protects Skywalker harm. While Luke Skywalker is engaging in a philosophical and mythological journey within the films, he is also moving from the obscurity of life on a "backwater planet" to become part of the broader galaxy as eventual hero of the Rebel Alliance.[16] It is here where Skywalker's description of Tatooine provides a counter-intuitive, yet revealing, point of access for an examination of the Rebel Alliance's juxtaposed relationship to the Galactic Empire.

In the *Star Wars* imaginary, Tatooine functions as both a literal and figurative "ghetto" of galactic civilization. Geographically, Tatooine is located on the Outer Rims, far from the centers of commerce, trade, and culture, and it is peopled by aliens, droids, and humans. For Tatooine's residents, this diverse populace necessitates a broadly multicultural and expansive understanding of the value of difference and the Other. Marguerite Waller, in "Poetic Influence in Hollywood: Rebel without a Cause and *Star Wars*," buttresses this observation with her description of Lucas' emphasis on aliens, difference, and human subjectivity:

> If the plot of *Star Wars* is predictable, however its imagery is not. Lucas has designed a non-anthropocentric universe that has a way of catching off guard anyone who trusts to much his own ego-centric perspective. Luke, for example in trusting his technologically sophisticated macrobinoculars while looking for "primitive" Sand-people is taken by surprise by the one which as crept up beneath his range of vision to attack him ... The bar-room scene at Mos Eisley almost makes its few human figures look out of place, dramatically displacing our sense of what life must look and sound like ... Three-pio and Artoo escape her captured spaceship successfully because the Imperial forces trust both their instruments, which indicate that there are no "life forms" aboard the androids' escape pod, and the thinking behind the design of these instruments, which makes an absolute distinction—in favor of itself—between organic and inorganic intelligence ... as the story unfolds it comes to seem mere bigotry to assume that, even where the distinction applies, humans are necessarily superior to machines. In the series of escapes that follow this one, each different, each successful because it makes and exploits connections which violate the expectations of the pursuers, Lucas's space, a space which represents no place we know, but is a space quintessentially of film, offers further embarrassing insights into the Imperial mind, a mind that may very much remind us of our own [65].

Skywalker understands his world to be far from "the bright center of the universe," because it is radically different from the sterile, homogeneous, "white" society which the Galactic Empire has identified with high culture and civilization. While Luke would like to leave Tatooine for better opportunities at the Imperial Academy, Skywalker's personality and ethos are heavily informed by his formative experiences on his home planet. Tatooine is rugged and demanding, and, as a symbolic proxy for the Old

West of America's national mythos, Luke's upbringing on this planet both necessitates, and helps to nurture, a sense of rugged individualism (Wright 120–5). In addition, Tatooine is a multicultural world where its human settlers have to navigate and negotiate an existence with their fellow alien denizens.

Because of his upbringing in this multicultural society, Luke Skywalker shows no discomfort in his interactions with the aliens of the Rebel Alliance. Luke's lack of high minded morality and human-centrism extends to his close friendship with the two rogues, Han Solo and Chewbacca, that help to spirit him off of Tatooine. While the Imperials assume that aliens are subject races and not worthy of respect, Luke (literally) embraces Chewbacca, and the two show great loyalty and friendship to one another throughout their journeys.

This sense of equality extends to the droids R2-D2 and C-3P0. While many humans generally, and the Galactic Empire as a matter of policy, view robots as machines that are interchangeable, the droids, both as a function of their central symbolic and narrative roles in the *Star Wars* meta-narrative, and because of their close relationship to Luke Skywalker, are fully developed personalities that have emotional value to the characters and which prove invaluable to the Rebel Alliance in its triumph over the Empire.

If we extend these cases to the narrative at large, in many ways, Luke Skywalker is the Rebel Alliance. Both cooperate with, and are tolerant of, alien and droid Others. Luke Skywalker is positioned as a literal and metaphorical sword (or lightsaber) of freedom against the tyrannical Empire, while the Rebel Alliance is the last vestige of the Old Republic. In total, Luke Skywalker is inseparably marked by experiences on Tatooine and is constituted as a radically "democratic" character, which David Meyer, in "Star Wars and *Star Wars*," frames to be:

> As a hero, Luke is drawn no more subtly than villain Darth Vader. He is passionate, youthful, impatient, and resolutely democratic. "Call me Luke" he tells C3 [*sic*] the protocol droid, who prefers to address his new owner as "Sir." ... The heroic rebels succeeded by virtue not of technological advantages, but through greater commitment, diversity, and justness of cause. Luke appeared to be both a common man and a master of science—much as Jimmy Carter (the peanut farmer and "nuculah" engineer) did in his presidential campaign. The heroes sought independence, not dominance, and personal affiliation was always a stronger motivation for action than obedience or ideology [101].

As a symbolic referent to his populism, Luke's inner circle is populated with humans, aliens, and droids, and while a nuanced point, the characters of the Rebel Alliance are in fact individual, unique, and irreplaceable.

For example, in contrast with the exclusively male Empire, and in keeping with its mythic pairing of prince and princess, Leia is the only prominent female character in the original trilogy, where she serves as a strong leader that drives the narrative forward while simultaneously avoiding the full trope of "the damsel in distress."[17] A swashbuckling rogue, Han Solo, and his companion, Chewbacca, accompany Luke on his journeys. The droids are loyal attendants to the core characters and the emotional center of the *Star Wars* saga. And fulfilling the role of guide and Zen master, Jedi Master Yoda speaks in his particularly distinct and memorable dialect ("Judge me by my size do you?") as he imparts the secrets of the Force to his young protégé.

This emphasis on discrete characters is as much a result of Lucas's utilization of archetypes as it is the desire to emphasize a contrast between the Rebel Alliance (the heroes) and the Galactic Empire (the villains). While the Galactic Empire treats humans as interchangeable cogs in the state apparatus, the Alliance utilizes all of its members' talents in a moral crusade against tyranny and oppression. The Rebels' ethos of cooperation and diversity pays dividends in *Return of the Jedi*, where an alien Other, one that defies superficial expectations regarding their ferocity and cunning in battle, proves instrumental in the Rebel Alliance's defeat of the Galactic Empire at the pivotal battle of Endor.

While *Return of the Jedi* (and the *Star Wars* saga in general) can be read as a crystallization of Lucas's worries regarding technology and society, there are other themes at work in the triumph of the Ewoks over the fearsome Imperial military (Henderson 151–157). Metaphorically, the Ewoks are presented as harmless, little "fur balls," and in keeping with Lucas's theme of appearances versus truth, their innocent appearance disguises ingenuity and tenacity (Fader 192–204). In an allusion to the fate that befell many imperial and colonial powers, the Galactic Empire's technology, while dominant on the battlefield, denies them the flexibility and the "vision" necessary to defeat a guerrilla force that is not blinded philosophically, nor literally imprisoned within, their technology. The rigidity of the Galactic Empire as a fascist and totalitarian State and its inability to place faith in the Force rather than in naked power, in combination with their hostility to non-humans, denies them the wisdom necessary to be victorious. Ultimately (and in clear contrast to the Rebel Alliance), the prejudice and bias of the Galactic Empire leads to defeat because their ideology as a Racial State does not permit them the philosophical or moral vision necessary to either cooperate with, respect, or embrace the alien Other.

By comparison, the Rebel Alliance values individuality, draws strength from the diversity of its members, and finds merit in tolerance and inclusion. The actions and personality of Luke Skywalker, as both the protagonist of the original trilogy, and as a symbol of the Rebel Alliance, embodies these populist and democratic values. In the *Star Wars* films and in science fiction and space opera more broadly, aliens and droids, and human's responses to them, serve as proxies and metaphors for the broader social values of multiculturalism and racial inclusiveness.[18] However, this question of representation is problematic for both the original trilogy and the *Star Wars* prequels because, while the *Star Wars* imaginary is populated by a multitude of alien species, there is scant racial diversity among the heroes of the films. How does this fact challenge a reading of the *Star Wars* meta-narrative as one that is an inclusive, tolerant, and diverse film imaginary? If we grant these critical readings of the original trilogy, how do we reconcile these perspectives with race critical readings of the *Star Wars* prequels?

"I Find Your Lack of Faith Disturbing": "Race Critical" Readings and the Star Wars *Universe*

The original trilogy has been labeled as a film series that is profoundly traditional in its values and themes. This is not surprising as Lucas formulated *Star Wars* as a modern day fairy tale where archetypal characters communicate long held truths regarding good and evil. Lucas's saga also emphasizes themes of fatherhood, trust, and security where young men confront their destinies, embark on journeys of emotional and spiritual maturation, and eventually take their rightful place in the world. The tradition to which *Star Wars* is moored is both conservative in its values as well as conservative (though not right wing or fascist) in its political ideology. As echoed by Peter Lev's, "Whose Future? *Star Wars, Alien,* and *Blade Runner,*"

> Men are active heroes. Princess Leia is a damsel in distress, good and evil are clearly separated, and Luke is guided by the benevolent father figure Obiwan Kenobi [*sic*]. The film is very consciously a break from the anti-heroes and anti-genres of many films of the early 1970s. According to Dale Pollack's biography of Lucas, the film's return to family entertainment and traditional morality was a conscious decision by its writer-director ... Pollack lists the values of the film as "Hard Work, self-sacrifice, friendship, loyalty, and a commitment to a higher purpose" [31].

In addition, the original trilogy, and *A New Hope* in particular, can be read as reinforcing conservative political values and has been identified by some observers as portending the rise of Reagan and the American right. In keeping with Reagan's skillful manipulation of nostalgia, his rhetoric of "renewing America," and the administration's trope of America as a beacon of democracy and a "bright city on the hill," the epic journey of an innocent, blue-eyed, (and American accented) farm boy from his rural roots to do battle in a war for freedom and independence both easily suited, and was easily manipulated by, the purposeful demands of Reagan-era conservatism. Tom Carson locates *Star Wars* within the political moment of Reagan's regime in the following terms:

> Lucas's invitation to the audience to return to the comforting simplicities of an earlier era of entertainment was as ideologically loaded as Reagan's summons to hark back to an earlier state of historical ignorance-as-bliss, because you can't uncritically revive the pulp narratives of an earlier age without also replicating their values.... In their separate realms, though, they both also expressed one of this country's most cherished conceptions of itself, benignly endorsing American exceptionalism in all its ahistorical innocence and sense of virtuous sanctified mission [70].

The most damaging claim against the *Star Wars* saga is that because of this double conservatism of morals, and its appropriation by conservative ideologues, that the original trilogy is ultimately a story about normalcy told from a particular historic and social vantage point that does not unsettle or challenge assumptions regarding power, hierarchy, or privilege. In the *Star Wars* imaginary, white men (and one woman) are "naturally" in positions of authority. White men are the protagonists, and they serve heroically and nobly in the service of a just cause. Again, returning to Lev's observations in "Whose Future? *Star Wars*, *Alien*, and *Blade Runner*," while the Rebel Alliance eventually overcomes the evil, tyrannical Galactic Empire, the victory is not "revolutionary":

> One should also remember that *Star Wars* rebellion in no way challenges gender, race, or class relations. White male humans are "naturally" in positions of authority. The boy Luke grows up and takes his place as a responsible leader ... the films dominant tone is reassurance, things change so that they can return to a comfortable norm [33].

The world returns to a natural state of balance where the heroes of the saga, with the late addition of Lando Calrissian, celebrate their victory in a racially homogenous space. The deeper narrative of *Star Wars*, with its emphasis on themes of security, stability, and familiarity, is fulfilled as the heroes and (the white) audience are reassured of a return to the normal, as white characters are unquestionably the centerpiece of the narrative and preside over a just resolution to the Galactic Civil War.

In the *Star Wars* saga, people of color are pushed to the boundaries and are not central to the drama. While Lando Calrissian is instrumental to the plot, the *Star Wars* saga is essentially rooted in a particularly "white" imaginary and nostalgia. The ideological component of this intersection of memory and race results in a problematic outcome that exists in tension with the themes of diversity and tolerance which penetrate the *Star Wars* narrative. While not malevolent in intent, Lucas's oversight to the social context in which his imaginary and nostalgia is embedded (as one rooted in a particularly narrow upbringing in a white, suburban California community) reveals the work that whiteness does in bounding and framing the confines of the creative imagination. People of color are marginalized in the *Star Wars* saga because Lucas's conceptual lens permits him the luxury of "seeing" race in a very particular fashion, where as a function of white privilege, race is rendered invisible and racial difference is erased as a meaningful referent.[19]

Ultimately, *Star Wars* is a vast and rich imaginary that is governed by a mystical energy field, detailed with fantastic technology, and populated by wondrous aliens, yet it is one in which people of color are conspicuously absent from the film. One would expect that this marginalization would contribute to a lack of popularity of the original trilogy and the broader *Star Wars* saga among audiences of color. However, *Star Wars* remains central to the black popular imagination. I would suggest that this importance is a result of the film saga's popularity among audiences generally, but more interestingly this centrality is also a consequence of the ways in which audiences of color have reframed and reinterpreted the themes and characters of the *Star Wars* film saga.[20]

Audiences, because of social relationships to power hierarchies, particular intersections of identity, and the ways in which popular culture circulates among diverse groups, construct and reconstruct their own systems of meaning around such objects as music, film, and art. These reinterpretations can serve counter-hegemonic purposes because they involve recoding and reorganizing the output of symbols, narratives, and meaning assigned to certain texts. For example, these oppositional readings of texts challenge the racial, gender, and other codings of a given cultural object in order to reveal new meanings or to critically engage the norms and assumptions that underlie the text.[21] Audiences can also apply the same principles to "read" themselves into a film imaginary from which they are excluded.

Black popular culture defies binary explanations and is fueled by the ability of the black creative imagination to borrow, reframe, and incorporate culture(s) from multiple locations into new aesthetic and conceptual formations. The *Star Wars* saga is a site of this re-reading and borrowing in a number of ways. Primarily, the black popular imagination has inverted the meanings attached to certain characters in the *Star Wars* imaginary. In *A New Hope*, for example, Darth Vader, "the dark father" of Lucas's imagination, is the only "black" character in the film.

He is a tragic figure and fallen angel that embodies the evil and fear (both external and internal) that Luke Skywalker must overcome. Adding an additional level to his "racialization," Vader also literally embodies what Leilani Nishime in her piece, "The Mulatto Cyborg: Imagining a Multiracial Future," describes as the "mulatto cyborg," a white person (Anakin Skywalker), encased within and sustained by black armor and voiced by the prominent African American actor, James Earl Jones (34–49). Lucas intends for Darth Vader to be the embodiment of evil and as such, to earn the audience's censure: Vader is the natural antagonist to the blue eyed, blond hero; in a subtle nod to the taboo of interracial sex, "black" Vader wants to possess the white, fair maiden; and Vader wages war against the heroic (and white) Rebel Alliance.

However, the black popular imagination, by reinterpreting and reframing meaning and intention, transforms Vader into a type of hero that transcends mere anti-hero status. Although Vader is literally black in color, he becomes a proxy for audiences of color as the "strong" character that leads the Empire in their war against a traditional, white, and homogenous Rebel Alliance. Darth Vader is transformed from the symbol of parental authority and youthful angst into something far different— he fulfills the "baadman" or "bad nigger" that is central to the black popular imagination.[22] In essence, as Elvis Mitchell asserts in the piece, "Works Every Time," Vader becomes "cool":

> And the bullying vigor of James Earl Jones's vocal presence—recognizable instantly to a black audience—giving a malevolent elegance to Darth Vader, begged another question. Although, to be frank, given that Vader was about the coolest thing going in the first *Star Wars*, it made the possibility that he was black perfectly acceptable [78].

Lando Calrissian, as the only black hero of the Rebel Alliance, also enjoys popularity because of his "cool pose."[23] While a rogue that both harkens back to Han Solo prior to his joining the Rebel Alliance and a character that initially chooses self interest over the greater good, Calrissian helped to anchor *Star Wars* within the black popular imagination and was read as a "mea culpa" on the part of Lucas for the racially homogenous *A New Hope*, a claim Mitchell supports:

> Williams's addition to the cast of *Empire* showed an admirable sensitivity on Lucas's part, an empathy that few filmmakers would've displayed.... Knowing—if he ever got to make his planned sequels— that a romance for Han and Leia was planned, Lucas didn't want the controversial, and probably non-commercial element of an interracial relationship ... To compensate for his moment of cowardice and the complaints of racism lodged against the first *Star Wars* ... Lucas conjured up the sleek Calrissian and contoured him to

Williams's contours ... The swell of pride in theaters when Lando sidled up onto the screen—I can testify to the reaction in Detroit when *Empire* first played—caused an attendant ripple of applause, the quieter version of a shout-out. By placing Williams in the picture, Lucas guaranteed that black audiences would connect with the *Star Wars* galaxy in a way that they never had with fantasy and science fiction before [78–9, 82].

The reframing of character and narrative by the black popular imagination is one example of the broader ways in the original trilogy was framed and interpreted by audiences in ways that helped to insulate it from criticisms and readings that focused on both its conservative politics and the lack of racial diversity among its human cast. To the present, the original trilogy remains central to the American popular imagination. While its ideological content remains at times problematic, this crisis in values is trumped within the American popular imagination by the film saga's universal values of friendship, loyalty, and the inevitable triumph of good over evil.

In contrast, despite its explicitly progressive and populist content, the *Star Wars* prequels have been met with charges that they communicate themes of racism, xenophobia, and intolerance. For example, the first film of the new installment was savaged for featuring a narrative in which a white, blue eyed boy, and a product of virgin birth, problematically symbolized an ideal in which whites are saviors, (in contrast to other films such as *The Matrix Trilogy* (1999 and 2003) in which people of color are prominent) and where despite the popularity of *Star Wars* among a global audience, white characters would "naturally" remain central to the film imaginary. In addition, the characters of Jar Jar Binks, Watto, and the Neimoidians of the Trade Federation were branded as racist and stereotypical caricatures of blacks, Jews, and Asians, stereotypes, which Greg Grewell in his piece, "Colonizing the Universe," comments upon:

> And with *Star Wars*' use of earth-type racialized beings, aliens have more familiar types: the evil Asian-like Federation of representatives trying to force a trade embargo on the mostly European-stylized Naboo, whose main urban-center is comprised of Greco Roman architecture; the cake-walking, dread-locked, Caribbean-like speaking Gungans, of who Jar Jar Binks is the type, and who as literal subalterns, live underwater and retreat to a jungle, "their sacred place," and go to battle with African-like spears and shields; the patriarchal Jedi, who will save the day, if not the universe [36].

Attack of the Clones was also criticized for communicating themes of racial bias and xenophobia. The primary complaint against this film was a response to the revelation that the Clonetroopers (the precursors to the familiar Stormtroopers of the original trilogy) are cloned from the enigmatic Jango Fett (played by the "racially ambiguous" and brown complexioned, Maori actor, Temeura Morrison) and the "father" of fan favorite, Boba Fett. This revelation, when mated with earlier concerns regarding *The Phantom Menace*, fueled a reading of the film in which the clonetroopers became metaphors for Mexican and Hispanic immigrants to the United States. In this reading, the armies of brown people being manufactured at the clone facilities on the planet Kamino represent deeply held fears of the Other in the American political subconscious, a worry regarding a "clash of civilizations" and the challenges posed to the West by illegal immigration.[24]

In both the original trilogy and the *Star Wars* prequels, aliens are both "the problem" and the "solution" in Lucas's film imaginary. In *A New Hope, The Empire Strikes Back*, and *Return of The Jedi*, aliens are a "solution" that represents diversity and tolerance. Here, the Other of droids and robots challenges narrow visions of humanity and the value of difference. In the *Star Wars* prequels, aliens are "the problem" in that their depiction is too closely rooted to the classic science fiction thematic where the alien Other is an embodiment of our earthly worries and anxieties.[25] Causally, the "erasing" of race in the original trilogy and the assertion that race and processes of racialization do pernicious work symbolically via the aliens of the prequels are claims which are both rooted in the whiteness of Lucas's nostalgic imaginary—an imaginary which is the source for his creative inspiration and that is often blind to the possible encodings of race and the problematic relationship of this nostalgia to broader social contexts. Carson echoes this critique in "Jedi Uber Allies," with his observation that

> you can't help wondering how this filmmaker can stay so blandly oblivious to the distasteful implications of what he's doing, if he really is. All this goes back to Lucas's sources—the adolescent fables of an age when white superiority was taken for granted and swashbuckling adventure in exotic lands dramatized the imperial mission at its sexiest, a genre whose stereotypes got transplanted lock, stock, and barrel to sci-fi [167].

Alternatively stated, this particular type of white imaginary cannot "see" how the character Jar Jar Binks can be read as a Steppin Fetchit, how the character Watto can be read as performing a particular type of "Jewishness," or how the Neimoidians with their "Asian" accents are reminiscent of offensive caricatures such as Charlie Chan. In the terrain of this intersection between whiteness and nostalgia, these characters are simply pieces of childhood memories that are disembodied from social context and necessarily disconnected from their problematic origins in racist popular culture. Carson echoes this formulation with,

Viewers without particular memories of Stepin Fetchit or Butterfly McQueen are probably serenely unaware of the offensive tradition that Jar Jar Binks revives.... Since his own nostalgia, like Reagan's, is partly a rebellion against the critical spirit that insisted on looking behind such things, Lucas may not recognize it either. What helps him get away with reviving stereotypes like these is that he seems to relate them purely as entertaining pop conventions, without the faintest notion of their import [168].

Given this divergence, how then do we explain the varied audience responses to the original trilogy and the *Star Wars* prequels? I would like to suggest that the "triangle" of film, fandom, and critics, was disrupted by the tepid and in some cases hostile reception on the part of some audiences to the *Star Wars* prequels. While the original trilogy was both problematic ideologically in its lack of racial diversity, the films' flaws were largely overlooked because of the appeal of their universal values, novelty, popularity and (coming) cult status. This triad of text, reception, and criticism worked both to sustain the popularity of the original trilogy and to prevent a mass resonance of race critical readings, whereas in the case of the *Star Wars* prequels, fan disappointment was simultaneously echoed and fueled by film critics. This synergy challenged Lucas's intentions for how audiences would (or would not) read race into the *Star Wars* saga and gave life to oppositional readings of the film.

What I posit to be a weakening in the relationship between the film, fandom, and critics has led to a triumph of "the particular" over "the universal" in the constructions of meaning around the *Star Wars* films. More broadly, the broad and epic themes that penetrate the *Star Wars* meta-narrative have been overtaken by complaints regarding inconsistencies in plot, worries regarding casting, and a focus on how new information that has been revealed by the *Star Wars* prequels challenges fandom's expectations for the film saga.[26] Of greatest consequence is how this move towards the particular has disrupted the broader *Star Wars* meta-narrative by weakening the continuity of the films with its focus on apparent inconsistencies that exist between the original trilogy and the *Star Wars* prequels.

In addition, this focus on the particular is highly problematic for the *Star Wars* narrative because it gives equal resonance to claims and critiques that are both "strong" and "weak."[27] This focus on the particular and the primacy given to "race critical," oppositional readings has helped to generate a blind spot where the progressive themes of the *Star Wars* prequels have been subsumed by other discourses. In the next section of this chapter (and as both a corrective as well as an intervention) I explore this tension by asking, how do we bring balance to the Force? What politically progressive themes are present in the *Star Wars* prequels that can help to resuscitate the *Star Wars* imaginary from the weight of these varied oppositional and particular readings of the *Star Wars* text? First, in responding to these questions, I return to my earlier emphasis on the ways in which color and visual images communicate meaning in Lucas's films. Second, I detail what I identify to be one of the more resonant and politically "progressive" narratives at work in the film series, where the symbolic politics of family does a particular type of thematic "work" in the films as metaphors for domestic and international political life under the post–September 11th Bush political regime.

"So This Is How Liberty Dies, with Thunderous Applause?": Star Wars, *Tyranny, and the Triumph of Democracy*

In the *Star Wars* prequels, Lucas crafted an explicitly political narrative. The rise and fall of the Republic and the political machinations that precipitate it are central to the plot and the characters in the films. By comparison, the original trilogy's politics were more subtle and helped to ground the narrative while existing as a secondary to the action sequences and characters. Ironically, Lucas's move towards a more political narrative may be partly responsible for the disappointment and confusion among more casual fans and critics, many of which were not prepared for such weighty fare nor equipped to contextualize these developments within a larger story arc (Lancashire 235–253).

As hinted at earlier, this deterioration in the triad of film, fandom, and critic, and the triumph of the particular over the universal in readings of the *Star Wars* saga has obfuscated their progressive and critical political content. Ironically, while the *Star Wars* prequels have suffered under pressure by race critical and oppositional critics, these films offer themes such as anti-corporatism, anti-militarism, and a cautionary warning to resist the ready impulse to trade freedom for security that are (1) highly critical of the same hegemonic processes that ground the progressive and radical imagination to which these critical epistemologies are heir, and (2) which exist as cautionary tales regarding the decline of democratic values and the rise of tyranny.

Lucas has been deeply concerned with the rise and fall of democratic institutions and of the relationship of individuals to society, technology, and the State. The *Star Wars* films were intended by Lucas to demonstrate how great and powerful democracies (e.g. Rome and the United States) do not fall from without but rather rot from within like an old tree because of greed, corruption, and fear. The *Star Wars* saga is also an explicit tale of how democracies fall, (often from a phantom menace) and then rise again through the corrective action of a rebellion by their people (as we see in *A New Hope*).

In a fashion similar to the films of the original trilogy, the *Star Wars* prequels utilize visual symbolism, metaphor, and narrative to communicate Lucas's cautionary themes and to ground the film in a post-September 11th, War on Terror, and Iraq Insurgency zeitgeist of dread and uncertainty, where freedom and democracy are challenged by threats from without, in the form of terrorism, as well as from within, in the creeping rise of militarism and the national security state. In *Attack of the Clones*, for example, there are several moments of deep pathos where color and the visual communicate the coming inevitability of war and tyranny to the Republic.

Following the battle of Geonosis, Count Dooku escapes the planet and returns to Coruscant where he meets Darth Sidious/Emperor Palpatine. Their rendezvous takes place far from the center of Coruscant in an abandoned, rust colored, industrial section of the city. Here the two political actors that are propelling the Republic to its destruction are symbolically bathed in red, the color of war and conflict. Almost simultaneous to these events, the visual focus shifts to a deftly edited sequence in which Anakin and Padmé are marrying in secret on her home planet of Naboo. While Padmé and Anakin fulfill their secret pledge to one another, Bail Organa, who is symbolically positioned as the moral conscious for the Republic, looks to the ground in disgust as the Grand Army of The Republic parades in front of politicos on its way to the Clone Wars. In both of the dialogue-less sequences, (an editing choice which forces an emphasis on the visual), the audience's attention is drawn to a pair of seemingly dissimilar events that will have the cumulative effect of destroying the Republic.

In *Revenge of the Sith*, visual symbolism works to communicate Anakin Skywalker's emotional and ethical tumult and to complement the narrative developments by grounding the themes of the film in the contemporary, post 9–11 political moment. In the former, Anakin Skywalker's moral failure in the internal struggle between good and evil results in his betrayal of the Jedi Order and the Republic. This failure results in the climactic battle on the volcanic planet Mustafar, where Anakin confronts Obi-Wan Kenobi in a battle to the death. As Lucas has noted, this battle results in Anakin making a metaphorical deal with the devil—a Faustian bargain, and taking a literal journey into hell from which he cannot emerge unscathed either spiritually or physically (Corliss and Cagle 56–68; Gavin 42–6). Here, as a symbol of Hades, the bubbling lava and explosive fire metaphorically capture Anakin's inner rage and the moral failings that Anakin, now christened and reborn as Darth Vader, cannot escape.

The act which seals the Faustian bargain, and that ultimately converts Anakin Skywalker from Jedi Knight (and defender of the Republic) to a fascist enforcer (Darth Vader) is Anakin's execution of Order 66 where he returns to the Jedi temple and kills his former allies. Communicating Lucas's worries regarding how post September 11th angst and fear has permeated American political life, the Jedi Temple is shown burning on the horizon in a visual that is eerily reminiscent of the World Trade Towers prior to their collapse. Powerless and evoking the position of the American public as spectator on September 11th, Padmé looks toward them and painfully realizes her husband's role in its destruction and that her world, as well as that of the Republic's, have been forever changed by one act of violence.

The *Star Wars* saga is Anakin Skywalker's story. His fall from grace and eventual redemption through Luke Skywalker's love are at the heart of the narrative. As such, *Star Wars* is a story of fathers and sons. Accordingly and expectedly, traditional viewings of the films focus on the relationship between Darth Vader and Luke Skywalker and the revelation of Luke's parentage (the iconic moment of, "Luke I am your father") which has become ingrained in American popular culture. However, I suggest that in our efforts to look for deeper political meaning in The *Star Wars* meta-narrative and to resuscitate progressive meanings around the *Star Wars* prequels, that we broaden our analyses beyond the dyad of Luke Skywalker and Darth Vader to include the character of The Emperor/ Darth Sidious and his relationship to Anakin Skywalker. When viewed as a triad, the characters, and their relationship to one another, take on a more clearly defined symbolic and metaphorical political meaning.

Prior to *Revenge of the Sith*, The Emperor has been primarily understood as Vader's Sith Lord and Master, a dark side version of Jedi Master, Yoda. As the *Star Wars* prequels develop, the films communicates how Darth Sidious is not "merely" Anakin's master but also a mentor and a Manichean figure that tempts the young Jedi into making destructive choices. The final film in the prequels, *Revenge of the Sith,* imparts subtle information that adds additional detail and context to Anakin's relationship to his older mentor.

Revenge of the Sith features several moments of praxis where Palpatine tempts young Anakin Skywalker ambitions with the promise of power and security. In one of these instances, Palpatine sits alone with his protégé and tells him the story of Darth Plagueis, the wise, a Sith Lord that was so powerful he could defeat death and create life through his ability to manipulate the Force. Palpatine implies that he has this power and that no Jedi is able to teach Anakin this archaic and forbidden knowledge. This sharing of information is crucial within the context of the *Star Wars* narrative because Anakin's parentage has never been revealed, and until this point, he was a Jesus figure of a virgin birth, one that would bring balance to the Force.

I suggest that this conversation can also be read as Darth Sidious' claim of parentage to Anakin Skywalker. Anakin and Palpatine have always enjoyed a father and son relationship, where the former used Anakin's devotion in order to corrupt him. However, the revelation that Sidious could in fact be Anakin's father (by willing him into existence through the Force) changes the relationship from metaphorical and emotive to actual and real as Palpatine the tyrant literally becomes the father of Vader, a fascist and failed democrat.[28]

Because of his attachment to the material world, intolerance of ambiguity, and his deep yearning for control, Anakin is a "wobbly" democrat with deep suspicions regarding democratic rule and the legitimacy of the Republic. In *Attack of the Clones*, Anakin frolics with Senator Amidala on the planet Naboo where, in what Robert Kaufman identifies as a "high camp" style of dialogue and narrative, Skywalker clearly tells Padmé of his deep suspicions regarding democracy and of his belief in efficient and powerful leaders that serve the public good (33–5). Anakin's cynicism toward democracy grows deeper as the narrative progresses towards an inevitable crisis of faith and an inevitable choice that, by the end of *Revenge of the Sith,* will push Anakin towards evil and the abandonment of his democratic values.

In the climax of *Sith*, the dialogue is particularly revealing as Anakin, now reborn as Darth Vader and intoxicated by blind power and rage, is warned by Obi-Wan, the protagonist of the film and "voice" of Lucas in this scene (with dialogue that is reminiscent of President Bush's famous phrase, "evil-doers" in reference to terrorists and those that oppose American power), that he should not believe in absolutes.[29] Ultimately, Obi-Wan warns Anakin that his desire for power and order will lead him to his destruction. Anakin, as a metaphor for a corrupted and fearful polity, is vulnerable to seduction by ideologues that are able to oversimplify and reduce the terms of political discourse to a set of binary options ("you are either with us or against us") and where those who dissent (Obi-Wan, Padmé, the Jedi Order) are labeled as traitors and enemies of the State.[30] Defeated in battle, Darth Vader/Anakin, the failed democrat, pays a high price for his confrontation with Obi-Wan Kenobi (who symbolizes justness of cause and the Old Republic which is hinted at by his exchange with Anakin, "I have the high ground"), as he is severely wounded and forced to live within his iconic black armor, armor that works symbolically to communicate Lucas's warnings regarding how technology is a threat to individuality and how Vader literally becomes a part of the Galactic Empire's technocracy, a living cog in its war machine.

Luke Skywalker, the third part of the triad, the "grandson" of Palpatine, and son of Anakin, is used by Lucas to complete the cycle in which democracies become tyrannical and are eventually returned to health by a citizens' rebellion. In the *Star Wars* narrative, Luke brings balance to the Force and fulfills the prophecy through his redemptive love for his father. As noted earlier, Luke is a populist democrat who is a leader of a multi-species alliance that is determined to restore the Old Republic and its democracy. Luke, as a symbol for the moral superiority of democracy and in keeping with Lucas's mythic themes of temptation and choice, is challenged by the appeal of power without responsibility that the dark side provides. In their confrontation at the end of *The Empire Strikes Back*, Vader verbalizes these temptations with the famous passages of "join me ... with our combined power we can rule the galaxy as father and son" and "with our combined strength we can end this destructive conflict and bring order to the galaxy." Luke resists these urgings from Vader, and in *The Return of the Jedi*, eventually confronts the true tyrant, Emperor Palpatine.

In this confrontation, which occurs on the symbolically resonant location of the second Death Star, Luke (the populist) faces Vader (the fascist) for Palpatine's (the totalitarian), amusement. As the battle climaxes, Palpatine attempts to goad the younger Skywalker into joining him as an apprentice by making appeals based on fear and worry regarding Luke's attachment to his friends and loved ones—the very fears which tempted Anakin to join the dark side. As a good democrat, Luke refuses to kill his father and symbolically throws away his lightsaber. Luke would prefer to win a moral victory and choose martyrdom rather than join the tyrant Palpatine in his crusade.[31] In response, Palpatine launches an overwhelming assault on the morally righteous democrat for his defiant and principled stand ("So be it Jedi") as Skywalker pleads for help from his father Darth Vader.

Emperor Palpatine's manipulation of the circumstances and of Anakin's vulnerability has been made clear. Vader in a moment of moral clarity chooses to kill the Emperor. Mortally wounded, Darth Vader, now (re)born again as Anakin Skywalker, has broken this cycle of family dysfunction. As Meyer in his article, "Star Wars, *Star Wars*," describes, this action possesses symbolic resonance as the failed democratic is morally recuperated by the political maturity, courage, and sacrifice of his son, the democratic populist:

> The real story is that Luke recognizes that his achievements have come through recognizing other ways of doing battle.... Although he is able to demonstrate considerably more saber skill in *Return*, the climactic battle is won with moral suasion. The Emperor is defeated by rallying the conscience of his servants, not by beating him or those

servants down.... We recognize Luke's political maturity when he
realizes ... even more deft swordsmanship are not marks of maturity, rather maturity is marked by the ability to lay weapons down....
Contrary to the Emperor's expectations, Luke's compassion proves
not to be his vulnerability, but the strength which makes it possible
to topple the Empire [114].

Together, Anakin and Luke were able to combine their efforts and
destroy the evil embodied by Emperor Palpatine, their tyrannical father,
and grandfather. In a closure to Lucas's cycle of the decline of democracies and their eventual resurrection, Vader removes the helmet that literally and metaphorically blinded him to truth and justice and "sees"
Luke Skywalker, the son and stalwart democrat, with his own eyes.

Conclusion: Bringing Balance to the Force

In this chapter, I have suggested that race, and questions of racial
encoding, provide helpful theoretical frameworks for reading both how
meaning is constructed around the *Star Wars* trilogies as well as for interpreting the ways in which these films can be understood to be complex
(and often contradictory) political narratives. For example, the original
trilogy can be read as being a space that is in many ways tolerant and
inclusive and where, despite the absence of characters of color, *A New
Hope*, *The Empire Strikes Back*, and *Return of The Jedi*, resonate within
the black popular imagination because of the ways that audiences reframe
and reconstitute meaning around objects of popular culture. In comparison, the *Star Wars* prequels have been interpreted as being racially
regressive, although they implicitly critique intolerance and xenophobia
as values that corrupt healthy States. By mining these tensions between
a text, its reception, and the thematic and visual ways that race, and the
construction of the Other, does work within these films, we as critics can
gain new insight into the *Star Wars* meta-narrative. In total, this chapter has also suggested that while oppositional and "race critical" readings of the *Star Wars* trilogies provide powerful theoretical lenses for
reading the *Star Wars* film text, these interpretations are not "merely"
or "simply" about race.

Alternatively stated, this chapter has hinted at how our readings of
Star Wars are not "simply" about race or the ways that norms of
difference are constructed within the films, per se. Rather, the problematics surrounding race, and our discussion of themes of tolerance and
inclusion in the saga, represent a broader set of questions regarding particular and universal readings of the films. A race critical, oppositional
reading of the *Star Wars* films encourages us to look to the larger crisis

in fandom surrounding the Star Wars prequels and their relationship to the *Star Wars* meta-narrative, where questions of racial encoding both hint at, as well as represent, deeper fissures surrounding the films and their reception by audiences. By looking to these criticisms, and by leveraging the diverse ways in which audiences reframe and reinterpret the *Star Wars* saga, we as critics can highlight the *universal themes* that transcend *the particular,* and generate new questions and terrain for the study of the *Star Wars* trilogies and their relationship to the American popular imagination.

Notes

1. For example, see: William Brooker's *Using the Force: Creativity, Community and Star Wars Fans*; Kevin S. Decker and Jason T. Eberl's *Star Wars and Philosophy*; Steven A. Galipeau's *The Journey of Luke Skywalker: An Analysis of Modern Myth and Symbol*; Michael J. Hanson and Max X. Kay's *Star Wars: The New Myth*; Mary Henderson's *Star Wars and the Magic of Myth*; and Glenn Kenny's *A Galaxy not so Far Away.*

2. Helping to fill this void, see: Kevin J. Wetmore Jr.'s *Empire Triumphant: Race, Religion and Rebellion in the Star Wars Films.*

3. Acknowledgements: this chapter has benefited from conversation with a number of individuals, and any and all shortcomings or errors are mine alone. I would like to thank my fellow galactic traveler Leigh Golden for his patience, insight, and humor in our some twenty year long conversation regarding all things *Star Wars*. I would also like to thank Professor Harold Forsythe for his helpful editing and insightful comments. Also, I am indebted to the Department of Political Science at The University of Chicago and my dissertation committee for encouraging my research into the many ways that popular culture intersects with the politics of race in America. Finally, I would like to thank my mother and (late) father for encouraging my intellectual creativity and for letting their young son fall in love with the *Star Wars* universe that summer of 1982 at The Strand Theater in Hamden, Connecticut.

4. While this complaint has been widespread, see in particular: Patricia J. Williams's "Diary of a Mad Law Professor: Racial Ventriloquism"; John Leo's "Fu Manchu on Naboo"; Andy Seiler's "Something to Offend Everyone: Minority Groups Say Hit Films Fill Screens with Stereotypes"; Brent Staples's "Shuffling Through the Stars"; and Jessica D. Thorpe's "Black and White and Strained All Over."

5. See: C. Condit's "The Rhetorical Limits of Polysemy"; bell hooks's *Reel to Real: Race, Sex, and Class at the Movies*; L. Steiner's "Oppositional Decoding as an Act of Resistance"; and T. Nakayama's "Show/Down Time: 'Race,' Gender, Sexuality, and Popular Culture."

6. See: John Fiske's *Understanding Popular Culture*; Simon Frith's *Performing Rites: On the Value of Music*; Frith's *Popular Music: Critical Concepts in Media and Cultural Studies*; Dick Hebdidge's *Subculture: The Meaning of Style*; John Street's *Politics and Popular Culture*; and Dominic Strinati's *An Introduction to Some Theories of Popular Culture.*

7. In regards to this question of "arbitration" and meaning, see Brooker's "Readings of Racism: Interpretation, Stereotyping, and *The Phantom Menace.*"

8. While this chapter focuses on the *Star Wars* films, I also acknowledge the varied storylines that have been produced under the banner of *The Star Wars Expanded Universe*. While ranging in quality, many of the these *Expanded Universe* materials, including comics, role-playing games, video games, and novels (and excluding slash, i.e. fan generated stories and fan films from the extended universe category), have contributed greatly to the longevity and entertainment value of *Star Wars* by offering additional levels of understanding and narrative depth to events that occur outside of the formal boundaries of the officially sanctioned films. The *Expanded Universe* occupies a precarious position in the *Star Wars*

imaginary because they are not always considered to be authentic representations of the *Star Wars* meta-narrative and imaginary. However, while only those events in the films are canonical, Lucas has also mined *The Expanded Universe* for ideas and included elements that are in agreement with his vision of *Star Wars*. In this chapter, I acknowledge this balancing act by privileging the original trilogy and the *Star Wars* prequels in my analysis, but by also referencing *Expanded Universe* materials that both reinforce the themes of, and which do not contradict any specific events, depicted in the officially sanctioned films.

9. For example, see: Decker's "By Any Means Necessary: Tyranny, Democracy, Republic, and Empire"; Koenraad Kuiper's "*Star Wars*: An Imperial Myth"; Anne Lancashire's "*Attack of the Clones* and the Politics of *Star Wars*"; Peter Lev's "Whose Future? *Star Wars, Alien,* and *Blade Runner*"; David S. Meyer's "Star Wars, *Star Wars* and American Political Culture"; Michael Ryan's *Camera Politica: The Politics and Ideology of Contemporary Hollywood Film*; Marguerite Waller's "Poetic Influence in Hollywood: *Rebel Without a Cause* and *Star Wars*"; and Will Wright's "The Empire Bites the Dust."

10. See the film documentary: *Empire of Dreams* (2004) that was included in the *Star Wars* DVD box-set released that year. Also, see Peter Biskind's *Easy Riders, Raging Bulls: How the Sex-Drugs-and-Rock 'n' Roll Generation Saved Hollywood*; and Dale Pollack's *Skywalking: The Life and Films of George Lucas*.

11. In this chapter, I use "imaginary" to signal to the reader the idea of a "*Star Wars Universe*"—a set of iconic films that resonate in the popular imagination, as well as the events and characters that are depicted within the two film trilogies.

12. See: Joe Feagin's *Racist America: Roots, Current Realities, and Future Reparations*; George Lipsitz's *The Possessive Investment in Whiteness: How White People Profit from Identity Politics*; Melvin L. Oliver and Thomas M. Shapiro's *Black Wealth/White Wealth: A New Perspective on Racial Inequality*; and Michael Omi and Howard Winant's *Racial Formation in the United States: from the 1960s to the 1990s*.

13. Interestingly, at the conclusion of *The Revenge of the Sith*, the viewer "sees" the world through Darth Vader's eyes as his samurai inspired helmet is lowered onto his head and the internal lenses are revealed to be red in color. Here, Vader literally sees the world in a reddish hue, and his perceptions of that world are symbolically "colored" by rage, war and anger.

14. The policies of the New Order and Governor Tarkin's "Doctrine of Terror" where the systems of the Galactic Empire are kept under control by threat of pre-emptive military force are described at, "The *Star Wars* Databank—The Empire." The *Star Wars* role-playing guides also contain information on the policies of the Galactic Empire. See: Bill Slavicsek, Steve Miller, and Owen K.C. Stephens's "Aliens and the New Order."

15. For a summary, see "The Galactic Empire and *Star Wars*: Xenophobic Racism and the Empire."

16. Again see: Henderson, *Star Wars: The Magic of Myth*.

17. For an alternative reading of Leia's gendered role and the role of gender in *A New Hope*, see: Kathleen Ellis's "New World, Old Habits: Patriarchal Ideology in *Star Wars: A New Hope*."

18. See: Greg Grewell's "Colonizing the Universe: Science Fictions Then, Now, and in the (Imagined) Future"; and David Bernardi's *Star Trek and History: Race-ing Toward a White Future*.

19. For an example of the literature on critical whiteness studies from which this observation is drawn see: Joe Kincheloe's *White Reign: Deploying Whiteness in America*; and Christopher Deis's "Talking About Whiteness and American Politics."

20. For a broad discussion of the relationship of *Star Wars* to black popular culture see: Henry Allen's "Planet Rock: *Star Wars* and Hip Hop"; and Elvis Mitchell's "Works Every Time."

21. For example see: David Golumbia's "Black and White World: Race, Ideology, and Utopia in *Triton* and *Star Trek*"; Lynne Joyrich's "Feminist Enterprise? *Star Trek: The Next Generation* and the Occupation of Femininity"; Sue Kim's "Beyond Black and White: Race and Postmodernism in *The Lord of the Rings* Films"; and Brian L. Ott and Eric Aoki's "Counter Imagination as Interpretive Practice: Futuristic Fantasy and *The Fifth Element*."

22. See: John W. Roberts's *From Trickster to Badman: The Black Folk Hero in Slavery and Freedom*.

23. As a continued effort to feature at least one prominent black character, Lucas introduces the character of Mace Windu in the *Star Wars* prequels. This Jedi is one of the leaders of the Jedi Order, one of its most powerful warriors, and is portrayed by the actor Samuel Jackson whom as a character actor, embodies the notion of "coolness" as famously conveyed by his memorable performances in Quentin Tarantino's films, *Pulp Fiction* (1994) and *Jackie Brown* (1997). Jackson's character is also pivotal to the plot of the films through his pivotal confrontation with Darth Sidious in *Revenge of the Sith*, and by Anakin Skywalker's decision to betray the Jedi order that is symbolized by Skywalker's attack on his former Jedi ally and council leader, Mace Windu.

24. See: Michael H. Hodges's "Critics Say 'Clones' Has Racial Stereotypes."

25. See again, Grewell and Bernardi.

26. I would include several recurring complaints and points of confusion surrounding the *Star Wars* prequels in this category. The broader plot and its emphasis on questions of politics and trade have been criticized as uninteresting and flat. The casting choices of Hayden Christensen, Jake Lloyd, and Natalie Portman have been questioned, and Lucas's general direction has been critiqued as being suspect. The character of Jar Jar Binks was received with consternation by much of fandom. Narratively, there has been much complaint and confusion regarding the birth of Luke and Leia and the latter's ability to "remember" her mother, Padmé Amidala. Also, the inclusion of midi-chlorians in the lore surrounding the Force has been met with disappointment because it supplies a "scientific" explanation to what had been long understood to be a matter of faith. For a range of reactions see the websites, *The Force.net* (www.theforce.net); *Ain't It Cool News* (www.aintitcool.com); *Supershadow.com* (www.supershadow.com); and the film review archive, *Rotten Tomatoes* (www.rottentomatoes.com).

27. For example, there is a strong and persuasive case for reading of race in *The Phantom Menace* that resonates because it is representative of the broader "problems" of nostalgia, whiteness, and race in Lucas's film saga. However, this focus on the particular, which was heralded by the breakdown in the triad of fandom, film, and critic, allows "weaker" readings of the film to find traction. For example, the observation that *Attack of the Clones* is xenophobic and racist because the clonetroopers are "raced" is a weak claim because it ignores the species diversity in the films and, more subtly, is ignorant of particular subtleties of fandom and the *Star Wars* imaginary. For example, Boba Fett has a cult following within fandom. As one of the most popular characters in the *Star Wars* universe, the revelation that he is a person of color, in much the same fashion as Lando Calrissian's addition to *The Empire Strikes Back*, can be read as a signal on the part of Lucas to fandom of an acknowledgement of the problematic nature of the racially homogeneous casting of his earlier films. The revelation that the clonetroopers and the stormtroopers are "brown" and linked to the most popular anti-hero in the films can be understood to be a popular and positive one among fans. For a discussion of Boba Fett's appeal to, and place in, *Star Wars* fandom, see: Tom Bissell's "Pale Starship, Pale Rider: The Ambiguous Appeal of Boba Fett."

28. See: Kuiper for a discussion of the theme of family and empire as it relates to the *Star Wars* meta-narrative.

29. Lucas expresses his concerns for democracy and the effect of the United States's foreign policy on freedom in Joe Williams's "George Lucas senses a Dark Side rising in the United States."

30. Conservatives and the conservative press reacted strongly to the implication that George W. Bush was embodied by Darth Vader, while predictably, liberals and others agreed that Vader's fall was a metaphor for American domestic politics in the post-9/11 moment. See: Chuck Baldwin's "Darth Vader and G.W. Bush: A Common Vision of Empire"; Morton Kondracke's "Tales from Dark Side Don't Live up to Hype"; "Star-Crossed: Partisans Imagine Politics Among The Jedi Knights"; and David Halbfinger's "*Star Wars* Is Quickly Politicized."

31. See: John Lyden's "The Apocalyptic Cosmology of *Star Wars*" for an extensive discussion of the religious undertones, Luke Skywalker's moral choices, and the biblical symbolism in the *Star Wars* imaginary.

Works Cited

Allen, Henry. "Planet Rock: *Star Wars* and Hip Hop." *A Galaxy Not So Far Away*. Ed. Glenn Kenny. New York: Henry Holt, 2002. 153–9.

Baldwin, Chuck. "Darth Vader and G.W. Bush: A Common Vision of Empire." *The Humanist* July/August 2005: 4–5.

Bernardi, David. *Star Trek and History: Race-ing Toward a White Future*. New Brunswick: Rutgers University Press, 1998.

Biskind, Peter. *Easy Riders, Raging Bulls: How the Sex-Drugs-and-Rock 'n' Roll Generation Saved Hollywood*. New York: Simon and Shuster, 1999.

Bissell, Tom. "Pale Starship, Pale Rider: The Ambiguous Appeal of Boba Fett." *A Galaxy Not So Far Away*. Ed. Glenn Kenny. New York: Henry Holt, 2002. 10–40.

Brooker, William. "Readings of Racism: Interpretation, Stereotyping, and *The Phantom Menace*." *Continuum: Journal of Media and Cultural Studies* 15.1 (2001): 15–32.

_____. *Using the Force: Creativity, Community and* Star Wars *Fans*. New York: Continuum, 2002.

Carson, Tom. "Jedi Uber Allies." *A Galaxy Not So Far Away*. Ed. Glenn Kenny. New York: Henry Holt, 2002.

Condit, C. "The Rhetorical Limits of Polysemy." *Critical Studies in Mass Communication* 6 (1989): 103–122.

Corliss, Richard, and Jess Cagle. "Dark Victory." *Time Magazine* 29 Apr. 2002: 56–68.

Decker, Kevin S. "By Any Means Necessary: Tyranny, Democracy, Republic, and Empire." *Star Wars and Philosophy*. Eds. Kevin S. Decker and Jason T. Eberl. Chicago: Open Court, 2005. 168–180.

_____, and Jason T. Eberl, eds. *Star Wars and Philosophy*. Chicago: Open Court, 2005.

Deis, Christopher. "Talking About Whiteness and American Politics." *Readings in American Political Issues*. Eds. Franklin D. Jones and Michael O. Adams. Iowa: Kendall Hunt, 2004. 35–46.

Ellis, Kathleen. "New World, Old Habits: Patriarchal Ideology in *Star Wars: A New Hope*." *Australian Screen Education* 30: 135–138.

Empire of Dreams: The Story of the Star Wars Trilogy. Dirs. Edith Becker and Kevin Burns. Lucas Film Limited. 2004.

Fader, Shanti. "'A Certain Point of View:' Lying Jedi, Honest Sith, and the Viewers Who Love Them." *Star Wars and Philosophy*. Eds. Kevin S. Decker and Jason T. Eberl. Chicago: Open Court, 2005. 192–204.

Feagin, Joe. *Racist America: Roots, Current Realities, and Future Reparations*. New York: Routledge, 2000.

Fiske, John. *Understanding Popular Culture*. New York: Routledge, 1992.

Frith, Simon. *Performing Rites: on the Value of Music*. Cambridge: Harvard University Press, 1996.

_____, ed. *Popular Music: Critical Concepts in Media and Cultural Studies*. New York: Routledge, 2004.

"The Galactic Empire and *Star Wars*: Xenophobic Racism and the Empire." *Wikipedia.com*. 5 Oct. 2005. <http://en.wikipedia.org/wiki/Galactic_Empire_%28Star_Wars%29#The_Empire_and_xenophobic_racism>.

Galipeau, Steven A. *The Journey of Luke Skywalker: An Analysis of Modern Myth and Symbol*. Chicago: Open Court, 2001.

Gavin, Edward. "The Cult of Darth Vader." *Rolling Stone* 2 Jun. 2005: 42–46.

Goldberg, David Theodore. *The Racial State*. Cambridge: Blackwell, 2002.

Golumbia, David. "Black and White World: Race, Ideology, and Utopia in *Triton* and *Star Trek*." *Cultural Critique* 32 (Winter 1995–1996): 75–95.

Grewell, Greg. "Colonizing the Universe: Science Fictions Then, Now, and in the (Imagined) Future." *Rocky Mountain Review of Language and Literature* 55.2 (2001): 25–47.

Halbfinger, David. "*Star Wars* Is Quickly Politicized." *The New York Times* 19 May 2005: Arts and Culture, Final.

Hanson, Michael J., and Max X. Kay. *Star Wars: The New Myth*. Xlibris Corporation, 2002.

Hebdidge, Dick. *Subculture: The Meaning of Style*. London: Methuen, 1979.

Henderson, Mary. *Star Wars and the Magic of Myth*. New York: Bantam, 1997.

Hodges, Michael H. "Critics Say 'Clones' Has Racial Stereotypes." *Detroit News* 18 May 2002: Entertainment Section.

hooks, bell. *Reel to Real: Race, Sex, and Class at the Movies.* New York: Routledge, 1996.

Joyrich, Lynne. "Feminist Enterprise? *Star Trek: The Next Generation* and the Occupation of Femininity." *Cinema Journal* 35.2 (Winter 1996): 61–84.

Kaufman, Roger. "High Camp in a Galaxy Far Away." *Gay and Lesbian Review Worldwide* 9.5: 33–5.

Kenny, Glenn, ed. *A Galaxy Not So Far Away.* New York: Henry Holt, 2002.

Kim, Sue. "Beyond Black and White: Race and Postmodernism in *The Lord of the Rings* Films." *Modern Fiction Studies* 50.4 (Winter 2004): 875–907.

Kincheloe, Joe, L., et al., eds. *White Reign: Deploying Whiteness in America.* New York: St. Martin's, 1998.

Kondracke, Morton. "Tales from Dark Side Don't Live Up to Hype." *Chicago-Sun Times* 5 June 2005: Editorial.

Kuiper, Koenraad. "*Star Wars*: An Imperial Myth." *Journal of Popular Culture* 21 (Spring 1988): 77–86.

Lancashire, Anne. "*Attack of the Clones* and the Politics of *Star Wars*." *Dalhousie Review* 82 (Summer 2002): 235–253.

Lipsitz, George. *The Possessive Investment in Whiteness: How White People Profit from Identity Politics.* Philadelphia: Temple University Press, 1998.

Leo, John. "Fu Manchu on Naboo." *U.S. New and World Report* 12 Jul. 1999: 14.

Lev, Peter. "Whose Future? *Star Wars*, *Alien*, and *Blade Runner*." *Literature/Film Quarterly*, 26.1 (1998): 30–37.

Lyden, John. "The Apocalyptic Cosmology of *Star Wars*." *The Journal of Television and Film* 4.1 (April 2000).

Meyer, David S. "Star Wars, *Star Wars* and American Political Culture." *The Journal of Popular Culture* 26.2 (1992): 99–115.

Mills, Charles W. *The Racial Contract.* New York: Cornell University Press, 1997.

Mitchell, Elvis. "Works Every Time." *A Galaxy Not So Far Away.* Ed. Glenn Kenny. New York: Henry Holt, 2002. 77–85.

Nakayama, T. "Show/Down Time: 'Race,' Gender, Sexuality, and Popular Culture." *Critical Studies in Mass Communication* 11 (1994): 162–179.

Nishime, Leilani. "The Mulatto Cyborg: Imagining a Multiracial Future." *Cinema Journal* 44.2 (Winter 2005): 34–49.

Oliver, Melvin L., and Thomas M. Shapiro. *Black Wealth/White Wealth: A New Perspective on Racial Inequality.* New York: Routledge, 1995.

Omi, Michael, and Howard Winant. *Racial Formation in the United States: from the 1960s to the 1990s.* New York: Routledge, 1994.

Ott, Brian L., and Eric Aoki. "Counter Imagination as Interpretive Practice: Futuristic Fantasy and The Fifth Element." *Women's Studies in Communication* 27.2 (Summer 2004): 149–176.

Pollack, Dale. *Skywalking: The Life and Films of George Lucas.* New York: Da Capo, 1999.

Roberts, John W. *From Trickster to Badman: The Black Folk Hero in Slavery and Freedom.* Philadelphia: University of Pennsylvania Press, 1989.

Ryan, Michael. *Camera Politica: The Politics and Ideology of Contemporary Hollywood Film.* Bloomington: Indiana University Press, 1988.

Seiler, Andy. "Something to Offend Everyone: Minority Groups say Hit Films Fill Screens with Stereotypes." *USA Today* 28 Jun. 1999: Life section, final edition.

Slavicsek, Bill, Steve Miller, and Owen K.C. Stephens. "Aliens and The New Order: An Excerpt from *The Rebellion Era Sourcebook*." *Wizards of the Coast.* 5 Oct. 2005. <http://www.wizards.com/starwars/article.asp?x=sw20010823c_rebellion&c=rpg>.

Staples, Brent. "Shuffling Through the Stars." *The New York Times* 20 Jun. 1999, late edition-final.

"Star-Crossed: Partisans Imagine Politics Among the Jedi Knights." *Pittsburgh Post-Gazette* (Pennsylvania) 21May 2005: Editorial, Sooner edition.

"The *Star Wars* Databank—'The Empire.'" *Star Wars.com* 5 Oct. 2005. <http://www.starwars.com/databank/organization/theempire/?id=eu>.

Star Wars Episode I: The Phantom Menace. Dir. George Lucas. Screenplay by George Lucas. Twentieth Century Fox, 1999.

Star Wars Episode II: Attack of the Clones. Dir. George Lucas. Screenplay by George Lucas and Jonathan Hales. Twentieth Century Fox, 2002.

Star Wars Episode III: Revenge of the Sith. Dir. George Lucas. Screenplay by George Lucas. Twentieth Century Fox, 2005.

Star Wars Episode IV: A New Hope. Dir. George Lucas. Screenplay by George Lucas. Twentieth Century Fox, 1977.

Star Wars Episode V: The Empire Strikes Back. Dir. Irvin Kershner. Screenplay by Leigh Brackett and Lawrence Kasdan. Story by George Lucas. Twentieth Century Fox, 1980.

Star Wars Episode VI: Return of the Jedi. Dir. Richard Marquand. Screenplay by Lawrence Kasdan and George Lucas. Story by George Lucas. Twentieth Century Fox, 1983.

Steiner, L. "Oppositional Decoding as an Act of Resistance." *Critical Studies in Mass Communication* 5 (1988): 1–15.

Stover, Matthew Woodring. *Star Wars: Episode III: Revenge of the Sith.* New York: Del Ray, 2005.

Street, John. *Politics and Popular Culture.* Philadelphia: Temple University Press, 1997.

Strinati, Dominic. *An Introduction to Some Theories of Popular Culture.* New York: Routledge, 1995.

Thorpe, Jessica D. "Black and White and Strained All Over." *The Buffalo News* 5 Nov. 2000: Entertainment section.

Waller, Marguerite. "Poetic Influence in Hollywood: Rebel Without a Cause and *Star Wars.*" *Diacritics* 10 (Autumn 1980): 57–66.

Wetmore, Kevin J., Jr. *The Empire Triumphant: Race Religion and Rebellion in the* Star Wars *Films.* Jefferson: McFarland, 2005.

_____. "The Tao of *Star Wars,* or, Cultural Appropriation in a Galaxy Far, Far Away." *Studies in Popular Culture* 23.1 (2000).

Williams, Joe. "George Lucas Senses a Dark Side Rising in the United States." *St. Louis Post-Dispatch (Missouri)* 18 May 2005: Everyday, Late Edition.

Williams, Patricia J. "Diary of a Mad Law Professor: Racial Ventriloquism." *Nation* 5 July, 1999: 9.

Wright, Will. "The Empire Bites the Dust." *Social Text* 6 (Autumn 1982): 120–5.

5

Feminism and the Force

Empowerment and Disillusionment in a Galaxy Far, Far Away

DIANA DOMINGUEZ

Is There Feminism in Star Wars?

In May of my seventeenth year, I sat in a darkened theater, watching a classic fairy tale scene unfold in a space setting. Luke Skywalker, donning a white uniform, enters a prison cell to discover a white-robed, beautiful princess lying asleep on a black slab. He stands in mute admiration of her as the background music turns romantic and soft. It was *Snow White*, set "a long time ago in a galaxy far, far away..." (*Star Wars Episode IV*).

At first, the scene seems to exemplify the traditional "dynamics of female adolescence" as described by Carol Gilligan:

> In the world of the fairy tale ... the adolescent heroines awake from their sleep, not to conquer the world, but to marry the prince, [so] their identity is inwardly and interpersonally defined.... The sex differences depicted in the world of fairy tales ... indicate repeatedly that active adventure is a male activity, and that if a woman is to embark on such endeavors, she must at least dress like a man [13].

What happens next in the scene, however, is not only a turning point in the film but a turning point in my life. Princess Leia awakes on her own, rather than because of a kiss, and utters: "Aren't you a little short for a storm trooper?" This catches Luke off guard, but he finally takes off his helmet and victoriously announces, "I'm Luke Skywalker. I'm here to rescue you," to which she responds in a bemused and amused tone, "You're who?" (*Star Wars Episode IV*). With those words, George

Lucas instantly shatters the familiar fairy tale trope of the fair unknown knight or prince in shining armor who comes to save the silent but eternally grateful damsel in distress and whisk her off to safety and a life of happily ever after.

Fast forward twenty-eight years to another darkened theater in May of my forty-fifth year. I sat in stunned silence and growing disillusionment as I watched the final scenes of Lucas's *Episode III: Revenge of the Sith* unfold. Had we gone back in time? Twenty-eight years into the future, I felt catapulted back into the world of traditional fairy tales and medieval romances where damsels wasted away and died of broken hearts, pale and weepy, unable to live for themselves if their knights abandoned them. The tracking shot of Padmé's funeral procession and casket brings to mind Sir Thomas Malory's and Alfred, Lord Tennyson's tale of Elaine of Astolat/Lady of Shallot, the beautiful maiden who dies of a broken heart after being rejected by Sir Lancelot and floats down the river to Camelot in a flower-strewn boat.

Padmé's tragically beautiful demise is reminiscent of Ophelia's in *Hamlet* and calls to mind Mary Pipher's use of her as a figure that represents the "destructive forces that affect young women" (20):

> As a girl, Ophelia is happy and free, but with adolescence she loses herself. When she falls in love with Hamlet, she lives only for his approval. She has no inner direction; rather she struggles to meet the demands of Hamlet and her father. Her value is determined utterly by their approval. Ophelia is torn apart by her efforts to please. When Hamlet spurns her because she is an obedient daughter, she goes mad with grief. Dressed in elegant clothes that weigh her down, she drowns in a stream filled with flowers [20].

Pipher describes that adolescent girls, like Ophelia, feel the dual and conflicting pressures of parental and societal expectations at the very time in life when their physical and psychological development is undergoing the most upheaval. On the one hand, Pipher says, adolescence is a time for pulling away from parents and family to develop an independent self and personality; on the other hand, "adolescence is when girls experience social pressure to put aside their authentic selves and to display only a small portion of their gifts" (22). Pipher continues: "This pressure disorients and depresses most girls. They sense the pressure to be someone they are not" (22). Ophelia's madness and suicide is a dramatic metaphor for Pipher's claim that "adolescent girls are saplings in a hurricane" (22). The devolution of Padmé's character throughout the prequel trilogy seems an eerie parallel to this adolescent loss of self, especially in terms of her death in *Episode III*, with its visual echoes to Victorian representations of Ophelia's and the Lady of Shalott's flower-strewn, tragically romantic deaths.[1]

Because Lucas shattered the damsel-in-distress trope with his characterization of Leia in the original trilogy and, in the first two episodes of the prequel trilogy, gave audiences a Padmé who exhibited the same kind of feistiness, outspokenness, and rebelliousness as her screen daughter, the unraveling and disintegration of her spirited character in *Episode III* was not only a disappointment, but smacked of betrayal as well. The traditional tropes and stereotypes that he so ably and consistently (and, I firmly believe, deliberately) subverted and questioned in five of the *Star Wars* films, he seems to have put firmly back in place in *Episode III*, which severely dilutes Padmé's character and sets up an automatic (and unfavorable) comparison with Leia's character. I could not help but be reminded of Melanie Wilkes's tragic but beautiful death scene in 1939's *Gone with the Wind* as I listened to Padmé's dying words to Obi-Wan Kenobi: "There is good in him. I know there is still" (*Star Wars Episode III*). I never much liked Melanie Wilkes; I always thought it was much more exciting to be Scarlett O'Hara.

This essay analyzes the central female characters in the two sets of *Star Wars* trilogies in terms of their status as role models for, especially, the young women in their respective audiences. In the original trilogy, Leia's character served as a spunky, no-holds-barred role model for an emerging generation of young women trying to break into still overwhelmingly male-dominated work places and social/political arenas—an exemplar to follow, a woman who strove and learned to "have it all" as so many women did in the late 1970s and early 1980s. Although it is easy to criticize and dismiss Padmé's character in *Episode III* as weak and a negative role model for young women (as relevant and appropriate as that criticism is) and leave it at that, further, deeper analysis reveals the slow deterioration of her character from an outspoken, risk-taking queen in *Episode I: The Phantom Menace* to a woman who loses the will to live when her man betrays her in *Episode III*. She can thus be read as an alarming reflection of the complex, confusing, and contradictory messages today's young women receive from society and the media.

I have divided the essay into two distinct parts. In the first section, I analyze Leia's character in the original trilogy (*Episodes IV, V, VI*: 1977, 1980, 1983) and show how she stands out as a strong feminist role model, in spite of her status as the "token female" in what most critics and scholars have termed a classic male hero journey tale—essentially, Luke's story. The second section focuses on Padmé's role in the prequel trilogy (*Episodes I, II, III*: 1999, 2002, 2005) as a feminist role model, with disappointing results. Also cast as the "token female" in what is Anakin's "anti-hero" journey to the dark side, Padmé fares considerably less favorably than her screen daughter twenty-two years earlier. Both analyses include examinations of important social aspects that significantly affect women, especially young women, and that, therefore, also have strong bearing on both the portrayals of each character and reactions from the audience to those portrayals.

Outspoken and Unpunished: Princess Leia

Although much has been written about the original trilogy, especially in connection with its classical mythical, or monomythical, aspects as defined by Joseph Campbell in *The Hero with a Thousand Faces*, surprisingly, not a great deal of that scholarship has focused on Princess Leia's character herself. Her character has often been included in articles and essays that seek to place her role in relation to the hero development of Luke, where she is often cast as the archetypal "goddess/muse" that helps the hero to fulfill his destiny (Campbell 109–20). Using the predominantly male-centered hero cycle as her starting point, Kathleen Ellis focuses on Leia's character but sees her as co-opted by a traditional patriarchal framework in which, ultimately, only males can be truly heroic and independent. According to Ellis:

> The underlying assumptions of the world depicted in *Star Wars* are very similar to the norms and values of twentieth century planet earth, particularly in terms of gender representation. A close examination of *Star Wars: A New Hope* reveals the patriarchal ideology Lucas unconsciously adopted. Early in the movie when Princess Leia Organa (Carrie Fisher) is taken prisoner by Darth Vader (David Prowse, voice by James Earl Jones) she exercises power; she stands up to Vader, defies his mind probes and then lies about the location of the rebel base. However as Luke Skywalker (Mark Hamill) and Han Solo (Harrison Ford) become involved, this is quickly forgotten. She is thereafter the traditional damsel in distress and it would appear that her "femaleness" is what prevents her from saving herself [135].

While Ellis's analysis makes several valid points, I dispute her contention that Leia's strength is forgotten once Luke and Han come on the scene or that she falls into the "traditional damsel in distress" role, either in *Episode IV* or in the entire original trilogy. Lois Hatton, writing in a *USA Today* article supports Leia's character as a stereotype-shattering figure: "Traditionally, beautiful princesses are helpless creatures who need to be rescued. Dressed in a beautiful white flowing gown, Leia belied her fairy tale costume to combine beauty, intelligence and bravery. Even though Luke came to her rescue, it was Leia who engineered their escape from the prison bay of the Death Star."

The writer who uses the pseudonym lazypadawan on the web-based

Saga Journal, an academic *Star Wars* fan journal, analyzes Leia's character in the original trilogy as a version of the woman warrior archetype in the April 2005 issue. She writes that, while Leia encompasses aspects of that traditional archetype, she transcends it by incorporating "a modern understanding of women's roles in society." She aligns Leia with such historical and mythological warrior women as Joan of Arc and the Greek Amazons, but shows in her essay how she goes beyond these ancient female warriors: "'(The princess in peril) is the one we have seen time and time again in fairy tales and legends of knights in shining armor with their damsels in distress; this is Leia's starting point. This is the one we thought she was until she opened her mouth'" (Meluch, qtd. in lazypadawan).

Indeed, until the "rescue" scene described in the opening paragraphs of this essay, Leia is something of an illusion, like those waiting damsels in the traditional fairy tales so many of us grew up with. Although viewers are given hints of her non-traditional personality earlier in scenes with Darth Vader and Grand Moff Tarkin, the film takes pains through the first half of the story to focus audience attention on Luke's perception of her: a holographic "vision in white" asking for help in an impassioned and almost breathless voice that Luke becomes enchanted with. He wants to know who she is the first time he sees her image, adding, in a scene reminiscent of a classic fairy tale: "She's beautiful."

From the "rescue" scene onward, however, Leia becomes a full-out rebel: outspoken, unapologetic, sarcastic, even bossy, and, shooting and killing without hesitation with the same skill as all the tough guys around her; in other words, she doesn't act at all like a damsel and, certainly, not one in helpless distress. [L]azypadawan expresses it succinctly: "As Carrie Fisher has put it, Leia isn't so much a damsel in distress as she is a distressing damsel." And, yet, there is no mistaking that she is female, female enough for both Luke and Han Solo to think of her in more than "buddy" terms, leading the audience to assume that competition for her favors is on the horizon—an assumption confirmed in the next two films of the trilogy.

For me, the best part of the original trilogy is that her sassy personality is neither tamed nor punished, as is the case in traditional in fairy tales and most other stories featuring initially outspoken or strong women. Leia presented (and still presents) an alternative femininity to the one I had most often been exposed to in my life. The two models of "womanhood" most obviously available while I was growing up are best exemplified by the character Sandy in the film version of *Grease* (1978): the age-old dichotomy of virgin or whore. One either grew up to be the "good" girl who learned to keep house, cook dinner, and raise clean, well-mannered children, like Carol Brady, *The Brady Bunch* (1969–74); Mrs. Cunningham, *Happy Days* (1974–84); or Mrs. Walton, *The Waltons* (1972–1981). Or, one became the girl with the "reputation" like *Grease's* Rizzo, the leather-clad Sandy at the end of that film or Joanie Cunningham's often talked-about friend, Jenny Piccolo.

Two television shows in the 1970s, touted as break-through shows by many feminists, attempted to resist that traditional dichotomy of the good/bad girl with mixed results: *The Mary Tyler Moore Show* (1970–77) and *Charlie's Angels* (1976–81). While it is true that Mary Richards (Mary Tyler Moore) stood (and still stands) as a feminist role model in many ways, both Lou Grant and Murray Slaughter often treat her as the "little girl" playing at a grown-up job—an updated version of Lucy Ricardo who is humored, but not truly taken seriously. While she seems competent and logical, for the most part, it should be noted that she is the only female character who displays those kind of traits—Rhoda is marriage-obsessed; Sue Ann Nivens is a home-wrecker and sexually voracious; Phyllis is flighty. Cast alongside them, Mary can only look better. However, she is often called upon to smooth feathers, to put things right, to repair relationships, or, conversely, to make decisions that the men have to come and repair; in other words, she often performs the very tasks that women are expected to handle (or not handle, as the case may be). And while she is cast as an independent woman whose single lifestyle includes being involved in the dating scene, viewers never see her really grapple with having to choose between her job and a serious relationship that could put that job in jeopardy. It is notable that by series' end in 1977, Mary is still single and has not succumbed to the "all women are desperate to be married" syndrome; however, it should also be noted that the show never focuses seriously on Mary's seeming lack of serious marriage opportunities. I always wondered what would happen if that did become an issue. My bet is that Mary would have been the one to have to concede as domestic responsibilities increasingly encroached upon her job. Such a situation would effectively reduce her to another casualty of the marriage vs. career battle, giving fuel to the edict that women don't belong in the workforce because it distracts them from their "natural" vocations. While, on the whole, I did (and still do) find *The Mary Tyler Moore Show* empowering (especially as I studied and worked in journalism after college), I was and am unsettled by the frequent moments that reduce Mary to the stereotype of the "befuddled little girl." This same aspect of infantilization permeates and weakens the overall empowering message of the other break-through show of the 1970s.

While *Charlie's Angels* has garnered both avid praise and passionate criticism from feminist circles for its sexualized portrayal of the three main characters, it is not the objectification that bothers me the most about the series. It is empowering, to an extent, to watch stereotypical "bimbos" solve crimes in a professional manner, as far-fetched as the schemes sometimes seem. One important element to note about *Charlie's Angels*, however, is that the characters never actually *use* sex to solve their cases; these are not modern-day Mata Haris who sleep with the enemy to get his secrets. Most of the episodes feature one or more of the "angels" as an "overeager hyper-sexualized female body" (Wurtzel, 25), and there often seems to be the promise or threat of a sexual situation, but none of the characters ever has to follow through. The series capitalizes on the *appearance*, not the actuality, and in doing so, turns the three women into iconic sex objects rather than independent sexual subjects. On the one hand, this aspect of the characters exemplifies the concept of the "male gaze" explained in Laura Mulvey's 1975 essay "Visual Pleasure and Narrative Cinema": women serve as the objects of the male's gaze or look, whether that male is the protagonist in the film or the spectator in the theater (1448–49). They are objects of desire or downfall, objects to be either possessed and tamed or punished and rejected by the male protagonists, and, by proxy, the male spectators (1450). On the other hand, their "sexual" disguises can be seen as an empowering move, an enactment of Luce Irigaray's "mimicry" (deliberately adopting a stereotype) as a means of resisting and dismantling a suppressive social system (76). She says: "One must assume the feminine role deliberately. Which means already to convert a form of subordination into an affirmation, and thus to begin to thwart it" (76). The original "angels" are symbolic of "the pretty girls, girls who learned to manipulate, girls whose hearts always belonged to daddy" that Elizabeth Wurtzel says learned to play the "game," those who are rewarded and condemned at the same time for playing it (25), and they often use this behavior to their advantage, leading their rivals to underestimate them. The objectification, which troubles many feminist critics of the show, however, does not bother me as much as the fact that these three competent crime-fighters always revert to "daddy's little girls" by the end of every episode. They are treated like infantile "angels" by Bosley and especially by Charlie. There is always some piece of the puzzle they can't figure out, that Charlie has to explain over his speaker box while the "girls" listen in rapt attention, breaking out into cute smiles of admiration for their "wise father." The beginning of each episode sets the stage: "Once upon a time, there were three little girls." In the end, although both *Charlie's Angels* and *The Mary Tyler Moore Show* claimed to cast their female protagonists as smart, capable, and independent women, both shows ultimately infantilize their characters, giving women in the audience mixed messages.

But, in May of 1977, finally, I saw, larger than life on the screen, the woman I wanted to become. Here was a woman who could play *like* and *with* the boys, but who didn't have to *become* one of the boys and who could, if and when she wanted to, show she *liked* the boys, a woman who is outspoken, unashamed, and, most importantly, unpunished for being so. She also isn't a flirty sex-pot, tossing her hair seductively to distract the enemy, but Han's first remark about her sets up the possibility of flirtation: "Wonderful girl. Either I'm going to kill her or I'm beginning to like her." She doesn't play the role of the "maternal caretaker," although she does display caring and compassion, or the "sweet innocent damsel" who stands passively by while the men do all the work, but does step aside to let them do what they're good at when it is wise to do so. She isn't a "freak" with special powers, like Jamie, *The Bionic Woman* (1976–78), or Diana Prince, *Wonder Woman* (1975–79), who could then be "excused" from being a "real" woman but who still must hide her real identity and strength. And, she isn't a "tomboy," dressed like a man, who wants to "hide" that she is a "girl" so she'd be accepted—she just IS. Leia is a *hero* without losing her gendered status; she does not have to play the cute, helpless sex kitten or become sexless and androgynous to get what she wants. She can be strong, sassy, outspoken, bossy, and bitchy, and still be respected and seen as feminine.

Her first appearance in *Episode IV* is visually symbolic of this merging. She wears a long, flowing white dress and is referred to as a princess, reminiscent of Snow White and other fairy tale princesses, but she carries a blaster and can shoot with deadly accuracy. Additionally, although it has been the recipient of much ridicule, parody, and criticism, it should be noted that her hairstyle (the so-called cinnamon buns) is modeled on the traditional hairstyle of the Hopi Indian Corn Maiden, who symbolizes both fertility and wisdom and which was worn by Pancho Villa's soldaderas (female warriors) during the Mexican Revolution of the early 1900s, as Lucas himself commented in a 2002 *Time* magazine interview (Cagle). While Han Solo does attempt to disparage her by calling her advice "female" (implying inferior) after they have escaped the garbage hold, it needs to be pointed out that both Han and Luke continue to follow her advice as the story continues (Ellis 136). Shortly after this scene, perhaps to flex his wounded "manhood," Han chases a group of storm troopers to highlight to Chewbacca that there's nothing to be afraid of. This elicits the backhanded comment from Leia, "he has courage, I'll give him that much," prompting Luke to respond, "yeah, but what good will it do us if he gets himself killed." Luke's comment voices the wisdom of being more cautious in the face of such danger that Leia has been advocating.

In *Episode V: The Empire Strikes Back*, Leia displays the traditional traits of the soldier who never leaves his or her post in the first part of the film: she must be forcibly removed from her post as the rebel base's command center literally falls down around her. Later, when Han is encased in carbonite and is being loaded onto Boba Fett's ship, Leia exhibits the kind of determined, single-minded behavior one would expect from a traditional action hero like Sylvester Stallone or Arnold Schwarzenegger: she stands at the doorway and shoots her blaster, face stoic, ignoring the possible danger to herself, in direct opposition to the kind of hysterical "falling apart" that has been traditionally portrayed as "female" behavior.

Of course, no analysis of Leia can avoid a discussion of the famous metal bikini scene in *Episode VI: Return of the Jedi*. The scene and the outfit have become both iconic and controversial, for the scene seems to unfairly single out the primary female character in the trilogy for sexualization and objectification, which I have to admit, was my first reaction to the scene when I first saw the film, as it seems to be a textbook case for Mulvey's "male gaze" concept (see above). However, although the scene is rife with titillation for the primarily young male audience of the films, it can be read as a moment of great empowerment for the females in the audience. The powerless and sexually enslaved female uses the very elements of that enslavement to kill a captor that understood too late that he dangerously underestimated his prey. In addition, although it is true that Leia is the only character to be put into a specifically sexualized "victim" position, this may simply be a reflection of the fact that women are particularly vulnerable to such victimization as a means for torture and humiliation. I would argue that Han's carbon-freezing enslavement serves an almost equal function: he is kept immobile, trapped so that he cannot fight back, suspended in a half-dead, half-live state, and put on display like a trophy; he becomes a "body" just as objectified as Leia's body is in her metal bikini. Leia's victim-to-victor transformation anticipates, perhaps, shows like *Buffy, the Vampire Slayer* (1997–2003), *Alias* (2001–06), and *Xena, Warrior Princess* (1995–2001) more than twenty years after Leia, which also capitalize on the apparent vulnerability of the female protagonists who get the upper hand because their enemies seriously underestimate them.

In addition to exhibiting non-traditional feminine behavior—and not getting censured for it—Leia demonstrates a strength that comes from principles and convictions and exemplifies what Gilligan calls a universal "ethic of care" (74), which stands in direct opposition to traditional (and stereotypical) theories of female psychological and moral development. Traditional theories of moral development are based on early psychoanalytical studies dating back to Freud that focused primarily on males, who develop decision-making skills based on a sense of justice; morality imposes restrictions on what one can do (6–7). Girls and women, on the other hand, seem to focus their moral development on the basis of responsibility to/for others, of establishing and maintaining relationships, which, according to traditional psychological analysis, meant that women had a less developed sense of justice than men, or a "problem" in their moral development (7–8). Gilligan proposes that, instead, psychology needs to acknowledge the differences in men's and women's development so that women are not seen as "lacking" in moral development (17–19). A moral development based on the central concept of relationships and responsibility to others follows a parallel trajectory to the traditional "justice oriented" development of boys/men (in which they increasingly learn to acknowledge and respect the rights of others through laws and rules) (17–19).

Gilligan defines three sequences or stages in a woman's development of this ethic. The first stage could be called the selfish stage. There is "an initial focus on caring for the self in order to ensure survival" (74). In the second stage, there is a "new understanding of the connection between self and others which is articulated by the concept of responsibility" (74). This second stage, however, often leads to a sort of "martyrdom" to others' needs. "At this point, good is equated with caring for others," often at the expense of self (74). The final stage "focuses on the dynamics of relationships and dissipates the tension between selfishness and responsibility through a new understanding of the interconnection between other and self," and "evolves around a central insight, that self and other are interdependent" (74).[2]

In *Episode IV*, Leia seems to exhibit qualities that fit squarely into stage three. She has a highly developed sense of responsibility to the cause of the Rebellion, but she also has a strong sense of self (and self-preservation) and allows for others to follow different paths toward different goals. After Luke shows disappointment at Han's decision not to join the Rebellion, Leia tells Luke: "Everyone must follow his own path; you can't force them." In an earlier scene, when the captured Leia is confronted by Darth Vader and his mind probe in her cell, the audience sees the fear in her eyes, but she does not yield to her fear; she does not scream, and we find out later that she does not divulge her secrets. A personal attack does not break her down; it is only Grand Moff Tarkin's threat to her home planet with the Death Star that finally makes her divulge the location of the Rebel base. This "alternative method of persuasion," as Tarkin calls it, exploits her sense of responsibility to others, this awareness of the connection to others, but it is also a testament to her own need not to lose her loved ones—a form of self-preservation. She exhibits care in this scene as explained by Gilligan: "Care becomes the self-chosen principle of a judgment that remains psychological in its concern with relationships and response but becomes universal in its condemnation of exploitation and hurt" (74). She is committed to the Rebellion but not at the expense of the lives of her loved ones.

However, elements of stage two (the martyrdom stage) are subtly present in her refusal to mourn for her lost family and planet once she arrives at the Rebel base and in her rejections of both Luke's and Han's attempts at "romance." This particular element—rejection of romance or love—is made more apparent in *Episode V* when she forcefully denies having any feelings of affection for Han and when she desperately avoids having any physical contact with him when they are stranded on the Millennium Falcon inside what turns out to be the giant space slug. For Leia, at this point, there is only the cause of the Rebellion, to the exclusion of any personal gain or happiness—a psychological or emotional form of martyrdom. Personal safety can also be sacrificed for the cause, as Leia displays at the beginning of *Episode V*; while the base is literally falling down around them as the Imperial forces are attacking, she remains at her post, fully aware of the fact that she could die if she does not leave—literal martyrdom. Gilligan states: "when only others are legitimized as the recipients of the woman's care, the exclusion of herself gives rise to problems in relationships, creating a disequilibrium," which eventually leads to "a reconsideration of relationships in an effort to sort out the confusion between self-sacrifice and care inherent in the conventions of feminine goodness" (74).

This "sorting out" takes place toward the end of *Episode V* when Han is about to be lowered into the carbon-freezing chamber. While Han's response to Leia's admission that she loves him is most often seen as "comic relief" in what is a highly charged dramatic scene, his "I know" can also be seen as acknowledgement of her having taken the final step into a true universal "ethic of care." Her mission after this pivotal scene is no longer simply risking all for the Rebellion. While she will not abandon the larger cause, rescuing Han has become momentarily more important—a plot point that opens *Episode VI*. Once Han has been rescued, the larger mission can continue. And, in the final scenes of *Episode VI*, it is Leia that voices this marriage of self and responsibility when she tells Han that she loves him, but she is committed to helping Luke reestablish a new interplanetary alliance after the fall of the empire.

This ethic of care coincides with attempts at re-defining a heroic mythic "pattern" in feminist terms—or, "transforming the male myth" cycle, to quote the subtitle of Nadya Aisenberg's 1994 book, *Ordinary Heroines*. Aisenberg defines female heroism as follows:

> Beyond the great importance the heroine attaches to the individual life, she is deeply committed to a more humane society. She is forward-looking, since she is looking to forge something which doesn't exist yet. She remains a responsive leader of the society from which she has emerged, an ordinary woman endeavoring, nevertheless, to tackle extraordinary problems. In all these ways, she distinguishes herself

from the hero. Significantly, she substitutes moral courage and a moral voice for the hero's physical courage and sense of predestination [13].

Similarly, Carol Pearson and Katherine Pope state that the female hero "does not presume to kill dragons for others, and therefore they are not expected to become her followers or subjects. Others are both actually and potentially her equals, and she encourages them to undertake their own journeys" (14). Leia embodies these heroic qualities and learns that she does not have to "give up her life for others" and, therefore, "has no reason to entrap them, make them feel guilty, or dominate them. When she refuses to sacrifice her own self to others, she becomes more, rather than less, able to aid others in their search for fulfillment" (15). Leia's non-traditional, white-robed princess is a catalyst for both Luke and Han to find their own goals and reach them, but she also enabled me to begin my own journey toward fulfillment.

However, I would argue that the truly ground-breaking aspect of Leia's character is the fact that she transcends all of the stereotypes and archetypes: she is a princess, but not a damsel in distress; she is a warrior, but does not live solely by the sword or gun; she is a sister and, eventually, a wife and mother, but she never stops being a rebel; and, she exemplifies both traditional and feminist qualities of the hero, fighting dragons (or storm troopers) bravely and treating others equally. This same transcendence of types is reflected in the way the Kenner toy company marketed the Princess Leia action figure between 1977 and 1985. Sherrie Inness writes in "'It's a Girl Thing': Tough Female Action Figures in the Toy Store" that, prior to Leia, action figures like the Bionic Woman and She-Ra were sold with fashion accessories and designer clothing, like Barbie (83). The Bionic Woman, in fact, carried a purse with make-up and a photo of her boyfriend, Steve Austin, "which lessened her tough image" (82). "It is hard to run down the bad guys when wearing an evening gown and high heels, something that never concerned or worried the Six Million Dollar man, who did not even own a tuxedo," Inness comments (82). Leia, on the other hand, "wore relatively utilitarian outfits" (83) and "seemed more interested in saving the universe from Darth Vader than in shopping" (84).

Leia was a more grown-up version of my childhood hero, Dorothy, of L. Frank Baum's *The Wonderful Wizard of Oz* (1900). Pipher says of those girls who survive the storm of adolescence: "Strong girls know who they are and value themselves as multifaceted people" (265). Leia was someone I could identify with at seventeen. She was part of that crowd of girls who said what they felt, when they felt it, and put people in their places when they needed to be—the ones who dropped houses on wicked witches or shot a few storm troopers if necessary—and even managed to get the good-looking guy in the end, who didn't seem to mind it so much if she was a little bit bossy.

Diminished and Silenced—Padmé Amidala

If not very much has been written about Princess Leia in academic scholarship, there is even less to be found in academic circles about Padmé and nothing specifically about her role as a feminist model. Fans, of course, have had a tremendous amount to say about the prequel trilogy and its characters on fan forums and blogs, which I consulted for this essay in order to gauge the reaction to Padmé's character arc. I was pleasantly rewarded with the extensive and quite thoughtful discussions, especially, about Padmé's role in *Episode III*, which so disillusioned me. Those discussions, frankly, led me to explore her role and characterization beyond that knee-jerk reaction. Disillusionment and even a sense of betrayal are still quite present in my analysis, but her role and character arc can be read from a much deeper social perspective.

Audiences are introduced to Padmé in *Episode I* in a way that parallels our introduction to Leia in 1977: she is something of an illusion, easy to underestimate in her royal makeup and ceremonial robes. When she joins the Jedis on their search for Anakin on Tatooine, now disguised as the queen's maidservant, the non-traditional "damsel" aspect is revealed, again, in the same way it is with Leia in *Episode IV*. In all three episodes of the prequel trilogy Padmé exhibits a combination of traits that emphasizes her non-traditional characterization. She is only an adolescent in *Episode I*, but she is also the elected queen of her planet, exhibiting wisdom beyond her years. In keeping with her age, she exhibits stubbornness and an eagerness to satisfy curiosity and seek excitement, but she understands the responsibilities of leadership and takes appropriate measures to protect herself. In *Episode II: Attack of the Clones*, she displays the confused emotions of a young woman falling in love with the "wrong" man, but shows considerable focus and determination in the larger political concerns of the Republic. She continues to demonstrate stubbornness and courage in the face of imminent danger, not waiting for someone else to rescue her, for instance, in the Geonosis arena when she, Anakin, and Obi-Wan are to be executed, but she also reveals a depth of understanding and compassion when she comforts Anakin after he confesses he has slaughtered an entire village of Sand People on Tatooine after his mother's death.

Although it can be argued that Padmé becomes almost one-dimensional in *Episode III*, reduced to a weepy stereotype of a woman coming undone, she does have moments in which she exhibits flashes of her previous traits: she expresses wisdom born of years of diplomacy and political skill when she advises Bail Organa to go along with the senate vote on the Empire until the time was right to fight back and a stubborn refusal to simply accept what others tell her when she takes it upon herself to find Anakin and try to talk some sense into him. Early in the film, when Anakin comes home triumphantly after having rescued Palpatine in the opening battle scenes, Padmé appears wearing Leia's famous "cinnamon bun" hairstyle, which, because she announces to Anakin that she is pregnant, invokes the ultimate blend of traits: a warrior-maiden who announces impending motherhood. For me, as it must have for countless other Leia fans, that scene sets up a promise that is never fulfilled, for Padmé never becomes the warrior-mother I was expecting.

However, Padmé's character is not a female hero in the tradition of her screen daughter, Leia, who serves as a hopeful role model to young girls and women. A close analysis of Padmé's story arc in the prequel trilogy reveals that she serves as a different kind of "hybrid" archetypal female figure: a tragic heroine with warrior-hero traits. The trajectory her character follows is something akin to Jocasta's in the classic Greek play *Oedipus* (Sophocles) with an important difference. In *Oedipus*, Jocasta is a character who is most definitely acted upon; audiences are not allowed to see any of the decisions or activities she may have had a say in (if she did at all) during her life and marriage to Oedipus. In Padmé's case, audiences are given a character who has a considerable mind of her own rather than a side-lined character who is simply acted upon, which is perhaps why her death as a result of "losing the will to live" feels like such a betrayal.

Lazypadawan provides a truly insightful analysis of Padmé's story arc in the tragic heroine tradition in the August 2005 issue of *Saga Journal*, which addresses the complaint from many fans that Padmé's character devolved into a supremely weak figure. While lazypadawan stops short of calling her death heroic (unlike some fans on the fan forums), she astutely connects the trajectory of Padmé's character with the changing environment of the Republic as it devolves into a tyrannical empire. She explains the symbolism of Padmé's death in the following passage:

> There is a literal way of looking at Padmé's death and a symbolic way. Padmé was as much a symbiont [*sic*] with her time and place as she was with Anakin. When the Republic era passes, she passes. In a cut scene from *Attack of the Clones*, the lesson in Padmé's story about the refugees she tried to help as a child was that those who cannot adapt die. She cannot adapt to this new galaxy. Moreover, she refuses to adapt. She tells Anakin he is going down a path she cannot follow. She bitterly utters, "So this is how liberty dies, with thunderous applause," after Palpatine crowns himself Emperor before a cheering Senate. When [Anakin] in a rage cuts off her

breathing, it symbolizes that the Empire, as personified by Anakin, is killing her.

She suffers not only the death throes of the Republic and its ideals, she also suffers with the physical and spiritual pain Anakin endures in his transformation into the Darth Vader we know from the classic trilogy. The film intercuts between Vader's agony on the operating table and Padmé's dying moments as she gives birth. When Vader's transformation is complete, she dies.

As symbolic and classically tragic as Padmé's character can be read, however, many fans saw her role in *Episode III* as highly diminished and weakened. On the *Star Wars* official site fan forums, several forum threads were devoted to a discussion of Padmé's death and the weakening of her character. Representative of the comments is this one by a fan who uses the screen name Starwarsfan77–05: "I think another type of paradox could have been established, while still maintaining who she was. I think she would have fought to the bitter end to save [Anakin] and her children. She would have been DETERMINED to try, no matter what anyone else told her. As written, her death may be poetic and sadly beautiful, however it doesn't fit Padmé." The *Star Wars* films fan forum on the *Empire Online* magazine also devoted several threads to Padmé's character arc and death, which garnered comments like this one by DeviatedPrevert: "How Lucas could take the [prequel trilogy's] sole female character and make her into a simpering, weak-willed 50s housewife is beyond me. And it's unforgivable in this day and age." He compares Padmé's giving up the will to live at the end of *Episode III* unfavorably with Leia's actions after watching her planet being blown up by the Death Star in *Episode IV* and watching Han being encased in carbonite in *Episode V*: "Yet Padmé has kids, names them, then just gives up! Sorry kids, I love you, but your bastard father betrayed me, so I'm going to show my strength by dying and abandoning you.... Nice one, Padmé" (DeviatedPrevert). While the situations described in this post are not directly parallel, their emotional content is similar. Padmé has nearly been killed by Anakin (the love of her life), finds out that he slaughtered all the "youngling" Jedi apprentices, believes Anakin is dead, and has ostensibly witnessed the end of the Republic and all the Jedis, all at the same time—events that would devastate most people. Leia, in *Episode IV*, must have experienced excruciating emotional pain to watch her entire home world simply disappear, and, at that moment, she is unaware that help is on its way—she is, as far as she knows, completely alone. In *Episode V*, she has no way of knowing whether Han (the love of her life) will survive inside the carbonite casing, she is about to be handed over to Darth Vader by Lando Calrissian, and she doesn't know anything about Luke's whereabouts; he might be dead—again, as far as she knows, she is alone. Yet, Leia turns her emotional despair into successful action; Padmé, at least in the final minutes of *Episode III*, lets her despair kill her. It is clear that many fans were expecting a stronger, more outwardly heroic role and ending for Padmé, based on her traits and actions in the first two episodes of the prequel trilogy. I can certainly understand and sympathize with their feelings and comments. I remember my reaction during *Episode I* when Padmé arrives on Naboo with Anakin and Qui-Gon Jinn in order to try to save her people and draws her gun. I turned to my friend and said "Now we know where Leia gets it!" Her death, frankly, is a dreadful let-down.

The "weakening" of Padmé's character in *Episode III* can certainly be read in the way jobloffski interprets it on the *Empire Online* fan forum: "Padmé's trajectory is from being an all conquering hero queen, to 'mere' senator, to being 'only human' and having the frailty that goes with that. So the 'reducing' of her character didn't just come out of the blue." The point is valid, and, read this way, Padmé's demise is simply a vital part of the storytelling process. However, whether her diminished role is a product of Lucas's commentary on the loss of identity, part of the story arc of failure in *Episode III*, or a weakening of her iconic status as an overt comment on or, conversely, an unconscious reflection of the vocal and often virulent backlash against feminism in this country in the past few years, the effect is the same: she fails to serve as a positive female role model at a time when they are most needed. Furthermore, in an era of an explosion of female heroes who are popular with both male and female audiences—Xena, Buffy, *Alias*'s Sydney Bristow, Lara Croft, Eowyn and Arwen of *The Lord of the Rings* (2001–03) trilogy, to name a few—it is notable that Padmé's character should seem to revert to such a traditional trope, a reversal that is worthy of more serious analysis. Are there important social parallels to be uncovered in the devolution of Padmé's character from strong, level-headed, intelligent, and morally-concerned queen to sad, tragic young woman who loses the will to live and (figuratively/literally?) dies of a broken heart?

One aspect of Padmé's character that must be kept in mind is her age in the trilogy; she begins the story arc as a 14-year-old, and it must be assumed she led a sheltered life as a child and then moved into a position of high ceremony and heavy responsibility at a time of great psychological and hormonal upheaval—adolescence. When we next see her in *Episode II*, she is twenty-four, but, again, it seems clear she has led a protected and rigidly controlled life; as a senator, it can be safely assumed that she would not have been allowed to date freely or have much of an un-chaperoned social life. Her relationship with Anakin thus becomes increasingly secretive and isolated, leading to a marriage that further isolates her from any kind of support network. Finally, in *Episode III*, as a

27-year-old, trying to balance her political duties and her still secretive marriage, she must then keep her pregnancy hidden, and her whole world is reduced to, essentially, Anakin who becomes increasingly controlling, paranoid, and obsessive.

Read through that lens, Padmé's character is disturbingly symbolic of the rising statistics of domestic and relationship abuse among young women in this country—the CDC (Center for Disease Control) reports that, in 2003, 5.3 million women age 18 or over experienced Intimate Partner Violence (CDC). It especially concerned me to read several posts on two of the more popular *Star Wars* fan forums from fans that identified themselves as teenagers (under eighteen) or young adults (under twenty-five) that saw the ending as highly romantic because it showed just how deeply Padmé loved Anakin. As one young fan wrote: "She just lost it; she gave up; now that's love people. To love someone so much that to live with out them would be death anyway. She lived long enough to give birth and name her children that were made with the love of anakin and her [*sic*]" (Angelhonest).

Padmé's giving up the will to live after Anakin's betrayal is alarmingly analogous to the countless stories of women who lose their voices, independence, and their very souls in order to "keep" their lovers or husbands. Vanessa Bush, in her 2002 *Essence* article, reports that "approximately one in five girls ages 14 to 18 has experienced physical or sexual violence while dating" and "an astonishing 40 percent of girls between the ages of 14 and 17 knew someone their age who has been hit or beaten by a boyfriend." Young girls with little or no experience with relationships (like Padmé, it must be assumed), consider dramatic, excessive emotions on the part of a boyfriend (like jealousy or an obsessive desire to always be in touch with her to "protect" her) to be expressions of his overwhelming, consuming love for her (Bush). Psychologist Jill Murray says of the rising statistics of teen relationship abuse: "What is most alarming is that the signs of potential abuse [from their boyfriends] are also behaviors that young women find most flattering" (7), like wanting to spend all his time with her and eventually isolating her from her friends and even family, which she often interprets as love (9). Given how many comments I read on the fan forums that were similar in tone to Angelhonest's post (see above), it seems that this definition of love is an all too-popular one.[3] That kind of love leads to a loss of identity and autonomy, as Padmé's character so strikingly symbolizes.

From her study of adolescent girls and the pressures they face, Pipher offers a dramatic way to read Padmé's character: "At first blush, it seems things should be better now. After all, we have the women's movement. Hasn't that helped? The answer, as I think about it, is yes and no" (12). Although, as Pipher says, many older women (middle-aged, middle-class—the Leia generation) have opportunities their own mothers would have never dreamed of, "girls today are much more oppressed. They are coming of age in a more dangerous, sexualized and media-saturated culture. They face incredible pressures to be beautiful and sophisticated, which in junior high means using chemicals and being sexual. As they navigate a more dangerous world, girls are less protected" (12). While the prequel trilogy seems to take pains not to show Padmé in overtly sexual situations or as a highly sexualized figure (i.e. like Leia's bikini episode), much of Anakin's language regarding his love for Padmé is centered on her beauty and the image she portrays.

The pressures for women don't end when adolescence ends, as Kristin Rowe-Finkbeiner shows in her 2004 book *The F-Word: Feminism in Jeopardy*. The issues facing young women that she describes and analyzes in her book are disturbingly mirrored in Padmé's situation in the prequel trilogy, but in *Episode III* especially. Young women of today—the so-called third wave feminists—have advantages their first and second wave feminist grandmothers and mothers did not, but "they also have unprecedented new pressures related to education, career, relationships, home, family, and personal life in a culture that still isn't supportive of combining these roles" (3). One of the comments repeated several times on the fan forum sites as a reason for Padmé's moving into the background was her pregnancy. The general character of these messages—which often generated some impassioned responses—was that her marriage and pregnancy precluded her from partaking in senate or Republic matters because she now had more "important" things to think about (being a wife/mother), or that it somehow made her less physically/mentally able to deal with senate matters. Given the story line, that her marriage and pregnancy had to remain a secret, there is a legitimate reason for her taking a less visible role in the senate, but a number of these posts did not focus on this plausible explanation for this aspect of the plot. Instead, the tone of these posts (something along the line of "well, she's pregnant," as if that explains it all) implies that pregnant women have no business trying to maintain a career outside the home, or, that it somehow saps their intelligence and other skills.[4] As Rowe-Finkbeiner states, "many of the rights, freedoms, and opportunities for women to define their own lives and sexuality, along with the chances for women to be who they want to be without compromise or hidden penalties, are often taken for granted. Truthfully, those rights haven't been around for all that long. And all that can be taken away" (3). The erosion of Padmé's central role in the affairs of the Republic is an eerie reflection of the still constant struggle women have today to balance the many roles they are expected or want to play.

An analysis of Padmé's character based on Gilligan's universal "ethic of care" (74), described above in the section on Leia, reveals a sense of backsliding and psychological dysfunction. While Leia moves from caring only about others at the expense of self, giving "rise to problems in relationships, [and] creating a disequilibrium" to a true understanding of the interconnections between self and others—a true "ethic of care" (74), Padmé never fully moves out of the second, "martyrdom," stage. While it could be argued that *Episode II* finds her struggling between the larger, moral concerns of the Republic and her personal needs and desires, the moment she decides to wed Anakin *secretly*, she moves away from that "ethic of care" to a more selfish stage (stage one) that also encompasses putting others' needs before her own (stage two)—Anakin's troubled psyche that, like many women who find themselves in doomed or abusive relationships, she feels her love can "fix." Throughout *Episode III*, she is focused mostly on Anakin's needs, almost to the exclusion of the problems of the Republic and completely to the exclusion of her own compromised career and status. Her death is both a supreme form of martyrdom (her last words and thoughts are about Anakin's innate goodness) and a supreme form of selfishness (she dies only thinking about how she cannot live without Anakin, dismissing the children she has just given birth to). By the end of *Episode II*, Padmé has taken a terrible step backward from the highly desirable and healthy final stage of moral and psychological development—the universal "ethic of care" that "evolves around a central insight, that self and other are interdependent" (74).

Padmé's character, especially in *Episodes II* and *III*, enacts the very paradox of adolescent girls' psychological development described by Lyn Mikel Brown and Gilligan in their remarkable book *Meeting at the Crossroads: Women's Psychology and Girls' Development*, in which they record their findings based on a five-year in-depth study with nearly one hundred girls between the ages of seven and eighteen. Their findings are both enlightening and disturbing. Brown and Gilligan write about what they call the "crossroads" that girls face when they enter adolescence:

> As these girls grow older they become less dependent on external authorities, less egocentric or locked in their own experience or point of view, more differentiated from others in the sense of being able to distinguish their feelings and thoughts from those of other people, more autonomous in the sense of being able to rely on or take responsibility for themselves, more appreciative of the complex interplay of voices and perspectives in any relationship, more aware of the diversity of human experience and the differences between societal and cultural groups. Yet we found that this developmental progress goes hand in hand with evidence of a loss of voice, a struggle to authorize or take seriously their own experience—to listen to their own voices in conversation and respond to their feelings and thoughts—increased confusion, sometimes defensiveness, as well as

evidence for the replacement of real with inauthentic or idealized relationships ... these girls are in fact not developing, but are showing evidence of loss and struggle and signs of an impasse in their ability to act in the face of conflict [6].

As I watch Padmé's inevitable spiral toward her death in *Episode III*, I can only cry at the knowledge that she is, unfortunately, all too symbolic of the many young girls and women who end up traumatized, with their wholeness truncated because of the pressures our culture places on them (Pipher 12). In a dramatic way, Padmé represents the "series of disconnections that seem at once adaptive and psychologically wounding: between psyche and body, voice and desire, thoughts and feelings, self and relationship" (Brown and Gilligan 7) that too many girls do not survive as they move into womanhood; she reflects all too tragically those girls that, like Shakespeare's Ophelia, do not weather the storms of adolescence and young womanhood (Pipher 281). Unlike her screen daughter Leia, Padmé loses her voice, her self, and her life.

It is gratifying to note how many fans did express outrage at the devolution of Padmé's character because it implies that there is conscious awareness of the negative and damaging messages such a characterization sends to, especially, impressionable young women in the most vulnerable stages of their lives. However, it is alarming and disturbing to see how many comments there were among, especially, younger fans about how "perfect" such an ending was—romantic, tragic, the ultimate expression of true love—because, sadly, it seems to give credence to Pipher's, Brown and Gilligan's, and Rowe-Finkbeiner's contentions about how dangerous and destructive our current culture is to girls and women. While Padmé cannot be said to be a positive role model, she can serve as a strong warning bell to pay closer attention to the messages that girls of this generation are being exposed to and heeding.

Finding Lessons of Empowerment

Are there lessons and influences we can take from the primary female characters in what is debatably one of the most influential film franchises of the late twentieth/early twenty-first century? Princess Leia is still a highly iconic figure for many women, for those who came of age with her when she first appeared, as well as for those who were introduced to her through the videos, a twentieth anniversary theater re-release of the original trilogy, and the new DVD sets. Twenty-eight years after she exploded on the screen, larger-than-life, she still has the power to inspire girls and women to seek their own heroism. It is, however, disheartening to note how little true academic research has been devoted to this powerful character, especially when so much scholarly work has been devoted to such female heroes as Ellen Ripley—of the *Alien* (1979–1997) series) and Sarah Connor (of the *Terminator* (1984–2003) series—and now Xena and Buffy. Only time will tell whether the same kind of longevity and popularity will accompany Padmé and whether the prequel trilogy and her role in it will inspire serious scholarship in the area of film, popular culture, and women's studies.

Leia's impact cannot be dismissed. Teenagers like me in the late 1970s were the first group of girls on the verge of womanhood who could hear their parents say, "you can be anything you want," and have it be true. The problem was we had few visible role models to follow into that wide "anything" world. Our mothers may have been the pioneers of the contemporary women's movement, burning bras, taking birth control pills, and breaking all-male barriers down, but we were the first generation to have to fulfill the promise of "business as usual." We were no longer "door-busters," but we weren't really status quo yet. Lucas's portrayal of Leia as a no-nonsense, outspoken, unquestioned leader, who happens to be female, a princess, and *unpunished* for pushing the traditional boundaries of gender, shattered, for me at least, the unspoken assumption of what waited in my future.

It is sad to say that, twenty-eight years later, the same cannot be said of Padmé. Like Pipher's adolescent girls who lose their voices and souls in trying to fit into society's often damaging expectations for them (20), the strong, courageous, principled Padmé of the first two episodes becomes lost in the cacophony of female images in today's media, with an overwhelming number of them conveying the message that a woman is nothing if she is not with a man. Padmé's role in *Episode III* is also sadly reflective of the rash of recent stories of women overwhelmed by the responsibilities of marriage and motherhood that have lost their support networks and suffer in silence until they snap in horrifyingly public ways. Her situation also calls to mind those of mothers-to-be who suffer harm or death at the hands of husbands or lovers who crack under the pressure of impending fatherhood. The erosion of Padmé's overt heroic traits feels like a betrayal because, as Starwarsfan77–05 writes on her blog site: "We also didn't like [the weakening of her character], b/c Padmé is the 'Leia' of this generation. She is a role-model for young girls, and that was virtually thrown away in this film." Ultimately, rather than a role model to try to emulate, the prequel trilogy's audiences are given a character that sends a depressing message: love can be deadly, but you should want it at any cost.

There is a ray of hope on the horizon, however; this story and essay need not end on a sour, depressing note. Now that the *Star Wars* saga is complete, and can be viewed in its proper chronological order (*Episodes*

I—VI), the title of *Episode IV: A New Hope* becomes prophetic. In the saga that unfolds in this new viewing order, Leia transcends her mother in the same way that Luke transcends his father—tempted and almost killed by the dark side, only to emerge as the new order of Jedi who understands the balance of light and dark. Leia emerges as a new order of female hero, one who can balance the personal and the universal, romantic love and moral principles, marriage/motherhood and sociopolitical concerns. She is a woman we can all aspire to be: a woman who can shoot her enemies and tuck her children into bed; a woman who can cook her husband a romantic dinner and rescue him from the bad guys; and a woman who can be strong, wise, outspoken, sexy, and soft all at the same time, and, most importantly, *unpunished* for being so.

Notes

1. In Victorian England, both Ophelia and the Lady of Shalott became popular symbols of female madness and lovelorn women driven to suicide when their men abandoned or rejected them. Both became frequent subjects of the Pre-Raphaelite painters, notably John Everett Millais, whose 1852 painting of a drowned Ophelia, and John William Waterhouse, whose well-known 1888 painting of the Lady of Shalott almost serve as blueprints for Padmé's funeral casket scene. Thorough discussions of the so-called Ophelia phenomenon in the art and literature of the Pre-Raphaelite and late English Victorian period can be found in Elaine Showalter's *The Female Malady*; Sally Mitchell's *The Fallen Angel*; Nina Auerbach's *Woman and the Demon*; Gudrun Brokoph-Mauch's article "Salome and Ophelia: The Portrayal of Women in Art and Literature at the Turn of the Century"; and Bram Dijkstra's *Idols of Perversity: Fantasies of Feminine Evil in Fin-de-siecle Culture*.

2. Gilligan is not without her critics, the most vocal among them Christina Hoff Sommers (*The War Against Boys*), who accuses Gilligan of not providing enough (or any) empirical data for her conclusions and of having almost single-handedly started and perhaps even created what Sommers calls the "girl crisis" that has prompted feminist activists to privilege programs and advantages for girls to the detriment of boys in this country. Other critics in what might be called the Sommers' camp are Carol Tavris (*Mismeasure of a Woman*), Judith Kleinfeld ("The Myth That Schools Shortchange Girls"), and Michael Gurian (*The Minds of Boys*). All argue against Gilligan's (and Lyn Mikel Brown's and Mary Pipher's) claims that girls are in crisis in our society.

3. Although the romantic notion of finding one's soul mate and true love has been around for quite awhile, at least in Western society, it has been coupled in the last couple of decades or so with an increased portrayal of women as desperate, sex-crazed, and willing to do almost anything to "get" a man and keep him. Popular music lyrics, sung by both male and female singers, routinely express the idea that life is not worth living once a loved one has left—in 2005 alone, some of the most popular songs/videos boldly state that the speaker will do anything to bring the lost love back (Mariah Carey's "We Belong Together," Rob Thomas's "Lonely No More," and The Backstreet Boys' "Incomplete," as the most recent examples). On television, meanwhile, viewers are steadily assaulted with portrayals of women, especially on the so-called reality shows, willing to debase themselves for fame, money, or finding "love" (*The Bachelor* [2002–], *Joe Millionaire* [2003], *For Love or Money* [2003–] to name just a few). Theatrical films in recent years have increased their level of sexual content, often tied to violence or aggression, which only serves to promote aggression as an erotic component, and many comedies fall into the sex-crazed teen genre, which depicts both male and female teens scheming for ways to get into bed with the opposite sex (the *American Pie* series of films [1999–2003] being a prime example). Romantic comedies, meanwhile, consistently send out the message that being alone is a

"crime against nature," helping to fuel the idea that, women especially, *must* find a partner at any cost (the recent, and very popular, *Must Love Dogs* (2005), for instance). Given this onslaught of mixed messages, it is easy to see how younger fans might see Padmé's "soul" attachment to Anakin and her death as highly romantic rather than tragic.

4. It should be noted that during the fifth season (1999–2000) of the highly popular *Xena: Warrior Princess*, the main character (and the actress, Lucy Lawless) was pregnant. The character still continued her warrior duties, albeit slightly reduced, and it was reported that Lawless continued with her own stunts until well into her seventh month of pregnancy. During the fifth season (2005–06) of ABC's popular series *Alias*, both the character Sydney Bristow and the actress playing her, Jennifer Garner, are pregnant, but not "sitting out" of the action entirely (Sydney Bristow still goes on quite a few missions). And, finally, the critically acclaimed Sci Fi Channel series *Farscape* (1999–2003), featured a pregnant Aeryn Sun (the main female protagonist, played by Claudia Black, who was *not* pregnant herself) during its final regular season and in its follow-up 2004 four-hour mini-series. In that mini-series, Aeryn Sun not only gives birth, but actively helps to avert a war between two warring factions in her part of the universe; in fact, she and her husband, John Crichton, are forced to battle invading forces while Aeryn is in labor. Given these examples, it does not seem that much of a stretch to assume that Padmé might have been a little more active in her role, in spite of her pregnancy.

Works Cited

Aisenberg, Nadya. *Ordinary Heroines: Transforming the Male Myth*. New York: Continuum, 1994.

Angelhonest (pseudonym). "Padmé's Death in Episode 3." Online Posting. 2 June 2005. *Star Wars: Message Boards: Episode III*. 10 Aug. 2005 <http://forums.starwars.com/thread.jspa?threadID=211073>.

Auerbach, Nina. *The Woman and the Demon: The Life of a Victorian Myth*. Cambridge: Harvard University Press, 1982.

Baum, L. Frank. *The Wonderful Wizard of Oz*. New York: Dover, 1960.

Brokoph-Mauch, Gudrun. "Salome and Ophelia: The Portrayal of Women in Art and Literature at the Turn of the Century." *The Turn of the Century: Modernism and Modernity in Literature and the Arts: International Conference Papers*. Eds. Christian Berg, Frank Duriuex, and Geert Maria Jan Lernout. Walter De Gruyter, 1995.

Brown, Lyn Mikel, and Carol Gilligan. *Meeting at the Crossroads: Women's Psychology and Girls' Development*. New York: Ballantine, 1992.

Bush, Vanessa. "A Thin Line Between Love & Hate: Dating Violence Strikes One in Every Five Teenage Girls. Could a Young Woman You Know Be at Risk?—The War on Girls." *Essence* Nov. 2002. 10 Apr. 2004 <http://www.findarticles.com/p/articles/mi_m1264/is_7_33/ai_94384286/print>.

Cagle, Jess. "So What's the Deal with Leia's Hair?" *Time Online Edition* 29 Apr. 2002. 9 Oct. 2004 <http://www.time.com/time/covers/1101020429/qa.html>.

Campbell, Joseph. *The Hero with a Thousand Faces*. 2nd ed. Princeton: Princeton University Press, 1968.

Center for Disease Control (CDC). "Intimate Partner Violence: Fact Sheet." *National Center for Injury Prevention and Control*. 30 Nov. 2004. 5 Sept. 2005 <http://www.cdc.gov/ncipc/factsheets/ipvfacts.htm>.

DeviatedPrevert (pseudonym). " Padmé's Death." Online Posting. 28 June 2005. *Empire Online Film Forums: Star Wars*. 10 Aug. 2005 <http://ubb.empireonline.co.uk/show flat.php?Cat=&Number=1144418&page=&view=&sb=5&o=&fpart=1&vc=1>.

Dijkstra, Bram. *Idols of Perversity: Fantasies of Feminine Evil in Fin-de-Siècle Culture*. New York: Oxford University Press, 1986.

Ellis, Kathleen. "New World, Old Habits: Patriarchal Ideology in *Star Wars: A New Hope*." *Australian Screen Education* 30 (Spring 2002): 135–138. *Academic Search Premier*. EBSCO-host. Oliveira Memorial Lib., Brownsville, TX. 9 Oct. 2004 <http://pathfinder.utb.edu:2048/login?url=http://search.epnet.com/login.aspx?direct=true&db=aph&an=9459090>.

Gilligan, Carol. *In a Different Voice: Psychological Theory and Women's Development.* 1982. Cambridge: Harvard University Press, 1993.

Gurian, Michael, and Kathy Stevens. *The Minds of Boys: Saving Our Sons from Falling Behind in School and Life.* San Franciso: Jossey-Bass, 2005.

Hatton, Lois. "*Star Wars* Heroes Slay Stereotypes." *USA Today* 1 July 2005: 13a. *Academic Search Premier.* EBSCOhost. Oliveira Memorial Lib., Brownsville, TX. 10 Aug. 2005 <http://pathfinder.utb.edu:2048/login?url=http://search.epnet.com/login.aspx?direct=true&db=aph&an=J0E161651458505>.

Inness, Sherrie A. "'It's a Girl Thing': Tough Female Action Figures in the Toy Store." *Action Chicks: New Images of Tough Women in Popular Culture.* Ed. Sherrie A. Inness. New York: Palgrave Macmillan, 2004. 75–94.

Irigaray, Luce. "The Power of Discourse and the Subordination of the Feminine." *This Sex Which is Not One.* Trans. Catherine Porter. Ithaca: Cornell University Press, 1985. 68–85.

jobloffski (pseudonym). "Padmé's Death." Online Posting. 28 June 2005. *Empire Online Film Forums: Star Wars.* 10 Aug. 2005 <http://ubb.empireonline.co.uk/showflat.php?Cat=&Number=1144418&page=&view=&sb=5&o=&fpart=1&vc=1>.

Kleinfeld, Judith S. "The Myth That Schools Shortchange Girls: Social Science in the Service of Deception." *The Women's Freedom Network.* May 1998. 15 Oct. 2005. <http://www.womensfreedom.org//wp2.PDF.>

lazypadawan (pseudonym). "The Perils of Padmé: The Short Life and Fast Times of a Tragic Heroine." *Saga Journal* 1.8 (Aug. 2005). 15 Aug. 2005 <http://www.sagajournal.com/lptheperilsofpadme.html>.

_____. "Princess Leia and the Woman Warrior." *Saga Journal* 1.4 (Apr. 2005). 15 Aug. 2005 <http://www.sagajournal.com/lpwomanwarrior.html>.

Mitchell, Sally. *The Fallen Angel: Chastity, Class, and Women's Reading, 1835–1880.* Bowling Green: Bowling Green University Press, 1981.

Mulvey, Laura. "Visual Pleasure and Narrative Cinema." *The Critical Tradition: Classic Texts and Contemporary Trends.* 2nd ed. Ed. David H. Richter. Boston: Bedford, 1998. 1444–1453.

Murray, Jill. *But I Love Him: Protecting Your Daughter from Controlling, Abusive Dating Relationships.* New York: Regan, 2001.

Pearson, Carol, and Katherine Pope. *The Female Hero in American and British Literature.* New York: R. R. Bowker, 1981.

Pipher, Mary. *Reviving Ophelia: Saving the Selves of Adolescent Girls.* New York: Ballantine, 1994.

Rowe-Finkbeiner, Kristin. *The F-Word: Feminism in Jeopardy: Women, Politics, and the Future.* Emeryville: Seal, 2004.

Showalter, Elaine. *The Female Malady: Women, Madness, and English Culture, 1830–1980.* New York: Pantheon, 1985.

Sommers, Christina Hoff. *The War Against Boys: How Misguided Feminism Is Harming Our Young Men.* New York: Simon and Shuster, 2000.

Sophocles. "Oedipus the King." *The Three Theban Plays: Antigone, Oedipus the King, Oedipus at Colonus.* Trans. Robert Fagles. New York: Penguin, 1982. 155–252.

Star Wars Episode I: The Phantom Menace. Dir. George Lucas. Screenplay by George Lucas. Twentieth Century Fox, 1999.

Star Wars Episode II: Attack of the Clones. Dir. George Lucas. Screenplay by George Lucas and Jonathan Hales. Twentieth Century Fox, 2002.

Star Wars Episode III: Attack of the Clones. Dir. George Lucas. Screenplay by George Lucas. Twentieth Century Fox, 2005.

Star Wars Episode IV: A New Hope. Dir. George Lucas. Screenplay by George Lucas. Twentieth Century Fox, 1977.

Star Wars Episode V: The Empire Strikes Back. Dir. Irvin Kershner. Screenplay by Leigh Brackett and Lawrence Kasdan. Story by George Lucas. Twentieth Century Fox, 1980.

Star Wars Episode VI: Return of the Jedi. Dir. Richard Marquand. Screenplay by Lawrence Kasdan and George Lucas. Story by George Lucas. Twentieth Century Fox, 1983.

Starwarsfan77–05 (pseudonym). "Padmé's Death in Episode 3." Online Posting. 26 May 2005. *Star Wars: Message Boards: Episode III.* 10 Aug. 2005 <http://forums.starwars.com/thread.jspa?threadID=211073>.

_____. "Summary of Why Leia Remembers Padmé, and Some of Our Thoughts on Padmé's Death–What SHOULD Have Happened." Online Posting. 28 June 2005. *Star Wars: Blogs.* 10 Aug. 2005 <http://blogs.starwars.com/starwarsfan77–05/1>.
Tavris, Carol. *Mismeasure of a Woman.* New York: Simon and Shuster, 1992.
Wurtzel, Elizabeth. *Bitch: In Praise of Difficult Women.* New York: Doubleday, 1998.

6

Seduced by the Dark Side of the Force

Gender, Sexuality, and Moral Agency in George Lucas's Star Wars *Universe*

VERONICA A. WILSON

Throughout his popular *Star Wars* films, writer-producer-director George Lucas repeatedly links, through rhetoric, ideology, and symbolism, womanhood, femininity, and male homoeroticism with the destructive power of the dark side of the Force. This malign psychic energy, responsible for the demise of Anakin Skywalker and his symbolic reincarnation into the Sith Lord Darth Vader; the slaughter of the Jedi Knights; the rise of the ancient Sith order to take dominion over countless worlds; and the collapse of galactic representative democracy, is both "feminine" and "feminizing." The dark side fuels and empowers the machinations of Sith Lord Darth Sidious, who becomes the Emperor Palpatine, the truest villain of the saga. This essay explores how Lucas's ultimately misogynist theme—associating femininity with darkness, deception, and moral decay—is dramatically expressed through the Anakin/Vader character and his problematic desires. It is the dark side, personified by the sexually ambiguous Palpatine/Sidious, that "seduces" Anakin into joining the Sith, murdering the Jedi, and helping establish the Galactic Empire. Throughout the films, and despite his Jedi training, Anakin/Vader rarely acknowledges moral self-responsibility and instead makes fateful decisions based upon possessive emotional "attachments" to his mother, his wife, and his mentor Palpatine. Finally, two decades after Vader's embrace of darkness, it is his attachment to his son Luke Skywalker—rather than any ideological change of heart—that redeems Anakin and destroys the Sith order for all time.

Scholars have discussed at length how George Lucas drew inspiration from Joseph Campbell's mythological analyses and from Jungian archetypes when crafting characters and situations for his *Star Wars* saga. Few, however, have analyzed ways in which Lucas's characters and narratives apparently reflect other sorts of cultural and authorial attitudes as well—assumptions so deeply embedded that they are largely unexamined, unconscious, and perhaps wholly unintentional. On first examination, in fact, the *Star Wars* saga appears to say little about women, and far less about misogyny or homophobia. While there are only a few female characters in the six films (a meaningful fact in itself), three of them—Princess/Senator Padmé Amidala, Princess Leia Organa, and Rebel Alliance leader Mon Mothma—are presented as strong, capable political leaders, compassionate spokespersons for democracy and galactic freedom. Furthermore, despite a few clumsy allusions to male-female attraction and romance, there are no obviously sexual characters in the films, except the (significantly) doomed Anakin and Padmé. Lucas has repeatedly stated that his targeted audience is young people and that he envisions the *Star Wars* saga as family-friendly films that downplay, usually to the point of ignoring, the fraught issue of sexuality and its potential consequences. Given that fact, the films are nevertheless overtly, nostalgically heterosexual in their orientation, and Lucas clearly never meant for them to say anything whatsoever about homosexuality or same-sex desire.

Yet regardless of Lucas's conscious creative intentions, the films contain a wealth of both implied and overt misogyny and homoeroticism. Moreover, the saga offers ultimately patriarchal and homophobic resolutions to the political and personal crises central to its essential plot. In addition, the characters most directly involved in the temptation, fall, and redemption of Anakin Skywalker/Darth Vader—Shmi Skywalker, Padmé Amidala, and Sidious/Palpatine—are multivalent, ambiguous figures which, in theorist Judith Butler's terms, possess a "signifiability" that cannot be wholly controlled by their creator, Lucas. They hence "continue to signify in spite of their authors, and sometimes against their authors' most precious intentions" (241). A close examination of these characters, and their impacts upon Anakin/Vader's life and choices, will explicate this signifiability and, in so doing, demonstrate the implicit, occasionally inconsistent yet omnipresent misogyny and homophobia at the heart of the *Star Wars* saga.

As a historian of cultural and gender politics, I analyze popular films for internal contradictions that illuminate modern American concerns and dilemmas. To a certain extent, nearly all cultural texts grapple with questions of gender relations and family matters, the tensions between individualism, and the human need for emotional connection to others.

Hence popular films, the *Star Wars* saga included, are sites for contemporary struggles over meaning and interpersonal politics. They are elements of ongoing cultural discourses about gender and sexuality, relationships of power between individuals and institutions. According to feminist scholar Jackie Byars, film analysis can help us see "the range of readings a single text can evoke," and expose "the hierarchies of power at work in and through texts," hierarchies "linked to race, class, sex, and gender differences" (61). In other words, close analysis of the *Star Wars* films can help us not only to examine the problems of a galaxy far, far away, but also to understand how the films reflect and potentially help shape cultural struggles over questions of gender and sexuality in contemporary American society. Texts can be, and are, read differently depending on time and place, but as Byars points out, they also "participate in the ideological process that constructs real, historical, gendered subjects—human beings" (61). To dismiss the *Star Wars* films out of hand as lowbrow adventure-romance films that cannot support any meaningful analysis, as some commentators have done, is erroneous and perhaps irresponsible. Given the saga's immense popularity, its potential cultural and psychological impact upon millions of viewers and their individual gender and sexual identities and beliefs should not be underestimated.

As with any text, the *Star Wars* films can be read for both dominant and competing ideologies: for themes that uphold mainstream cultural values and prejudices and themes that challenge or subvert them. In this essay, I analyze Lucas's saga and several of its offshoot novels, reading them in some cases against the grain, so to speak, interpreting these texts with my own set of negotiated readings centered around issues of sexuality and gender. Alternative readings are always possible, of course, including those that Lucas himself would surely prefer. My interpretation is meant to point out some of the competing messages concerning sexuality and gender in the *Star Wars* filmography and hence to offer oppositional readings that identify and challenge misogynist and homophobic messages contained in the films. In so doing, I hope that analyzing the *Star Wars* saga as a set of mainstream texts might open up, if not precisely a "feminist space," in Byars's words (169), at least an opportunity for non-patriarchal, non-homophobic, and more egalitarian interpretations.

Close examination of Anakin Skywalker's "seduction" by the dark side of the Force throughout the *Star Wars* films reveals that the troubled Jedi Knight's moral downfall is not only melodramatic and (in terms of Jedi and Sith beliefs in destiny, discussed in all six episodes) quite possibly fated, but also overdetermined. Once the audience learns that, according to Jedi wisdom, deep emotional attachments to other beings can pave the way to the dark side through possessiveness and fear of loss, it becomes evident that Anakin's core personality is quite problematic. In *Episode I: The Phantom Menace*, we see his deep emotional bond with his mother Shmi Skywalker, the only parent he has ever known. Theirs is a loving, close relationship, despite or perhaps because of the hardships of life under slavery, and one that obviously conditioned Anakin (unlike most Jedi children who know no parental figures save the Knights who rear them from infancy at the Jedi Temple) to expect and desire intimate emotional attachments to other beings. In the little we see of Shmi, it is clear that her life is centered around her young, precocious son, whom she selflessly encourages to leave her care, escape slavery on the harsh desert planet Tatooine, and pursue his destiny as a Jedi Knight in the galactic capital of Coruscant. Despite Shmi's self-sacrifice and Anakin's emotional security in her care, however, Lucas posits this loving mother-son relationship, strangely enough, as a primary cause or source of the events that will gradually transform Anakin Skywalker into the terrifying Sith Lord Darth Vader.

From his first arrival at the Jedi Temple, the nine-year-old Anakin is understandably concerned for his mother, left behind in slavery on a gangster-controlled Outer Rim planet thousands of light-years away. Not surprisingly, he also misses her, having presumably never been apart from her since his birth. Yet for the Jedi Masters who will decide his fate, Anakin's fears and melancholy are a source of grave concern. In Anakin's first meeting with the Jedi Council, we see the initial dramatic foreshadowing of the emotional dynamic that will later be responsible for Anakin's fall to the dark side. "Fear," admonishes Master Yoda, "leads to anger; anger leads to hate; hate leads to suffering." Fear for loved ones' well-being, fear of the sundering of emotional ties, is considered a primary route to the dark side. Hence, Anakin is immediately given the first and most important lesson he will never truly learn as a Jedi apprentice or Knight—that emotional detachment, compassion, and concern for all beings in the abstract, but no passionate attachments to particular persons, should govern the behaviors and attitudes of a proper Jedi Knight. Intense, passionate bonds of any sort are a potential path to selfishness, darkness, and evil.

Whether or not viewers agree with such logic, Yoda's concerns become quite valid in Anakin's case. In the course of events that make up *The Phantom Menace*, Anakin finds something of a substitute mother figure in Padmé Amidala, the young queen of Naboo whom Anakin's first Jedi mentors, Qui-Gon Jinn and Obi-Wan Kenobi, are attempting to protect from various political enemies. Responding to Padmé's maternal concern for his well-being, the precocious Anakin, despite his tender years, soon becomes interested in her romantically, convinced that they will one day wed—no matter Jedi prohibitions of such relationships. Separated from Shmi, he has already found another woman upon whom to focus his apparent deep need for emotional attachment. Over the intervening decade that separates the events of *The Phantom Menace* from those of *Episode II: Attack of the Clones*, Anakin's fixation on Padmé continues to grow until it becomes a full-blown and nearly irrational erotic obsession.

At this point, *Attack of the Clones* takes a dramatically misogynist turn, blaming both Padmé and Shmi for Anakin's violent possessive emotions and his subsequent blatant betrayal of Jedi rules and values. From nearly the first scenes of the film, viewers see Anakin's obsessive, nearly stalker-like fixation on Padmé, whom he has not seen in nearly ten years. Initially the young woman, now the Senator of Naboo and the target of repeated assassination attempts, discourages his hopes and advances but accepts his assistance as a protective escort to her home planet and soon rather inexplicably begins to welcome his overly-intense and forbidden attentions. Older than Anakin by several years, fully aware of the prohibitions placed upon Jedi, and committed to the success of her own senatorial career, Padmé nevertheless begins sending mixed signals, both protesting and encouraging Anakin's advances, alternatively reminding him of their respective duties and admitting her own growing—and, to most viewers, rather inexplicable—romantic attraction. Indeed, the more violently possessive and somewhat deranged Anakin behaves, the more Padmé is attracted to him, until the audience is left wondering half-seriously whether she has unknowingly fallen prey to some sort of psychic suggestion or Force persuasion on Skywalker's part. The alternative seems hardly less implausible in light of her relative sophistication and Anakin's disturbing behavior.

Given the age difference between them, and Padmé's initially successful rebuffs of Anakin's advances, it seems that Lucas assumes her most culpable for Anakin's decision to be with her no matter the consequences. This moral responsibility is particularly evident in *Episode II*'s most dialogically awkward and emotionally charged scene in which Anakin explains his desperate desire and Padmé tries to dash his romantic ambitions. Yet even as she insists they cannot betray their vocational callings and moral values to pursue a secret forbidden romance, she does so in a skin-tight, strapless black leather bodice which displays a generous amount of cleavage, as if she had dressed deliberately to arouse her suitor. The senator protests her innocence and resolve while simultaneously and disingenuously dressing the part of a *femme fatale*. In this rather confusing and clumsy scene, Padmé Amidala the clean-cut, responsible heroine is suddenly crossed with a worldly seductress out of *film noir*. It is little wonder that Anakin only grudgingly acknowledges her protests and continues to hope she will experience a change of heart.[1]

The crowning moment of this surreal courtship, and Padmé's temporary transformation into a sort of *femme fatale*, comes when she comforts Anakin, assuring him that "anger is only human," after he slaughters an entire encampment of Tusken Raiders on Tatooine in revenge for their sadistic murder of his mother Shmi. Understandably alarmed at his own dark, murderous fury, Anakin sobs out his confession to Padmé only to learn that she cares for him all the more despite (or, viewers may wonder, perhaps because of?) his destructive rage and its alarming consequences. Convulsed with grief, and wracked with guilt for abandoning Shmi ten years before, Anakin erupts into racist violence, and his growing ties to Padmé—more desperately necessary to him than even before—are soon cemented in her confession of love and their secret marriage at the conclusion of *Episode II*. Hence Anakin's emotionally fraught relationships to these two women lie at the heart of his growing darkness and willful, knowing betrayal of Jedi precepts and values.

After Shmi's death, Anakin's over-intense, possessive, and even violent passions, centered upon and encouraged by Padmé, continue to grow until they reach destructive crisis proportions in *Episode III: Revenge of the Sith*—with dire consequences for the entire galaxy. Just as Anakin was obsessed with fears of his mother's death for years before her actual murder on Tatooine, so too, once he learns that Padmé is pregnant, does he become fixated on the possibility that she might die in childbirth. Despite Padmé's placid assurances that she's in the best of health, Anakin sinks ever deeper into frantic fear and despair. Foregoing sleep and food (somehow without Padmé's notice: she seems too distracted by gestation to notice much of what's happening around her; more on that below), Skywalker grows increasingly irrational, convinced that her death (and perhaps that of their unborn child) is immanent and he must somehow prevent it.

At this point, the plot of *Episode III* and the explanation of Anakin's fall to the dark side become even more sexist, woman-blaming, and confusing. Skywalker fixates on the notion that only supernatural powers he does not possess, and which the Jedi cannot or will not teach him, can possibly save his wife from certain death. His extreme fear of loss combined with his emotional dependence upon Padmé push him over the edge. And while the strong-willed senator-queen Amidala of *Episodes I* and *II* may have been able to help him or jar him into his senses, the Padmé of *Revenge of the Sith* seems to have lost her forceful personality and much of her independent intelligence. A vivid illustration of Lucas's difficulty writing about and understanding women, Padmé, once she is a wife and expectant mother, becomes passive and ineffectual.[2] It is as if her sexual awakening and marital union to the fiery-tempered and obstinate Skywalker have transformed her from an independent, strong-minded politician and warrior-maiden into a docile, uninteresting, domesticated cipher.

Now far more a sexist stereotype than any sort of real archetype, Padmé is to blame for her husband's excesses insofar as she makes virtually no attempt to counter them. Lucas increases the cumulative impression of Padmé's uselessness by cutting from the film scenes deemed "unimportant" relative to Lucas's preferred action sequences and special effects: moments of her senatorial opposition to Supreme Chancellor Palpatine's growing dictatorial powers. Yet Lucas leaves intact minutes of footage showing her sitting or standing alone in her apartment, hands clasped and idle, staring rather blankly into her chambers or out the window, and otherwise doing nothing at all.[3]

No longer a convincing heroine or politician, nor even a seductress or *femme fatale*, the domesticated Padmé is now merely the object of Anakin's possessive need. Despite their age difference, her presumed sophistication and practicality, and her political and wartime experience, the senator is no longer really an agent of her own destiny, her husband's, or even, as we shall see, that of their unborn child. Indeed, she seems unwilling or unable to resist becoming a victim of Anakin's growing obsessive madness and gradual fall to the dark side. In response to Skywalker's frustrations with the Jedi, galactic corruption, and his wife's passivity in the face of possible immanent death, Padmé merely wishes they could return to a time (which seems not to have actually existed in the *Star Wars* chronology) when she and Anakin had "only their love," before political differences of opinion arose between them and before the Separatist conflict and Clone Wars divided the galaxy. This speech is so out of character for the once-strong-willed senator Amidala that the audience almost invariably titters or winces in dismay.

Indeed, Padmé's passivity seems largely to blame for Anakin's fall to the dark side. She only half-heartedly attempts and abysmally fails to dissuade him from seeking forbidden occult knowledge that may, no matter the personal or galactic cost, supposedly save her from an unlikely death in childbirth. She also seems completely unaware of how thoroughly Anakin is being seduced by the blandishments of Supreme Chancellor Palpatine, who soon reveals to Anakin his true nature as a Dark Lord of the Sith—with supposed supernatural powers over life and death.

Padmé has more political experience than her husband and has worked with Palpatine as a colleague for many years. She knows that Palpatine has politically mentored Anakin for more than a decade and that the Chancellor—whether in genuine concern for the Republic's security, or out of self-serving motives, or both—appears to be a grave threat to galactic civil rights and liberties. Yet never in the film, nor in the novelization of *Revenge of the Sith* based on the original screenplay, does Padmé

warn Anakin about Palpatine's possible hidden agenda or suggest that
the Chancellor may be using the Jedi Knight for his own sinister purposes. According to the novel (again, these scenes are deleted from the
film itself), Padmé joins a petition with several thousand other senators,
expressing concern about the Chancellor's dictatorial emergency powers. Yet, inexplicably, she does not discuss this with Anakin, who learns
about her activities from his mentor Palpatine and is angry and humili-
ated as a result. Perhaps she exercises exceptionally poor judgment in
not fully explaining her concerns to her husband (who, ostensibly, might
help effect changes in Palpatine's policies), or perhaps she already fears
Anakin and does not wish to risk his potentially violent reaction. Either
way, Padmé appears a far weaker and more timid personality than in the
two previous films, an ineffectual, hand-wringing woman and brow-
beaten wife, seemingly powerless to alter the course of events.

Only near the end of *Revenge of the Sith*, after it is too late and Anakin
has sworn loyalty to Palpatine/Sidious (in return for the promise of learning Palpatine's alleged dark side, sorcerous ability to defeat death), does
Padmé temporarily regain some of her old courage, intelligence, and
elan. Traveling to find Anakin on the volcanic planet Mustafar, where
he has just cold-bloodedly killed the leaders of the Separatist movement,
Padmé confronts him about his recent crimes: the carnage at the Jedi
Temple and the slaughter even of Jedi children, as commanded by
Anakin's new master, Sidious/Palpatine. Begging him to turn back from
the obvious precipice upon which his entire life now teeters, Padmé warns
Anakin that galactic domination is not her goal, that he is "traveling down
a path [she] cannot follow." He cannot precisely deny her accusations
and instead turns on Padmé for her supposed betrayal once he learns
that Kenobi—a secret stowaway aboard her ship—has come to Mustafar to duel him. At this point Anakin is clearly unstable, possessed by
jealousy and rage, perhaps driven mad by recent events. Like many an
abusive husband, in an all-too-ordinary outburst of domestic violence,
Anakin turns on his pregnant wife, the one he had vowed to protect and
save at all costs, and strangles her. Only the more attractive prospect of
destroying Kenobi distracts him from murdering Padmé in his irrational
fury. She has rediscovered some of her old spirit only to be nearly killed
for it in the end. Despite Padmé's growing ineffectiveness over the course
of the three films, Anakin clearly remains threatened by what limited
and dwindling power over him she still possesses and turns upon her
the dark murderous fury he had previously reserved only for Tusken
Raiders and, now, the Jedi Knights as well. Indeed, it seems as if much
of Anakin's rage stems from his resentment over the "control" Padmé
exerts over him without even intending to—the problematic and potentially "castrating" force of his excessive emotional dependence upon her.

Thus he tends to blame her, in the long run, for his own turn to darkness.[4]

The misogyny of *Episode III* continues to build until the very end, when, instead of surviving to deal with the consequences of her husband's actions, Padmé decides to die. For no reason medical droids can ascertain, she simply loses "the will to live" and chooses to perish rather than live without Anakin, knowing what he has done. This course of action, melodramatic and ludicrous to most viewers, does violence to the character concept of Padmé as portrayed in *The Phantom Menace* and even in *Attack of the Clones*. Instead of working to help educate the galaxy about and to save it from Palpatine's evil designs, Padmé chooses her personal pain over her political duty, placing self-centered emotional distress above all other considerations. Deciding to die rather than live and be of additional civic service, she also opts out of motherhood entirely, leaving her infant children Luke and Leia to be reared by other beings still dedicated to reestablishing Republican freedoms and the Jedi Knighthood—to reclaiming the galaxy from tyranny and Sith Imperial rule.

The Padmé we see in the first two films would have scoffed at the mere notion of such a fate. Strong-willed and courageous, fiercely dedicated to the cause of galactic democracy, *that* young woman would not have surrendered to despair, abandoning her love for and responsibilities to her children, her planet's peoples, and the Republic. Yet in *Episode III*, Lucas chooses to have her embrace a selfish and needless martyrdom and perish without having any influence upon her stronger daughter Leia, who will grow up to fight the Empire with all of her might. Had Lucas simply let Padmé survive the events on Mustafar, and left intact the excised political scenes mentioned above, he could easily have given audiences an admirable, independent female character for the new trilogy of *Star Wars* films. Yet for his own reasons, and perhaps to make Anakin a more sympathetic or unsympathetic character (because Anakin grieves Padmé's death, viewers might react either way), Lucas renders her a cinematic victim better suited to the serials and B-movies of his 1950s childhood than to a twenty-first-century audience. This is but one reason why the new film trilogy is relatively unsatisfying to many viewers when compared to the original *Star Wars* films.

Despite Padmé's erratic and disappointing characterization, however, Lucas makes it clear in *Episode III* that neither Padmé nor Anakin is fully responsible for Anakin's fall to the dark side and his subsequent rebirth as the Sith Lord Darth Vader. The ultimate villain of the saga, and the character most responsible for the creation of Vader, the destruction of the Jedi, and the oppression of the entire galaxy is the duplicitous, "feminized" and sexually ambiguous Palpatine/Sidious. From his first scenes as the apparently mild-mannered and humane senator from

Naboo to the end of his life as the wizened Emperor aboard the second Death Star battle station, Palpatine is, throughout the story arc of the *Star Wars* saga, seemingly the most one-dimensional of the major characters. More even than Vader, the traitorous former Jedi who willingly helped orchestrate the slaughter of the entire Knighthood and the end of galactic representative democracy, Palpatine is evil personified, devoid of mercy and compassion, and cynically obsessed with acquiring power for its own sake. Furthermore, he has created a patriarchal political system in which human males are fully in charge and other sorts of beings unimportant or expendable. Upon closer examination, however, Palpatine is more complicated—and more ambiguously gendered—than he initially appears. This too adds to the overall misogyny and homophobia of the *Star Wars* saga.

Let us first analyze the Sith—the ancient tradition of dark Force-users to which Palpatine/Sidious belongs. According to numerous *Star Wars* novels, reference books, and comics[5] in addition to Lucas's films, the Sith are a sect of heretic Force-users who long ago rejected Jedi ways, embraced darkness and its attendant primal and negative passions, and fused dark side powers with sorcerous and occult study. Millennia in the distant past, the Sith numbered in the thousands and controlled large sections of the galaxy. But over the course of centuries, wars with the Jedi and the Republic, as well as internecine sectarian strife, decimated Sith ranks. Eventually one man, Lord Darth Bane, arose to kill the remaining Sith and re-establish the order under new strictures, with only his child-apprentice as the next heir to the dark tradition.

Bane established the Only Two rule, which held sway for the next millennium, and under which, in any given generation, there were almost always only two Sith in existence—a master and an apprentice, living in secrecy, biding their time, sowing dark thoughts and precipitating evil events throughout the galaxy. Masters taught apprentices everything they knew in the way of sorcery and other dark side skills, as well as hatred of the Jedi Knighthood that remained ascendant and the Republic which the Jedi served. This tightly-knit pair, then, bound together in a charged, paradoxical combination of mutual dependence and distrust, isolation and mutual need, waited for the moment when the pupil would come of age and try to kill the master. If successful, the erstwhile student would then become the sole surviving Sith Lord and adopt an apprentice of his or her own, only to repeat the pattern years in the future.

For many generations this remained the Sith way, until Lord Darth Sidious emerged from obscurity to assume the role of an ordinary human politician—Senator Palpatine—and gradually take control of the galaxy through countless machinations, including war, assassinations, bribery, senatorial corruption, treachery, and deceit. Once he was elected Supreme

Chancellor, Sidious/Palpatine's centralization of galactic power acceler-
ated until, with the Sith-orchestrated Clone Wars, he managed to emas-
culate the Senate, seduce the gifted Anakin Skywalker to darkness and
make him his new Sith apprentice, destroy the Jedi Knighthood, and
declare himself Emperor of the galaxy. Thus was the eponymous
"revenge of the Sith" finally achieved.

Hence, throughout his career, Sidious, like countless Sith before
him, developed talents and traits that, according to George Lucas's con-
temporaries (i.e., late twentieth- and early twenty-first-century audiences), are usually seen as stereotypically "feminine," associated with
negative female qualities. As women frequently must do in patriarchal
societies, the Sith are obliged to operate in stealth and cunning, working behind the scenes, unacknowledged as galactic constituents, Republican citizens, or participants in power politics. Knowing he risks almost
certain annihilation if he works in the open, Sidious, true to his name,
instead works in secret prior to becoming Emperor, remaining "in the
closet" for many years and insidiously subverting Republican society
from the inside. Refusing to "fight fair" in the open, by the rules of his
dominant society and instead employing stereotypically "feminine" tools
of political rumor-mongering, seduction, and deceit, Sidious undermines
the Republic from within like the secret poison that is the murderess's
standard stock-in-trade.

The analogy fits in other ways as well. Just as Sith strategies mirror
feminine ways of fighting back in patriarchal societies, so is the Sith tradition evocative of European paganism and witchcraft—ancient belief
systems and religious practices that were discredited but not entirely
eradicated by the emergence of patriarchal, monotheistic Christianity in
the so-called Dark Ages. Similarly, in the "dark ages" of that long ago
and far away *Star Wars* galaxy, the Sith reigned supreme over large parts
of the future Republic: sorcerer-rulers with countless subject-worshippers
at their beck and call. In time, this "heretic" belief system, including its
cultural and political practices and occult-sorcerous-religious traditions,
was supplanted by Jedi dedication to the light side of the Force, and Sith
ways were mostly but never completely eliminated by their enemies. Just
as witchcraft and ancient pagan traditions continued to survive on Earth,
passed on usually in secret from teacher to pupil who always needed to
fear some possibility of official reprisal from the powers that be, so too
did the Sith tradition refuse extinction. Let us be clear—here I do *not*
mean to equate the dark, malevolent Sith with largely benign, nature-
oriented pre-Christian or modern-day paganism, or the Jedi with Christianity, or Force-users with religious practitioners of any sort found on
our planet Earth. My point is that, in terms of the history of paganism and
Christianity in Western society, the parallel cannot be entirely accidental,

even if Lucas did not consciously realize the analogy he created. In Lucas's universe, the Sith are the nightmare return of the repressed: an outlaw sect reasserting its dominion with bloody vengeance. Sithly behavior—occult, murderous, sometimes including human sacrifice and unholy conspiracies to topple all legitimate civil and religious authority—resembles the stuff of anti-pagan prejudices and fears held by many sincere Christians from medieval times until the present day.

And witchcraft, stereotypically, is usually associated with women. In countless witchcraft scares throughout European and American history, as well as in assumptions about witches in most patriarchal non-Western societies, witchcraft is and was regarded as a typically female crime: the mischief of society's disempowered and disfranchised, who seek influence, control, and even vengeance through occult and esoteric means. Prohibited and feared by the dominant power structure, witchcraft and sorcery offer esoteric alternatives to accepting the status quo. They are secret ways of exerting fearsome power, and their practitioners may, if very careful, remain undetected by the larger society. Throughout history, the punishments for supposed and "proven" witches, therefore, have often been quite severe—including torture and execution: reprisals by the dominant society for such treason and heresy.

This parallel between gendered stereotypes about witchcraft and Lucas's portrayal of the Sith is reinforced by other qualities that make Palpatine/Sidious seem rather sexually ambiguous. Drawing upon stereotypes (or, as he would claim, archetypes) of old, fearsome witches, Lucas made the Emperor of *Episode III*, *Episode V: The Empire Strikes Back*, and *Episode VI: Return of the Jedi*, the visual and visceral equivalent of an aged, withered crone. Desiccated by the ravages of time and malign sorcery, the dark ruler of the *Star Wars* galaxy appears lifted straight from the pages of the medieval witch-hunting manual, the *Malleus Maleficarum* ("The Hammer of the Witches," published by Heinrich Kramer and Jacob Sprenger in 1486 and modeled on Inquisition handbooks for witchcraft detection and prosecution). In addition to describing supposed witches as aged, dried-up, vengeful hags, the *Maleficarum's* monk authors characterize women and witches, which they tend to conflate, as "a foe to friendship, a natural temptation, a desirable calamity, a domestic danger ... an evil of nature ... the lust of the flesh ... an imperfect animal, [who] always deceives." They continue: just as witches "are more prone to abjure the faith; so through their second defect of inordinate affections and passions they search for, brood over, and inflict various vengeances, either by witchcraft, or by some other means" (qtd. in Russel 116). Liars by nature, according to this and similar literature, witches pose a grave threat to the social and religious order and must be destroyed.[6]

Such descriptions make apparent the numerous parallels between witchcraft stereotypes and Palpatine/Sidious's personality traits. Wielder of the occult, secretive dark side of the Force, Palpatine is also the bringer of galactic and personal calamity, a danger to the domestic tranquility of Anakin and Padmé's marriage and the Republic itself. In the *Star Wars* saga the dark side is fueled by, and its Sith disciples are extremely prone to, primal passions and destructive obsessions—violent angers and ambitions, jealousy, possessiveness, greed, murderous envy and resentment, lust for power and vengeance—that the Jedi abjure. Regularly employing lies and deceit to realize their dark ambitions, Palpatine and his pupils, Lords Maul, Tyranus, and Vader, routinely demonstrate these traits throughout the two film trilogies and in many of the official *Star Wars* universe comics and novels.

And then there is the matter of sexual attraction and desire. Ignored by Lucas as much as possible, the fraught issue of sexuality haunts the *Star Wars* films as a sort of unacknowledged specter, appearing sometimes in the most apparently unlikely places—especially the intense, emotionally charged relationship between Palpatine/Sidious and Anakin/Vader. Palpatine's political protégé, prior to Anakin's conversion to darkness, and his Sith apprentice afterward, Vader is intimately tied to the older man by a fraught combination of fear, need, loyalty, and resentment. Dependent upon Palpatine for his military and political position as the second-most powerful man in the galaxy, craving the occult knowledge the senior Sith possesses, and indebted to the ruler for saving his life after his duel with Kenobi, Vader longs to kill Palpatine, end his own dependency, and take control of the galaxy. Widowed at the end of *Episode III* and isolated in his life-supporting body armor and mask, Vader's sole emotional companion is Palpatine. Bound together by the terms of the Sith dyad and Only Two rule, Vader and Palpatine are by definition the only suitable mates for one another in the galaxy—until and unless one of them decides to seduce a new apprentice to darkness and eliminate his Sith counterpart.[7]

This emotionally charged, erotically fraught pairing is further underscored by the sort of emotions—ambition, lust, possessiveness—that fuel disciples of the dark side. Vader fantasizes about murdering the Emperor at the end of *Episode III* so that he and Padmé can rule in Palpatine's stead, but after Padmé's death, he refrains from doing so for another twenty years. Not until his newly discovered son, Luke Skywalker, confronts Vader and Palpatine aboard the second Death Star in *Return of the Jedi*, two decades after Vader's embrace of the dark side, does the younger Sith finally eliminate his formidable master (more on that below). In the meantime, Vader apparently discovers no suitable potential apprentice and decides to remain with Palpatine, continuing their dyad of mutual dependence and distrust, resentment, and need.

It is no accident that in the *Star Wars* saga, converting Force-users to darkness is nearly always spoken of as "seduction." Driven by lust for worldly and occult power, lust that can easily blend into desire for the masters who offer such reward, potential Sith acolytes (like Palpatine, who dwells at the center of the Republic but is also the ultimate outsider, the leader of a proscribed sect), are liminal creatures, caught on the threshold between love and hate, empowerment and enslavement, supernatural transcendence and spiritual abjection. Like the serpent in Eden urging Eve to eat from the Tree of Knowledge of Good and Evil, Palpatine seduces Anakin with the prospect of limitless knowledge and power, including the ability to prevent death. According to the novelization of *Revenge of the Sith*, additional temptations then ensue. In another scene Lucas unfortunately edited from the film, Palpatine, akin to Satan tempting Christ in the wilderness, promises Anakin cities, planets, star systems—rule over countless beings—in return for his conversion to darkness and oath of loyalty. The erotics of power are clear when Palpatine implores Skywalker to indulge his passions instead of repressing them. "Let yourself *out*, Anakin," he urges, and "I will give you *anything you want*" [emphasis in the original] (Stover 280).[8]

This dark, homoerotically charged dynamic is similarly illustrated in other *Star Wars* novels. In *The Mandalorian Armor*, H. W. Jeter explores the Sith relationship in nearly romantic terms. Immediately following the events of *Episode IV: A New Hope*, while debating how to deal with various bounty hunter and criminal organizations, the Emperor observes, "Sometimes, Vader, I think you'd prefer it if I trusted no one but you. I see into so many creatures' hearts, and all I find there is fear.... But when I look into yours, Vader, I see ... something else. Something almost like ... desire" (Jeter 88). As the double-entendres accumulate, astute witness Prince Xixor, Imperial nobleman and covert head of the galactic crime syndicate Black Sun, is inspired to overtly carnal musings. Palpatine continues, "If you are closer to what's left of my heart, Vader, if ... I place more trust in you than I do others, it's because of something beyond words" (89). Soon after this electric exchange, Palpatine relishes Vader's jealousy of anyone else who enjoys the Emperor's favor: "If you had no other value to me," he informs Xixor, "I would still require your presence, just for the ... *stimulating* effect you have on Lord Vader" [italics in the original] (90).

James Kahn explores Vader and Palpatine's homoerotic love-hate relationship in his novelization of *Return of the Jedi*. Awaiting the Emperor's arrival on the second Death Star, Vader's anticipation of being in his master's presence again merges with his lust to crush the Rebellion and enjoy total dominion with Palpatine. In this state of heightened desire, Vader's "breathing seem[s] to quicken, then resum[e] its measured pace, like the rising of a hollow wind" (332). In fact, something in Vader's chest always becomes "more electric" when he consults with the Emperor. In Palpatine's presence, he has a "feeling of fullness, of power, of dark and demon mastery—of secret lusts, unrestrained passion, wild submission.... These things and more" (371–72). Vader feels "complete at the Emperor's side. Though the emptiness at his core never [leaves] him," it becomes "a glorious emptiness" when he is penetrated by "the glare of the Emperor's cold light, an exalted void that could encompass the universe" (372). In sexually suggestive phrases, Kahn describes Vader's dark desires and satiety in Palpatine's presence. Awaiting an audience with Palpatine aboard the second Death Star, Vader ponders:

> it was an honor, and a noble activity, to kneel at his ruler's feet. He kept his eyes inward, seeking reflection in his own bottomless core. [Vader's] power was great now, greater than it had ever been. It shimmered from within, and resonated with the waves of darkness that flowed from the Emperor. He felt engorged with this power, it surged like black fire [383–84].

Vader goes on to relish the prospect of one day killing Palpatine, possessing all his knowledge and power, and then ruling the galaxy with his son Luke as his new Sith apprentice. But in the meantime, he is content to bask in the older man's dark glory and to be with the single soul who truly understands him: "The Emperor always knew the sense of what was in his heart; even if he didn't know the specifics" (373).

At the same time, Palpatine has "plans of his own": plans of erotic dominance, of "spiritual violation, the manipulation of lives and destinies." He savor[s] both Vader's subservience and the approach of his other conquest and potential new apprentice: "the final seduction of the young Skywalker" (Kahn 373). Yet Luke, as we shall see momentarily, is more properly masculine than his father and therefore more resistant to Palpatine's plans than the dark ruler has anticipated.

While Palpatine and Vader are both rather sexually ambiguous characters as demonstrated above, Vader's "emasculation" is more complete. Symbolically "castrated" (his loss of several limbs and dependence on prosthetic and life-support technology) upon his conversion to darkness, Vader is also subordinate to Palpatine and thus doubly "feminized" in his relationship to the sexually ambiguous elder Sith. Indeed, the Dark Lord comes to think of their dyad as a sort of unequal marriage in which Palpatine distinctly has the upper hand: "Married to the order of the Sith, you will need no other companion than the dark side of the Force" (Luceno 53), the Emperor teaches, and Vader feels he is "also married to Sidious, who dole[s] out precious bits of Sith technique as if merely lending them—just enough to increase his apprentice's power, without making him supremely powerful" (Luceno 314).[9]

With Luke Skywalker's arrival on the Death Star in *Episode VI*, Vader initially hopes to make his son his own apprentice and soon topple the ruler from his throne. Yet matters hardly proceed as Vader and his master anticipate. In response to Palpatine and Vader's combined barrage of threats and bribes, Luke almost turns, and nearly kills his father. Yet he pulls back at the last possible moment, rejecting the Emperor's inducements to destroy Vader and take his place as the new, younger, more physically intact and attractive Sith apprentice. The young Jedi is nearly seduced as his father was twenty years before, and by similar promises of endless power and galactic dominion. Palpatine's reactions to Luke's plight are overtly, symbolically sexual. As he revels orgasmically in Vader's son's "swelling" propensity for hatred, rage and violence, lovingly caressing the hilt of Luke's lightsaber, we see the most turgidly phallic and darkly homoerotic moment of the *Star Wars* film sextet and suddenly understand that this is surely how Palpatine must have thought about Vader too.

Free of the emotional neediness that defined and doomed his father and unencumbered by problematic ties to women, Luke is sufficiently independent and masculine to refuse Palpatine's offers in the end. Losing his previous love interest Leia Organa to her romance with Han Solo, and to the knowledge that she is actually his sister, Luke has no lover or wife to worry about. He never knew a mother to mourn. Padmé's death two decades before assured that fact. Although he comes closest to succumbing when Vader threatens to turn Leia to the dark side, Luke ultimately refuses to convert and informs both Sith that he is "a Jedi, like my father before me." This reminder of Vader's more virtuous and masculine past sends Palpatine into a cold rage and helps resurrect Vader's long-dormant goodness and capacity for parental love. When Palpatine turns his murderous, occult fury upon the young knight, Vader slays his master at long last, saving Luke at the cost of his own life and redeeming his own soul in the process. The ultimate message of *Return of the Jedi* and thus the entire *Star Wars* saga is that Anakin Skywalker's patriarchal affection trumps his destructive, homoerotic dyad with Palpatine, whose scourge is removed from the galaxy.[10] With this triumph of proper masculinity, Anakin joins his dead Jedi colleagues in the light despite the magnitude of his earlier crimes. As an additional reward (indicated by the 2005 edition of *Return of the Jedi*), Anakin has reclaimed his youthful unscarred pre-Vader appearance. It is up to Luke and Leia to restore the Jedi Knighthood and galactic representative democracy, and the Sith are supposedly eliminated for all time.

The intended moral of the *Star Wars* saga is essentially (if perhaps unconsciously) misogynist, homophobic, and conservative. Over-intense attachments to particular women, unseemly "feminine" emotional excess, and Palpatine/Sidious's destructive androgynous allure, seduce Anakin Skywalker to the dark side of the Force with hideous, oppressive, genocidal results for the entire galaxy. Yet this message, in the end, also contains the seeds of its own subversion. The ultimate *"femme fatale"* of the saga actually is not Padmé Amidala but Palpatine, and his illicit "marriage" to Anakin/Vader long outlasts the fallen hero's union with Padmé. Although this dark partnership rather inevitably ends in mutual destruction—a sort of murder-suicide—it endures for twenty years, as opposed to Anakin and Padmé's mere three years together, and grants the Sith two decades of dominion over the galaxy.

Indeed, the Sith are such intriguing, provocative characters that fans' responses to them, reflected in the sale of Lucasfilm products featuring Darths Sidious, Vader, Maul, and Tyranus, are measurably as positive as those elicited by the heroic characters of the books and films. Countless *Star Wars*-inspired Internet sites reveal widespread popular fascination with the Sith, as well as a rapidly proliferating fandom for "slash" amateur fiction featuring male *Star Wars* characters—Jedi, Sith, and otherwise—in homoerotic emotional or sexual relationships, no matter Lucasfilm's official disapproval and occasional threats of legal retaliation. Such popular reactions to the villains of the saga indicate that many viewers, on some level, are aware of the essential ambiguity of the *Star Wars* films and are intrigued by such potentially multivalent characters and messages.

In conclusion, I return to the ideas of film critic Jackie Byars. Although the themes and morals of the *Star Wars* films are clearly and primarily heterosexual and patriarchal, reflecting the ongoing hegemonic control and manipulation of power in the interests of heterosexism and male dominance, we can also see within the saga alternative messages and meanings. This discursive struggle between hegemonic themes and subversive interpretations can be found in all sorts of cultural texts, if audiences look for them, read against the grain, and "make unexpected meaning from the messages they create and consume" (Byars 55). This kind of resistant, critical meaning-making has the potential to help reshape our popular culture, values, and prejudices. Thus even the most seemingly conservative films, or those apparently least amenable to close scholarly analysis, as some commentators have accused the *Star Wars* saga of being, can bring forth fascinating insights about a culture's values, assumptions, and power relations. They can even offer, through critical and oppositional interpretations realized by audience members, the possibility of changing those social and political dynamics into more egalitarian alternatives.

Notes

1. For more on the cinematic trope of the femme fatale and the psychological and sexual dangers she poses for heterosexual male protagonists, see Mary Ann Doane's *Femmes Fatales: Feminism, Film Theory, Psychoanalysis* and E. Ann Kaplan's *Women in Film Noir.*

2. For examples of Lucas's difficulty identifying with women and writing about female characters, see Garry Jenkins's *Empire Building: The Remarkable Life Story of Star Wars.*

3. Ironically, shortly after the completed filming of *Episode III*, actress Natalie Portman described Padmé Amidala as a feminist character, specifically referencing the political scenes that Lucas soon excised from the movie. See Brett Rector's "Queen Mother of the Galaxy" (63).

4. In James Luceno's novel *Dark Lord*, which takes place immediately following the events of *Revenge of the Sith*, Anakin/Vader broods: "Padmé and Obi-Wan ... had sentenced him to his black-suit prison. Sentenced by his wife and his alleged best friend, their love for him warped by what they had perceived as [Anakin's] betrayal.... He had only wanted to save them! Padmé, from death; Obi-Wan, from ignorance. And in the end they had failed to recognize his power; to simply acede to him; to accept on faith that he knew what was best for them ... for everyone!" (76–77).

5. For detailed synopses of Sith history and sorcerous abilities, see Bill Slavicsek's and J.D. Wiker's, *The Dark Side Sourcebook: Star Wars Roleplaying Game* and Kevin J. Anderson's and Daniel Wallace's *Star Wars: The Essential Chronology.* The Sith are also explored in several book series produced by Dark Horse comics. Chronologically depicting Sith history, these are: Kevin J. Anderson, et al., *Tales of the Jedi: The Golden Age of the Sith*; Kevin J. Anderson, et al., *Tales of the Jedi: The Fall of the Sith Empire*; Tom Veitch, et al., *Tales of the Jedi: Dark Lords of the Sith*; Kevin J. Anderson, et al., *Tales of the Jedi: The Sith War*; and Darko Marcan, et al., *Star Wars: Jedi vs. Sith.* See also Matthew Stover's *Star Wars, Episode III: Revenge of the Sith* and James Luceno's, *Dark Lord: The Rise of Darth Vader.*

6. See also Andrew Sanders's *A Deed Without a Name: The Witch in Society and History.*

7. Exploring the thematic linkages between witchcraft, women, and homosexuality throughout western history, author Jack Fritscher argues that homosexual men, like strong-willed women, were often singled out for witchcraft accusations in the Middle Ages and early modern period. They both, he demonstrates, were alleged dangers to patriarchal power and control. Fears of secret sorcerous and treasonous societies, which led to numerous witch hunts, resemble similar fears of homosexual conspiracies to take over the world. Both are reflected in Lucas's portrayals of the Sith menace. See his *Popular Witchcraft: Straight from the Witch's Mouth.*

8. The homoerotic implications of joining a Sith dyad are made additionally clear in *Episode III* when Palpatine tells Anakin that the dark side of the Force offers many abilities and possibilities some beings "would consider unnatural."

9. Luceno further emphasizes this dark homoerotic dynamic through the viewpoint of doomed Jedi Roan Shryne. Fleeing the Empire's purge of the Jedi, Shryne encounters and duels Vader, who kills him. Shryne's dying words are, "[Y]ou and Palpatine are a perfect match" (296).

10. Writer and *Star Wars* fan Todd Hanson says of Palpatine as played by actor Ian McDiarmid throughout the films, "The Emperor is one of the very greatest characters in the *Star Wars* mythos.... [H]is every move, gesture, and weird half-speech-impediment-ish pronunciation oozing pure evil. As an audience, we react to the Emperor with visceral repulsion, mirroring the way people naturally react to the palpable presence of actual evil; our skin crawls at the sight of him" (194–95). See Hanson's "A Big Dumb Movie About Space Wizards: Struggling to cope with *The Phantom Menace.*" Viewers' largely unexamined "visceral repulsion" reaction to Palpatine, I believe, is also a result of the films' homoerotic/homophobic implications.

Works Cited

Anderson, Kevin J. *Tales of the Jedi: The Fall of the Sith Empire*. Milwaukie: Dark Horse Comics, 1998.

_____. *Tales of the Jedi: The Golden Age of the Sith*. Milwaukie: Dark Horse Comics, 1997.

_____. *Tales of the Jedi: The Sith War*. Milwaukie: Dark Horse Comics, 1996.

Anderson, Kevin J., and Daniel Wallace. *Star Wars: The Essential Chronology*. New York: Del Rey, 2000.

Butler, Judith. *Bodies That Matter: On the Discursive Limits of "Sex."* New York: Routledge, 1992.

Byars, Jackie. *All That Hollywood Allows: Re-reading Gender in 1950s Melodrama*. Chapel Hill: University of North Carolina Press, 1991.

Doane, Mary Ann. *Femmes Fatales: Feminism, Film Theory, Psychoanalysis*. New York: Routledge, 1991.

Fritscher, Jack. *Popular Witchcraft: Straight from the Witch's Mouth*. Madison: University of Wisconsin Press, 2004.

Hansen, Todd. "A Big Dumb Movie About Space Wizards: Struggling to Cope with *The Phantom Menace*." *A Galaxy Not So Far Away: Writers and Artists on Twenty-Five Years of Star Wars*. Ed. Glenn Kenny. New York: Henry Holt, 2002.

Jenkins, Garry. *Empire Building: The Remarkable Life Story of Star Wars*. Secaucus: Citadel, 1999.

Jeter, H. W. *The Mandalorian Armor: Star Wars: The Bounty Hunter Wars, Book 1*. New York: Bantam, 1998.

Kahn, James. *The Star Wars Trilogy: Special Tenth Anniversary Omnibus Edition*. New York: Del Rey, 1987.

Kaplan, E. Ann, ed. *Women in FilmNoir*. London: British Film Institute, 1980.

Kramer, Heinrich, and Jacob Sprenger. *Malleus Maleficarum: Hammer of the Witches*. 1486. Trans. Montague Summers. London: Hogarth, 1928.

Luceno, James. *Dark Lord: The Rise of Darth Vader*. New York: Del Rey, 2005.

Marcan, Darko, et al. *Star Wars: Jedi vs. Sith*. Milwaukie: Dark Horse Comics, 2002.

Rector, Brett. "Queen Mother of the Galaxy." *Star Wars Insider #82* Jul./Aug. 2005: 63.

Russell, Jeffrey B. *A History of Witchcraft: Sorcerers, Heretics, and Pagans*. New York: Thames and Hudson, 1980.

Sanders, Andrew. *A Deed Without a Name: The Witch in Society and History*. Oxford: Berg, 1995.

Slavicsek, Bill, and J.D. Wiker. *The Dark Side Sourcebook: Star Wars Roleplaying Game*. Renton: Wizards of the Coast, 2001.

Star Wars Episode I: The Phantom Menace. Dir. George Lucas. Screenplay by George Lucas. Twentieth Century Fox, 1999.

Star Wars Episode II: Attack of the Clones. Dir. George Lucas. Screenplay by George Lucas and Jonathan Hales. Twentieth Century Fox, 2002.

Star Wars Episode III: Revenge of the Sith. Dir. George Lucas. Screenplay by George Lucas. Twentieth Century Fox, 2005.

Star Wars Episode IV: A New Hope. 1977. Dir. George Lucas. Screenplay by George Lucas. Twentieth Century Fox. 1981.

Star Wars Episode V: The Empire Strikes Back. Dir. Irvin Kershner. Screenplay by Leigh Brackett and Lawrence Kasdan. Story by George Lucas. Twentieth Century Fox, 1980.

Star Wars Episode VI: Return of the Jedi. Dir. Richard Marquand. Screenplay by Lawrence Kasdan and George Lucas. Story by George Lucas. Twentieth Century Fox, 1983.

Stover, Mathew. *Star Wars Episode III: Revenge of the Sith*. New York: Random House, 2005.

Veitch, Tom, et al. *Tales of the Jedi: Dark Lords of the Sith*. Milwaukie: Dark Horse Comics, 1995.

PART III

TECHNOLOGY AND THE PUBLIC IMAGINATION

7

Kill Binks

Why the World Hated Its First Digital Actor

DAN NORTH

Introduction: Jar Jar Binks Must Die

Jar Jar Binks: beloved of few. Upon the release of *Star Wars Episode I: The Phantom Menace* in 1999, the Gungan outcast became the focal point of many critiques of the film itself, the lightning rod through which wildly abusive criticism could be channeled. The ferocity of the invective hurled at Binks is difficult to quantify, easy to illustrate.

In J. Hobermann's near-cataclysmic review of the film for *The Village Voice*, Jar Jar is "a rabbit-eared ambulatory lizard whose Pidgin English degenerates from pseudo–Caribbean patois to Teletubby gurgle" while his people, the Gungans, "suck the oxygen out of every scene" (5). Kenneth Turan's review hit a similar mark with his targeting of Jar Jar as "a large and ungainly sea horse ... who inexplicably speaks in a kind of Caribbean patois.... [He is] a major miscue, a comic-relief character who's frankly not funny" (17). James Berardinelli described Jar Jar as "a computer generated mistake included primarily for comic relief" who would "amuse children but annoy adults" (8). To Carlo Cavagna, seeing this "idiotic swimming donkey" in action made him wonder "what sidekick ideas did Lucas have to reject in order to reach the point where Jar-Jar actually seemed like a winning concept? A tree-dwelling walrus with a Russian accent? A playful Klingon? An animated crash-test dummy?" (11). He scooped the Razzie Award for Worst Supporting Actor 1999 (Wilson), topped *Entertainment Weekly*'s chart of the worst CG characters of all time, and has been included in a compendium of *Star Wars*–related atrocities in which columnist Tim de Lisle refers to him as "cloying, shrieky, barely audible, a gangling exhibitionist goat with an attention-deficit disorder" (31). When Kim Newman produced a list of twenty-five reasons "Why *Star Wars* is Rubbish," Jar Jar accounted for at least three of them. An episode of *South Park* (3—6, broadcast within a month of the release of *The Phantom Menace*) introduced the singularly irritating creatures the Jackovasaurs in a scorching, thinly-disguised Binks satire, while the British sitcom *Spaced* (1999–2001) featured running jokes about the struggle of its protagonist, *Star Wars* fanatic Tim Bisley (Simon Pegg), to come to terms with his disappointment: (Bilbo: "What about the Ewoks? They were rubbish—you don't complain about them." Tim: "Jar Jar Binks makes the Ewoks look like fucking *Shaft*").

There was no sanctuary for the character in cyberspace. A *Google* search for "Jar Jar Binks must die" returns nearly eight hundred hits, many of them sites dedicated to the digital desecration of his image in gruesome, graphic ways, allowing visitors to abuse his effigy with mouse-click assaults.[1] One newsgroup came up with over six hundred ways to kill the character, ranging from simple applications of cyanide, electricity, dynamite, acid, Ebola viruses, explosive decompression, drugs overdose, or somewhat more elaborate eviscerations by lightsaber while standing in for the piñata at a Jedi picnic; in a presumed nod to the question of Jar Jar's Afro-Caribbean heritage, *Newsweek* critic David Ansen called Jar Jar "a kind of extraterrestrial Stepin Fetchit"; the list included more than one suggestion that he should suffer the brutality of the LAPD ("Ways"). The "National Association for the Extermination of the Gungan Race" is, to this day, holding up resistance to the "Gungan despotic regimes." Even before *The Phantom Menace* went on theatrical release, Detroit rappers Damn Nation had unleashed their torrentially venomous track "Jar Jar Binks Must Die."[2] The hapless creature received precious little sanctuary online: a petition in his defense by the Jar Jar Binks Appreciation Society had notched up a paltry 61 signatures at the time of writing, far outnumbered by the threats and harangues issued by his cavilers (Craig); David Cassel noted that even in a webring for Binks fans, a poll indicated that 51% of posters nevertheless found him "annoying" (5).

It could be argued that these responses are prompted by the character's incongruity within a cinematic franchise whose borders are policed by fans in order to maintain the integrity of whatever communal identity it might have. Jar Jar might seem inconsistent with the worlds of *Star Wars* because of his interpersonal clumsiness, gesticulatory fervor, and childish persistence; he may seem out-of-place because his dialogue contains echoes of a quasi-Jamaican patois and other Earthbound colloquialisms that reminds us of our own planet rather than re-enforcing an authentic alienness; in his appeal to the youngest members of the film's audience he might be a jarring reminder firstly that *Star Wars* was always, you know, for kids (Krämer) and that merchandise and toy sales by far outstrip the box office takings of the films (Ahrens)[3]—perhaps Jar Jar is the most obvious example of ideas for toys *shaping* narrative events rather than *imitating* them.[4] So, is Binks despised as an unwelcome irritant, a racist stereotype, or the residue of a capitalistic stratagem and its ensuing creative compromises? There may be a combination of causes and circumstances to provoke such vitriolic condemnation, but I'd like to suggest that the exceptional level of animosity (and I appreciate that much of it is good-humored) directed at our hapless Gungan might be understood productively as the outgrowth of something else.

Crucially, Jar Jar Binks is an entirely digital character,[5] the first of his kind, embodying the potentialities of a technological paradigm while channeling the anxieties they provoke. He was to have stood as the glorious figurehead of an anticipated age of the synthespian, where digital characters would finally usurp the primacy of the human actors who once dominated the screen; though, his hostile reception might indicate that such an eventuality is not one which audiences are prepared to embrace without question. The possibility of creating virtual actors indistinguishable from their organic counterparts has been a potent aspirational object for special effects technicians throughout the development of computer-generated imagery (CGI) over the last decade. Lev Manovich argues that "throughout the history of computer animation, the simulation of the human figure has served as a yardstick for measuring the progress of the whole field" (196). Virtual bodies have appeared in numerous films as stunt performers, replacing human actors for impossible physical feats in *The Matrix Reloaded* (2003) (North), or as more prominent surrogate figures for the title characters of *Spider-Man* (2002) and *Hulk* (2003), for which the eponymous green id-monster was rendered entirely in CG. The character of Gollum in Peter Jackson's trilogy *The Lord of the Rings* (2001–03) was digitized using motion capture reference material from actor Andy Serkis. Such superheroic or sub/non-/post-human characterizations use their diegetic environments to explore the capabilities of spectacular bodies, but a film like *Hulk* in particular can be read as a testing ground for experimental digital anatomies and their reactions to certain environments. Just as *Hulk* is a film in which a transformed human body is pursued, threatened, contained and assaulted, meeting each danger with a new level of brute prowess, it is also a self-conscious text in which a digital form, animated partly by procedural programs which approximate and simulate the responses of objects to the spaces into which it is inserted (for instance, how might Hulk's flesh ripple when pummeled by rock, missile, or tank?), demonstrates the particularities of digital embodiment. As the synecdochic emblem of all such expectancy attending digital cinema, Jar Jar might have had a greater symbolic load to bear than Ang Lee's big green anti-hero. In *Hulk*, Bruce Banner's exploration of his new body becomes the motivation for spectacular demonstrations of the power of CGI, bonding the film's content and form into close co-dependents. Jar Jar Binks is permitted no such self-reflexivity and is required to deliver a fully integrated nuanced performance alongside human actors. His virtuality is not justified by narrative or thematic factors, and such a performance is out of reach of current computer graphics technologies. Accordingly, the results appear more like mistakes than exploratory steps towards imminent success.

In investigating the contested domain of digital animation and manipulation, this chapter will examine both the digitally modified *Special Editions* of the original *Star Wars* Trilogy (and the similarly adjusted DVD versions) and the CGI-saturated prequels. In doing so, the feelings of ambivalence which *Star Wars* expresses towards technology both within and without the film texts themselves will come into focus. The binaries of primitive/advanced, powerless/powerful, technologized/rudimentary which are narrativized in the story of a grassroots, spiritualized rebellion against an ultra-mechanized Imperial dictatorship are replicated (albeit on a less operatic scale) in the timorous reception of the films' use of digital visual effects. Jar Jar Binks can be shown to be the whipping boy for a broader debate about how digital technologies are to be deployed and the effects they might have on conventional modes of representation. His failure to harmonize with the *Star Wars* franchise, as indicated by the ferocious reactions to his inclusion, demonstrates that technical innovation is not always enough to dazzle and entice audiences. At the heart of this is a discussion of the special effects which have been such a vital component in each *Star Wars* film.

It has always been my contention that special effects, rather than being idiotizing spectacles which leave spectators numb with amazement, can operate actively as a component of the film text; as Barbara Klinger has noted, spectators do not passively absorb a film's narrative in isolation, but rather they augment the text with what she terms "digressions," external points of reference ranging from "generic or narrative intertexts that school the spectator in dramatic conventions, to a host of promotional forms ... that arm the spectator with background information" (4). Special effects can be seen as one such digression—the complexities of their fabrication, and the range of extra-diegetic materials relating to their achievement ("making of..." documentaries, DVD featurettes etc.), comprise a technological paratext which may be entirely unrelated to the film's narrative but may also complement and expand it. More succinctly, a film's narrative and thematic content can be complemented or expanded by consideration of the technological means by which it was manufactured.

Imperial Light and Magic

In an early response to *Star Wars*[6] written in 1978, Dan Rubey noted that the film articulated the "desires and ambiguities produced by living inside a machine-oriented technology," mixing such thematics with a romantic individualist credos:

> *Star Wars* embraces technology in order to enjoy the sensations of power and exhilaration which technology offers, and then falls back on heroic individual action and the metaphysical, non-rational Force to solve the problem of eroded values and depersonalized experiences which technology creates. The film combines traditional models of individual combat with the technology of electronic warfare ... [2].

Rubey summarizes a key aspect of the *Star Wars* environment—the interplay between serried ranks of brutal, gargantuan machinery and the pseudo-spiritual, mystically aspecific Force which the Jedi harness to transcend it. This site of conflict is accentuated by the film's mix of oldfashioned genres and tropes (westerns, classical mythology, saber duels) with science fictional elements usually associated with extrapolations of present day possibilities into futurological realizations (advanced technology, interplanetary travel); this is the common paradox at the centre of science fiction cinema which thematizes the threat of technological development while luxuriating in the ultramodern devices which can be deployed for the visualization of such seductive dangers.

If Lucas' trilogies express an ambivalent attitude towards technology, we can find that attitude built into Industrial Light and Magic, the institution which he inaugurated in 1975 for the design and execution of *Star Wars*' special effects sequences. Headed by motion control pioneer John Dykstra, the converted industrial warehouse at Van Nuys, California[7] covered 36,000 square feet and incorporated a studio facility, an optical house, a model shop and a design facility. It maintained close links between departments to create a space within which a cohesive and consistent vision of the film's galactic unity could emerge under Lucas' supervision (Vaz and Duignan 6; Smith 2).

The use of a purpose-built effects house was a dramatic shift of emphasis away from the contemporary state of play within the studio system, which had seen the majors disband their in-house effects facilities, employing freelance effects artists instead. John Brosnan calculated that in 1974 there were two hundred effects artists in Hollywood and nearly a hundred in the UK (10), and Thomas G. Smith adds that studios had changed "from self-contained production centers to mere soundstages controlled by landlords and suites of executive deal-makers" (2). Financial difficulties for studios had led the majors to rely more on the distribution of independent productions (by the beginning of the 1960s around two thirds of films released by the major studios were independently produced) and effects departments were disbanded in a process of overhead-reduction exacerbated by the increased use of stunts, pyrotechnics, and large physical effects performed on location (Rickitt 28). The crashing of real airplanes, instead of composited miniatures, for *The Great Escape* (1963), or *The Battle of Britain* (1969) is emblematic of how a trend for "live" spectacle was causing the widespread neglect of post-production special effects facilities. It was when the demand for destruction became truly hyperbolic that special effects technicians were once again called for on a regular basis, with disaster films such as *Airport* (1970), *The Towering Inferno* (1974), *Earthquake* (1974), *Airport 1975* (1974), *The Hindenburg* (1975) and *Airport '77* (1977) all requiring the use of miniatures and compositing for scenes which could not be staged full-scale.

The era of the blockbuster activated by *Jaws* (1975) and *Star Wars* was a lucrative period that saw huge investment in special effects production, research, and development, and by the 1980s, multiple effects companies were bidding for work. As Hollywood filmmaking became more capital intensive (with the majors becoming principally distributors of films made by smaller companies, such as the most successful of the 80s, Steven Spielberg's Amblin Entertainment), formulae for success emerged, which included youth-orientation, action, comedy, and special effects. While comic or action situations and themes could be recycled and turned into key components of multi-sequel franchises, special effects were relied upon for an injection of novelty and the impression of modernity.

In authorized publications, ILM is posited as an antidote to the formalization or corporatization of film production, especially in reference to their staff. Inspirited by their youthful vigor, Smith records that "they were children of the Sixties, and many rebelled against authority figures and traditional work rules" and later refers to them as "an irregular band of individuals" (2–3). In his introduction to Smith's book, George Lucas himself adds to the presentation of the ILM technicians as "more than machines and technical processes," with an "enthusiastic and wild spirit." In the unlikely event that they might be "tamed into corporate soldiers, the creative army would quickly lose its creative spark" (qtd. in Smith xi). This kind of press-agentry, cemented by the documentaries *The Making of Star Wars* (1977) and *From Star Wars to Jedi: The Making of a Saga* (1983), aims to construct and promote an image of frontiersmen resisting the dehumanizing capabilities of the very equipment they work with on a daily basis, part of a publicity drive to offset the perception of such craft as robotic drudgery. Further strengthening the image of ILM technicians as vintage artisans, they also deployed aged or modified equipment such as the Anderson optical aerial printer used at ILM from 1975 until 1993, but originally built for Paramount by Howard Anderson in the 1950s (Vaz and Duignan 9). Whether or not this kind of PR is a comfort to those at ILM who have seen many of their colleagues, their offices and their hardware extirpated to make way for computers is difficult to gauge; what is clear is that the increased use of computer interfaces in the production of visual effects delegates a certain amount of the representational graft to pre-packaged software and imprints on the resulting images an aesthetic inflected by particular properties borne out of digitalization. It is arguable that much of the "New Media" debate of the last few years has been focused on the issue of reconciling the place of human input within the nexus of new computer processes (Manovich, Harries, and Lister et al.).

Just as ILM's implementation brought special effects into a more central position within the production process, as it had been within the studio system until the early 60s, so *Star Wars* sought to return blockbuster film-making, in terms of construction and narrative to earlier modes, displaying a paradoxical urge to regress thematically and aesthetically while using advanced technology to achieve this. This extra-diegetic paradox is extensively demonstrated at the level of narrative content in the opposition set up between a super-technologized, brutish Empire and the more homespun armaments of the Rebel Alliance. The Rebel spacecraft are battle-worn and meager compared to the glistening, pristine arsenals of their fascistic Imperial enemies, whose machines seem to have been manufactured immediately prior to their appearance onscreen, signaling that the Empire commands the spectacle of manufactural and military display (the Death Star is the latest showcase of their engineering prowess). It would be misleading to brand *Star Wars* as a technophobic story, but it can be seen that the films posit a particular kind of machine identity as the embodiment of inhuman menace. Darth Vader's story arc sees him battling to redeem the human being trapped within a fearsome, mechanized chassis which sustains the remnants of Anakin Skywalker. His is the character which bears the weight of posthuman themes and contexts, a villain whose evil is signified by the abdication of humanity to machinery. Vader's imbrication within mechanical processes marks him as a conduit for the narrativization of technological discourse; his corruption and switch to the Dark Side is mapped onto his literal dehumanization and cyborgic reconstruction. His redemption comes when he over-rides his machinic obedience to the Emperor and acts to save the life of his son at the expense of the Empire. The mechanization of Anakin Skywalker, coincident with his mounting malefaction, makes a powerful statement about the connections between industrialization and corruption, while the thrill of audiences watching it happen is, whether deliberate or not, a summation of the fascination which power and evil can exert. As a product of digital imaging processes, the virtual form of Jar Jar Binks is partially affiliated with similar themes of ambivalence towards bodies shaped by technology, but his characterization as a rustic buffoon displays none of the self-reflexivity I have just attributed to the character of Darth Vader. As a result, Jar Jar lacks the cohesion between form and content which makes Vader such a productive component of the diegesis. There is no semiotic interplay between this clumsy amphibian and his alternate identity as a complex and astonishing collection of algorithmic virtuosity.

Special Additions

In 1997, in preparation for the production of the trilogy of prequels (1999–2005), Lucas remastered and augmented the original trilogy for theatrical distribution. This involved numerous cosmetic changes to the image and the soundtrack, sometimes inserting new shots, at other times altering dialogue or adding digital components to the frame.[8] This might seem like the work of a twitchy auteur driven to editorial fidgeting by the capacities of digital technology, but Lucas has been doctoring the films almost from the outset; *Star Wars* only became known as *Episode IV: A New Hope* when the sub-title was added to the opening crawl for a re-release in 1981, thus retro-fitting it as part of an ongoing saga, supposedly in keeping with his original intention for a much longer narrative; various lines of dialogue were altered for the same re-release in creating a new stereo soundtrack (Beru Lars was re-dubbed by a new actress, and some of C-3PO's dialogue was re-selected from alternate takes); the 70mm prints of *The Empire Strikes Back* contained many similar cosmetic differences from the more widely exhibited 35mm versions. These alterations, while numerous and perhaps pedantic (or assiduous, depending on one's interpretation) are far more obscure than the ostentatious modifications of the 1997 "Special Editions," which amount to a more foundational refurbishment of the trilogy, inscribing the signs of digital technology on the films in preparation for their subsequent coupling with a trio of CG-saturated prequels. The changes for these editions would, in turn, be supplemented by a second wave of alterations for the 2004 DVD releases, which more explicitly promoted continuities with the prequels. For *The Empire Strikes Back* (DVD version) Jason Wingreen's voice for Boba Fett is replaced by that of *Attack of the Clones* actor Temuera Morrison, and Ian McDiarmid's holographic image of the Emperor is inserted; for *Return of the Jedi*'s DVD edition, Sebastian Shaw's ghostly Anakin Skywalker in the closing scene is replaced by Hayden Christensen. Despite their intended goal of smoothing the joins and making the six films more visually continuous and compatible, some of the new sequences disrupt the text's received interpretations, and their canonicity is subverted by the efforts of keen-eyed fans intent on policing the maintenance of their beloved films.

For instance, the well-worn controversy over "Greedo shoots first" is illustrative of the problematic outcome of tampering with received interpretations of texts which have been as closely examined and hungrily consumed as *Star Wars*.[9] In the first releases of the film, one of Han Solo's earliest scenes sees him calmly shoot dead a bounty hunter who threatens to turn him in to his archenemy Jabba the Hutt. The scene marks Solo out as a cunning self-preservationist and brands him as the dangerous pirate who must eventually redeem himself from such selfish action in the final scenes by rescuing Luke and facilitating the destruction of the Death Star. In the 1997 Special Edition, we see Greedo shoot first, missing Solo's head (from an improbably close range) and thus rendering Han's killing shot an act of self-defense. This alteration adds a fraction of a second to the running time of the film but precipitated a sizeable amount of critical derision. Lucas may have felt that he was softening the tone of Solo's characterization, but his conception of these film texts as fluid and unfixed threatens to violate the aura of sacredness with which fans invest them. Perhaps in response, the 2004 DVD version of the film strikes up a compromise, with both characters firing simultaneously at one another.

Lucas has made it clear that the *Special Editions* are not alternative readings but replacement texts designed to become the official version: "The special edition, that's the one I wanted out there. The other movie ... doesn't really exist anymore" ("Lucas"). However, his alterations often seem to put the old text in dialogue with the new rather than paper over its defects. For instance, a scene in *Episode IV* sees Han Solo pursuing a small group of stormtroopers, only to round the corner and find himself ambushed by a dozen re-enforcements. In the *Special Edition* of the same scene, when Solo rounds the corner, he is confronted by the sight of a spacecraft hangar complete with serried ranks of hundreds of soldiers. The effect is to restore the element of surprise to a moment with which fans would already be familiar. In the most recent DVD edition of *Episode IV*, there is a well-known gaffe in which a stormtrooper bumps his helmet on a doorframe, but rather than being effaced or digitally altered, Lucas has amplified the noise of the accident on the soundtrack.

On the DVD of *The Empire Strikes Back*, a continuity error in Han Solo's costume has been corrected when his shirt collar was mis-matched between shots. What is it that marks the former out as a memorable moment and the latter as an embarrassing mistake? Certainly the sight of one of the Empire's crack troops struggling to negotiate the doorways of a fearsome battle-station is a sly, if momentary, undercutting of the professionalism of both the production team and the Imperial army, but why would it not be appropriate to simply adjust the offending helmet and allow the trooper a more dignified entrance? Perhaps Lucas is accepting that the revisions he makes are not auteurist hairsplitting, but can actually be part of a dialogue with audience preferences. Alternatively, I suspect that he is allowing the stormtrooper's blunderous moment to stand as a monument to human fallibility, while he continues to efface technical errors and antiquated special effects. Lucas is the foreman of a cluster of media companies (including Lucasfilm Ltd, Skywalker Sound, THX, LucasArts, Industrial Light and Magic) for whom the *Star Wars* films are calling cards of technical excellence, showcases for the high fidelity aptitude of their equipment. A minor pratfall by a background artiste is not an indictment of the film's production facilities in the same that visible wires or stilted animatronics might be. In short, it really doesn't matter that the soldier bumps his head as long as we see he does it in THX-Approved Dolby Digital 5.1 Surround Sound. From this point of view, it is easy to understand why Lucas's prioritization of image and sound precision at the expense of story and character might offend some devotees of the films who believe that the story should be served by Lucasfilm's gadgets rather than acting as a vehicle for their advertisement.

The manipulation of the framespace, in terms of its contents as well as its temporality, could be contested by viewers not merely on aesthetic grounds, but almost as a point of ethics. The alteration of fictional narrative films doesn't just conflict with the stable affection in which they are held by viewers, but also raises the specter of similarly augmented photographic evidence or news footage, feeding into a mistrust of mediated footage. This mistrust might constitute a healthy critical engagement with the composition of the images with which we are presented, or alternatively a devaluation of the integrity of the image as a historically specific, singular unit. Alarmism is not called for, but rather an energized awareness of how and why digital technologies operate. Digitalization did not invent trick photography nor promote propagandist sleights-of-hand by media institutions, but the ease with which computer software can aid such adjustments, and the imperceptibility of the subtle results, requires an informed response to its effects.

The augmentation of the *Star Wars* trilogy for the 1997 re-releases was an irrevocable push towards a digital aesthetic which would be imposed even on the pre-digital episodes of the eventual six-film saga. For fans, the re-releases and the prequels re-emphasized the ambivalent feelings towards technology upon which the *Star Wars* narrative thrives— Lucas's original vision was, as Kim Newman put it, "an exercise in nostalgia for old movies" (51), but now, somewhat perversely, the chance to see the films again theatrically, and the promise of three new films, would be traded off against the imposition of Lucas's modernization of those movies which had become nostalgic objects in themselves. By painting out markers of temporality such as "outdated" special effects and inadequacies of production forced by constraints upon budget, technology was used to deplete the contemporary and auratic resonances of the films. However, while new tools allowed Lucas to polish up his work, the same devices would transfer some of that power back to the spectators. The computer interfaces which enabled Lucas to give shape to Jar Jar Binks are directly related to the same technologies which empower their uses to distort, eviscerate, slice, and destroy the helpless Gungan's image. If his digital composition means that he heralds a new era of increased control over onscreen performers, a triumph over the inconvenient idiosyncrasies of human actors, it must also mean that that level of control is matched by the technology's cession of similar power to the techno-literate quarters of the audience.

The Amateur Auteurs' Alliance

A distillation of anti–Jar Jar sentiment can also be located in a series of challenges to the proprietorship of the *Star Wars* franchise as maintained by George Lucas. Just as Lucas has used the capabilities of digital technology to exert authorial control of the films and develop the framespace with updates and alterations, so rebellious fans have responded to such unwelcome incursions into the integrity spaces of *Star Wars'* visual spaces by exploiting the pliability of the same digital technologies to postulate counter-narratives and oppositional stances to Lucas' canonicity.

In 2001, a re-edited version of *The Phantom Menace* surfaced on the Internet. Revealed to be the work of editor Mike J. Nichols, the bootleg video removed most of Jar Jar's screen time, shortened political discussions, excised discussion of the Force in terms of "midi-chlorians," and re-organized shots in several scenes. It remains available on DVD and VHS—the DVD even includes an expository audio commentary from Nichols. The result is an example of how the consumption and interpretation of a film text can be driven by fans even when its central site of authorship is not in question.

If fandom is usually associated with committed but acritical allegiances to certain texts, or even with psychopathological obsessions, Sara Gwenllian Jones rejects these connotations to argue that:

> Fans make unauthorized and "inappropriate" uses of cultural texts, reading them in ways that seem alien to non-fans and threatening to a culture industry that has a vested interest in controlling the meanings that consumers make of its products. Fans combine conspicuous, enthusiastic consumption of official texts and spin-offs with their own creative and interpretive practices [172].

However, it seems to me that in the case of *Star Wars*, the reverse has happened, with fans seeming more protective of what they see as the coherent and immersive *Star Wars* universe—they police the texts, branding as abject those elements which seem either incongruous or destructive of that immersion. (Brooker; Hills)

As Gregory Solman points out, Lucas' fondness for adjusting the *Star Wars* master text "gives courage" to fans who might seek to propose their own orientation for the films. By reducing Jar Jar's and young Anakin's scenes and dialogue from their "Consumer's Cuts," fans such as The Phantom Editor excise "the adolescent aesthetics they're now embarrassed to confront" (Solman 22). Solman cites Ernie Fosselius's 1977 short film homage *Hardware Wars* (in which miniature spacecraft are replaced by household implements) as an early fan response to the franchise which is creative rather than reactive.[10] He also defends Jar Jar Binks as "in keeping with Lucas's digitization of cinema, in sync with the *Star Wars* series' steady accretion of synthetic, computer-generated imagery that has gradually overtaken first individual shots, then scenes, and now entire movies" (22). In this sense, Jar Jar might even be seen as the natural end product of the infantilization and the digitalization of *Star Wars*, two developments which remove it from the realms of nostalgia and naivety at the technological level while retaining an agelessness that doesn't sit well with aging fans. Solman proclaims that the *Star Wars* prequels pose the "Riddle of the Binks" (26), by forcing the issue of digital and its lack of anterior presence (the essential nature which connects representation to a real world referent), into full view. We are forced to work out the spectatorial relationships between digital and analogue elements, the illusory and the real (bringing to bear the problematic and unfocused definitions associated with both of those terms). It is what Paul Willemen has called the "waning of the indexical" (5), the severance of a causal link between photographic object and referent; the connective process between the two is transferred to digital media which build referents from the ground up to create digital figures.

The Edit-Suite Strikes Back

Aside from the unprecedented prominence of computer-generated characters, the main innovation embraced during the production of *The Phantom Menace* was what Ron Magid has called "edit-suite film-making," referring to a phase of post-production that not only situates shots in sequence but also edits spaces, characters, and objects within individual shots. Magid discusses a number of patching tricks which included: "splitting actors out of different takes of the same scene and recombining them in new plates to achieve the optimum performance from each character; adding lip movement to accommodate new dialogue; removing lip movement to edit dialogue; and adding characters to scenes in which they weren't originally scripted to appear" (118). For instance, a shot of characters including Padmé, Jar Jar, Shmi, and the droids celebrating with Anakin his pod-race victory, was entirely composed of "found" elements from other shots, pieced together when Lucas decided such a shot was required long after the close of principal photography.

A precedent for this technique was set by Lucas's TV series *Young Indiana Jones Chronicles* (1992–3); this show was, in part, a testing ground for a range of digital effects in the lower resolution environment of television (with the added constraints of smaller budgets and tighter schedules). In one case, a digital erasure removed a supporting player who had demanded increased payment for extra shooting hours (Sragow). As Manovich has described, this "modular" approach to film-making is in keeping with the properties of new media, whereby media elements are comprised of discrete components which exist independently of the final output in which they appear. Not only is this approach modular, it is also "variable," since the status of its output is not fixed—the modular product which is exhibited can be re-adjusted in the future (as the digitally altered DVD versions of the films demonstrate). Such techniques are rather like the "game patches" which some gamers use to customize certain computer games for individual preferences. The increased computerization of film-making processes and the ready availability of graphics software makes them more susceptible to amateur manipulation; even though the construction of films digitally results in their fixture within a fixed output such as a film reel, the film as a cultural entity is informed and reshaped by its association with computer interfaces.

Within the filmic space, the actor's body is also affected by the patches which are grafted onto it to impose an authorial stamp on what they might have considered to be their own idiosyncratic performance. For instance, compositor Tim Alexander casually remarked that in one scene "Shmi was turning the wrong way, so we actually sliced her head off and then reverse-printed it in the shot" (qtd. in Magid 120). It is this erasure of idiosyncrasy and spontaneity from human performance (the last line of defense for organic/analogic essence in visual media) which makes the body another prop, one more media element to be integrated with the all the other equally pliable components of the filmic space. Perhaps this is what inflects the film with a troubling hint of tyrannically fastidious authorship and prompts fans to respond with manipulated *Star Wars* images of their own, treating characters as arguable entities rather than as autonomous inhabitants of the narrative domain. For all that digital offers in the way of malleability, there will, for some time, be suspicion of how it impacts upon the function of human creativity and whether or not the obstacles which film poses for filmmakers are actually what create the dynamic interaction between its mechanical and its organic artistic elements.

Edit-suite film-making of this sort not only compromises the anterior presence upon which film relies for some of its affect but also detracts from a sense of liveness by creating shots that are built from different spatio-temporal units. The main difference between this and matte processes or other analogue compositional technologies is the ease with which digital interfaces enable it—the very act of combining elements from various sources within a single shot is perfectly in keeping with the modular nature of digital media. Manovich sees compositing as a process inherently aligned with postmodern principles of pastiche, play, and selection from extant cultural objects but not in the same way as earlier collage aesthetics which assembled montages from clearly delineated segments—computer-based compositing "supports a different aesthetic defined by smoothness and continuity" (142). Elements are fused to enforce the illusion that they occupy the same diegetic space. While Jar Jar Binks might be a showcase for the way computer-generated characters can be integrated smoothly into a diegetic space, the judgment passed on him by most fans and critics indicates that his integration is not wholly harmonious.

Criticisms of Jar Jar's gait and mien are precisely directed at the problems of his digitality—that is to say that his gesticular propensities mark him out as an attention-grabbing exponent of physical comedy with an almost vaudevillian monstration towards the viewer. In the immersive environments at which *Star Wars* excels, this reminder of spectatorial position is an uncomfortable one, just as it is a nod towards merchandising opportunities and Pepsi tie-ins which dissipates the sense of otherworldliness to which the films aspire. As visual effects supervisor Kim Libreri noted in 2004, although it would soon be possible to use new software to render totally photorealistic virtual actors, they would still be given away by their kinesic characteristics because "human beings don't move the same way that machines do." As such, what we see is a mechanized performance attempting to mimic the properties of organic bodies, even in the achievement of the precision chaos of physical comedy.

Goat, donkey, or frog, whatever animal we associate with Jar Jar, perhaps a more suitable reference point might be the eponymous hero of *Who Framed Roger Rabbit* (1987), a cartoon extracted from his customary surroundings and clashing tumultuously with real world spaces. Jar Jar is similarly at odds with his environment, constantly tripping, tumbling, aggravating or wrecking it, as if his digitality makes him an uneasy component of place and time. In his book *Film Performance*, Andrew Klevan notes the importance, for an actor, of establishing an "expressive rapport" with the filmic space, staying "in tune with the medium's encouragements" (3). He continues:

> Rather than obeying verisimilitude, the credibility of performance is created out of coherence and harmony with the film's environment— including the camera and other elements 'outside' the invisible fictional world—which then generates "truthful" analogy and metaphor [5].

If, then, the requirement for a virtual actor is to strike up an accord with the diegesis, interacting seamlessly with other performers and contributing to a harmonious screen space, we can see Jar Jar's eruptive mayhem as a contravention of that unspoken goal, but he seems torn between being just another character hoping for audience empathy and being a special effect, eliciting acritical, focused wonderment.

The need for congruity in interaction between human and digital figures points up what I see as a key principle of the introduction of virtual actors to mainstream cinema, and, by extension, of special effects more broadly. The human body stands as the measuring pole of verisimilitude, the standard against which machinic simulations must be assessed. Capturing the properties of skin, muscles and flesh, the astonishing detail and emotional responses of the human face (and provoking the corresponding intuitive responses in the spectator) in synthetic form has been a beguiling preoccupation driving many developments in computer graphics research and procedural programming. Scenes in which humans and synthespians share the screen make explicit this ongoing comparative feature of the way we consume visual effects sequences. As animation supervisor Rob Coleman states in the audio commentary of the DVD of *The Phantom Menace*:

> With computer graphics you want to make sure that it has all the weight and believability of a real object moving through 3-dimensional space because you're looking at Liam Neeson and Ewan McGregor and you're able to instantaneously compare Jar Jar's physicality to the humans' physicality.

The virtual actor represents a grey area of performance—it is, on the one hand, a special effect, designed to protrude from the diegetic space as a spectacular attraction and be viewed as a distinct object of technological wonder, while on the other it is required to integrate seamlessly with regular, pro-filmic elements such as sets and human actors. It is for this reason that a new kind of microspectacle predominates in CGI sequences and characters. Rather than the spectacular focus being predicated on ostentatious scale and splendor, the CGI object incites close inspection of its surface detail, texture, shading, and motion, the very elements which enforce the acceptance of real and virtual figures as occupying the same diegetic space. A prime example is when Liam Neeson grabs Jar Jar's tongue to stop him fidgeting: the forceful iteration of their co-existence showcases the craft involved in making them appear to be spatially co-dependent, and the spectator is challenged to perceive the point at which the simulation meets the solid. Given the dual tasks of ushering in new paradigms of virtual performance and simultaneously eliciting the same emotional responses from the audience as Ewan McGregor and Liam Neeson, it's little wonder that Jar Jar acts flustered and fraught. Once again we find a point of ambiguity in relation to technology in the *Star Wars* films in the digital character whose duty as spectacle requires him to reveal his mechanical basis, thus conflicting with the wish that he should act sufficiently organic to garner audience empathy.

Jar Jar Binks Must Have Died?

In *Episode II*, Jar Jar has become a minor character and is all but entirely absent from *Episode III*. If he was initially intended to have become a quasi-mythological "holy fool" character with imminent significance for the progress of the narrative, it is tempting to suggest that the chorus of disapproval for *The Phantom Menace* prompted Lucas to hasten his demotion. Binks's guileless naivety enables him to be manipulated into handing emergency powers to Senator Palpatine, thus precipitating the Clone Wars, the Rise of the Empire and the subjugation of the known universe. It seems that Senator Binks may have ended up deserving some of the premonitory antipathy hurled at him.

Many of the links to Jar Jar death sites are now dormant or deleted. The seething enmity has mellowed with the increased familiarity with CGI and the relegation of our Gungan apostate to that of a background artiste. It might be worth asking why, in light of the fierce criticism of Binks, the translation of one of the franchise's most beloved characters, Yoda, from a latex rod puppet to a fully computer-generated avatar was not met with such hostility; in the rankings of CG characters compiled by *Entertainment Weekly* in which Jar Jar was cited as the worst (see above), digital Yoda was listed as the best. For Yoda, the comparisons between rubbery puppet and digital double were obvious—in his computer-generated incarnation, loosed from the strictures of rods and cables, he could engage in athletic combat and could also, especially by the time of *Episode III*, withstand the scrutiny of extreme close-ups. The expressivity of these shots is clearly posited as an intertextual point of comparison between the capacities of the fluid digital body and the tethered inertia of the animatronic puppet, but here is an additional function of character development in Yoda's digitalization; we now deepen our engagement with the character by discovering abilities which we presumed were concealed from us all along, hidden away in his back-story. The digital Yoda is reigned in by a need to keep him consistent with the original characterization, whereas Jar Jar is packaged for us immediately as a digital wonder, an exhibit first and a character second.

The *Star Wars* special editions, and to a lesser, but notable extent *The Phantom Menace*, occupy a tricky mid-space between film as canonical, fixed text, and the digital object as endlessly mutable. Jar Jar Binks is the personification of that transitional phase, finding himself caught between the treasured nostalgic space of the *Star Wars* universe and the unripe aesthetic of congruous simulation. Torn between the ostentatious spectacular display of the former, and the need for seamless interaction of components that characterizes the former, he naturally ends up standing out like a swimming donkey.

Notes

1. See, for example: *The Death to Jar Jar Binks Page*: Other sites are gathered on *The Jar Jar Hate Webring* <http://adamrulz.com/jj/jjwr.html>.

2. The song can be downloaded free from Damn Nation's website: <http://www.damnnation.com/html/mp3.html>.

3. Ahrens reports that, as of May 2005: "The five *Star Wars* films have grossed nearly $5.7 billion in worldwide box office sales, with toy and merchandise sales adding $9 billion more in revenue, according to Lucasfilm. The company does not break out VHS, DVD, and video game sales, but Forbes magazine estimated those three categories have raked in an additional $4.3 billion."

4. The misjudgment of public feeling towards Jar Jar in the film's merchandising prompted the spoof online newspaper *The Onion*'s headline, "80 Billion Tons of Jar Jar Merchandise Now 70 Percent Off."

5. In a handful of shots, notably close ups of hands or feet, Jar Jar is represented by actor Ahmed Best, who also provides the voice. During production, tests were performed to ascertain whether it was more economical to shoot him in a costume with only his head replaced digitally, but it was agreed that it was simpler and more cost-effective to produce Jar Jar as an all-CG character.

6. The current title, *Star Wars Episode IV: A New Hope*, was not designated until the film's re-release alongside *The Empire Strikes Back* in 1981. Therefore, I retain the original

appellation when discussing the film as it was first released. Other films in the series, such as *The Phantom Menace* or *Return of the Jedi*, will be denoted by their episodic titles. In this chapter, "*Star Wars*" refers to "*Episode IV*" in the form in which it was released in 1977, except where the context indicates specific reference to the *Special Editions* or other re-release variant.

7. Along with the other divisions of Lucasfilm, ILM is, at time of writing, being relocated to the Presidio complex in San Francisco, presumably to allow greater synergy between production, post-production (of image and sound) and marketing.

8. A list of changes for *Star Wars* re-releases (including DVD versions) to date can be found in a Wikipedia entry "List of Changes in the *Star Wars* Re-Releases." John Campea of "The Movie Blog" also provides detailed shot comparisons between versions, most notably the DVD releases.

9. Several websites illustrate resistance to the changes. These include the online petition for a re-release of the films in un-altered form at *Han Shoots First.org*. One fan, Jason Hall, responds to the Greedo controversy in an online comic book entitled *Greedo Shoots First*.

10. A direct descendent of this film is *Grocery Store Wars*, a short film produced for the Organic Trade Association, using various organic vegetables in the lead roles (Obi-Wan Cannoli, Tofu Deetoo etc.).

Works Cited

Ahrens, Frank. "Final *Star Wars* Caps Moneymaking Empire." *The Washington Post* 14 May, 2005. 31 Jul. 2005. <http://www.washingtonpost.com/wp-dyn/content/article/2005/05/13/AR2005051301512_pf.html>.

Berardinelli, James "Review of *Star Wars Episode 1: The Phantom Menace*." *Reelviews* May 1999. 01 Sep. 2005. <http://movie-reviews.colossus.net/movies/s/sw99.html>.

Brooker, Will. "Internet Fandom and the Continuing Narratives of *Star Wars*, *Blade Runner* and *Alien*." *Alien Zone II: The Spaces of Science-Fiction Cinema*. Ed. Annette Kuhn. London: Verso, 2000: 50–72.

Brophy, Philip. "Clone Tones: Philip Brophy Sounds Off on *Star Wars*." *Film Comment* 38.4 (2002): 28.

Brosnan, John. *Movie Magic: The Story of Special Effects in the Cinema*. London: MacDonald & Jane's, 1974.

Campea, John. "*Star Wars Special Edition* vs. *Star Wars* 2004: A Shot by Shot Comparison of Lucas' Alterations." *The MovieBlog.com* 2 Aug. 2005. <http://www.themovieblog.com/archives/2004/08/star_wars_special_edition_vs_star_wars_2004_still_shot_comparisons_of_lucas_alterations.html>.

Cassel, David. "*Star Wars* Lovers Call for Jar Jar's Head." *Salon* 28 May 1999. 12 May, 2005. <http://archive.salon.com/tech/log/1999/05/28/jar_jar/>.

Cavagna, Carlo. "Review of *Star Wars Episode 1: The Phantom Menace*." *AboutFilm*. Jun. 1999. 1 Sep. 2005. <http://www.aboutfilm.com/movies/s/starwars1b.htm>.

Craig, Alastair. "Petition to George Lucas." *Support Jar Jar Binks*. 31 Jul. 2005. <http://www.petitiononline.com/jjbf5436/petition.html>.

The Death to Jar Jar Binks Web Page. 15 May, 2005. <http://www.mindspring.com/~ernestm/jarjar/deathtojarjar.html>.

De Lisle, Tim. "Space Invaders." *Guardian Unlimited* 6 May 2005. 1 Sep. 2005. <http://www.guardian.co.uk/arts/fridayreview/story/0,,1476958,00.html>.

Duncan, Jody. "Q & A: George Lucas." *Cinefex* 102 (2005): 57–64.

Ebert, Roger. "Review of *Star Wars Episode 1: The Phantom Menace*." *Chicago Sun-Times* 17 May 1999. 1 Sep. 2005. <http://rogerebert.suntimes.com/apps/ pbcs.dll/article?AID=/19990517/REVIEWS/905170301/1023>.

"80 Billion Tons of Jar Jar Merchandise Now 70 Percent Off." *The Onion.com* 4 Aug. 1999. 31 Aug. 2005.

Grocery Store Wars. Dir. Louis Fox. FreeRangeStudios.com 1 Sep. 2005. <http://www.storewars.org/flash/index.html>.

Hall, Jason, et al. *Greedo Shoots First.* 5 Aug. 2005. <http://willow.club. fr/Greedo_Comic/ Greedo_Comic_01.htm>.
Han Shoots First.org. 26 Aug. 2005. <http://www.hanshootsfirst.org/>.
Harries, Dan, ed. *The New Media Book.* London: British Film Institute, 2002.
Hills, Matt. "*Star Wars* in Fandom, Film Theory, and the Museum: The Cultural Status of the Cult Blockbuster." *Movie Blockbusters.* Ed. Julian Stringer. London: Routledge, 2003. 178–189.
Hobermann, J. "All Droid Up. *Phantom Menace*: Star Bores." *The Village Voice* 19 May 1999. 1 Sep/ 2005. <http://www.villagevoice.com/film/9920,hoberman,5854,20.html>.
"Jar Jar, E.T., and Draco Made Our List of Worst CG Characters." *Entertainment Weekly.* 18 May, 2005. <http://www.bbc.co.uk/films/2001/08/28/kim_newman_8_article.shtml>.
Jones, Sarah Gwenllian. "Phantom Menace: Killer Fans, Consumer Activism and Digital Filmmakers." *Underground U.S.A.: Filmmaking Beyond the Hollywood Canon.* Eds. Xavier Mendik and Stephen J. Schneider. London: Wallflower, 2002. 169–179.
Klevan, Andrew. *Film Performance: From Achievement to Appreciation.* London: Wallflower Press, 2005.
Klinger, Barbara. "Digressions at the Cinema: Reception and Mass Culture." *Cinema Journal* 28.4 (1989): 3–19.
Krämer, Peter. "'It's Aimed at Kids—The Kid in Everybody': George Lucas, *Star Wars* and Children's Entertainment." *Scope: An Online Journal of Film Studies* 20 Nov. 2001. 1 Sep. 2005. <http://www.nottingham.ac.uk/film/journal/articles/its-aimed-at-kids.htm>.
Libreri, Kim. "12 Predictions on the Future of VFX." *VFXWorld* 7 Dec. 2004. 12 Sep. 2005. <http://vfxworld.com/?sa =adv&code=57c5ed8a&atype= articles&id=2319&page=1>.
"List of Changes in the *Star Wars* Re-Releases." *Wikipedia.* 2 Aug. 2005. <http://en. wikipedia.org/wiki/List_of_changes_in_Star_Wars_re-releases>.
Lister, Martin, et al. *New Media: A Critical Introduction.* London: Routledge, 2003.
"Lucas on *Star Wars*, Filmmaking and His New DVD." *FOXNews.com* 19 Sep.2004. 14Sep. 2004. <http://www.foxnews.com/story/0,2933,132871,00.html>.
Magid, Ron. "Edit-Suite Filmmaking." *American Cinematographer* 80.9 (Dec 1999): 118–124.
Manovich, Lev. *The Language of New Media.* Cambridge: MIT Press, 2001.
The National Association for the Extermination of the Gungan Race. 5 Aug. 2005. <http://www. angelfire.com/ca3/jarjarburn/>.
Newman, Kim. "Review of *Star Wars Episode IV: A New Hope.*" *Sight and Sound* 7.4 (1997): 50–51.
_____. "Why *Star Wars* Is Rubbish." *BBC.* 4 Aug. 2005. <http://www.bbc.co.uk/films/2001/ 08/28/kim_newman_8_article.shtml>.
North, Dan. "Virtual Actors, Spectacle and Special Effects: Kung Fu Meets 'All That CGI Bullshit.'" *The Matrix Trilogy: Cyberpunk Reloaded.* Ed. Stacy Gillis. London: Wallflower Press, 2005. 48–61.
Pierson, Michele. *Special Effects: Still in Search of Wonder.* New York: Columbia University Press, 2002.
Rickitt, Richard. *Special Effects: The History and Technique.* London: Virgin, 2000.
Rubey, Dan. "*Star Wars*: Not So Long Ago, Not So Far Away." *Jump Cut* 41 (1996): 2–12+.
Schechner, Richard. *Performance Theory.* London: Routledge, 2003.
Smith, Thomas G. *Industrial Light and Magic: The Art of Special Effects.* London: Columbus, 1985.
Solman, Gregory. "Fancy Math." *Film Comment* 38.4 (2002): 22–26.
Sragow, Michael. "The Biggest Indie Film Ever Made." *Salon.* 20 May 1999. 1 Sep. 2005. <http://www.salon.com/ent/col/srag/1999/05/20/mccallum/index.html>.
Star Wars. Dir. George Lucas. Screenplay by George Lucas. Twentieth Century Fox. 1977.
Star Wars Episode I: The Phantom Menace. Dir. George Lucas. Screenplay by George Lucas. Twentieth Century Fox, 1999.
Star Wars Episode II: Attack of the Clones. Dir. George Lucas. Screenplay by George Lucas and Jonathan Hales. Twentieth Century Fox, 2002.
Star Wars Episode III: Revenge of the Sith. Dir. George Lucas. Screenplay by George Lucas. Twentieth Century Fox, 2005.

Star Wars Episode IV: A New Hope. 1977. Dir. George Lucas. Screenplay by George Lucas. Twentieth Century Fox. 1981.

Star Wars Episode IV: A New Hope. 1977. Dir. George Lucas. Screenplay by George Lucas. Twentieth Century Fox. Special Edition. 1997.

Star Wars Episode IV: A New Hope. 1977. Dir. George Lucas. Screenplay by George Lucas. Twentieth Century Fox. DVD Special Edition. 2004.

Star Wars Episode V: The Empire Strikes Back. Dir. Irvin Kershner. Screenplay by Leigh Brackett and Lawrence Kasdan. Story by George Lucas. Twentieth Century Fox, 1980.

Star Wars Episode V: The Empire Strikes Back. 1980. Dir. Irvin Kershner. Screenplay by Leigh Brackett and Lawrence Kasdan. Story by George Lucas. Twentieth Century Fox, Special Edition 1997.

Star Wars Episode V: The Empire Strikes Back. 1980. Dir. Irvin Kershner. Screenplay by Leigh Brackett and Lawrence Kasdan. Story by George Lucas. Twentieth Century Fox, DVD Special Edition 2004.

Star Wars Episode VI: Return of the Jedi. Dir. Richard Marquand. Screenplay by Lawrence Kasdan and George Lucas. Story by George Lucas. Twentieth Century Fox, 1983.

Star Wars Episode VI: Return of the Jedi. 1983. Dir. Richard Marquand. Screenplay by Lawrence Kasdan and George Lucas. Story by George Lucas. Twentieth Century Fox, Special Edition. 1997.

Star Wars Episode VI: Return of the Jedi. 1983. Dir. Richard Marquand. Screenplay by Lawrence Kasdan and George Lucas. Story by George Lucas. Twentieth Century Fox, DVD Special Edition. 2004.

Turan, Kenneth. "Review of *Star Wars Episode 1: The Phantom Menace*." *Los Angeles Times* 18 May 1999. 20 Aug. 2005. <http://www.calendarlive.com/movies/ reviews/cl-movie990517–1,0,6661504.story>.

Vaz, Mark Cotta, and Patricia Rose Duignan. *Industrial Light and Magic: Into the Digital Realm*. London: Virgin, 1996.

"Ways Jar Jar Binks Should Die." *Freaky Frea's Crazy Cosmos*. 19 May, 2005. <http://members.tripod.com/Freaky_Freya/diejarjar.html>.

Willemen, Paul. "Of Mice and Men: Reflections on Digital Imagery." *292: Essays in Visual Culture* 1.1 (1999): 5–20.

Wilson, John. "The Twentieth Annual Razzies." *Razzies.com* 18 May, 2005. <http://razzies.com/asp/content/XcNewsPlus.asp?cmd=view&articleid=71>.

8

"Your Father's Lightsaber"

The Fetishization of Objects Between the Trilogies

KEVIN J. WETMORE, JR.

The two trilogies that form the *Star Wars* saga are linked by story, characters, plot, themes, shared imaginative geography (Tatooine, Alderaan, etc.), and concepts. The two are also linked by the imaginative material culture of Lucas's invented universe. The objects of the *Star Wars* films overlap, forming a tighter connection between the two trilogies. The lightsaber is arguably the object that most unites the films and also is most fetishized by fans. Blasters, ships, droids, and personal properties, however, also link the two films. One might note that specific objects appear in both sets of films, forming a specific link between the prequel generation of characters and the original generation of characters. After viewing *Revenge of the Sith*, for example, one realizes that the lightsaber used by Luke in *A New Hope* and *The Empire Strikes Back* is the same one used by Anakin in *Attack of the Clones* and *Revenge of the Sith*. The Millennium Falcon makes an (admittedly brief) appearance in *Sith*, causing not only audience applause, but the recognition of the role it will eventually play in the destruction of not one but two Death Stars, the first of which is being construction at the end of *Sith*, the schematics of the Death Star of *A New Hope* having already been introduced in *Clones*. Lastly, C3PO (whom this author was shocked to learn was Darth Vader's childhood pet project) and R2-D2 are not only characters; they are constructed objects that link the two trilogies. The droid made by the father becomes the servant of the son; the droid that saved a queen and co-piloted a ship that destroyed the Trade Federation command ship in *Phantom Menace* is also the droid that saved a princess and co-piloted a ship that destroyed the Death Star in *A New Hope*.

In this essay, I will briefly consider the material objects that unite the two trilogies and then focus upon the lightsaber as uniting object *par excellence*. The lightsabers of the two trilogies, individually and conceptually, mark the significant moments of and unite the narrative of *Star Wars*. Lightsabers are fetishized in all senses of the word, and this fetishization serves not only to unite the six films together and generate meaning through the presence of lightsabers, but also to generate a relationship between the viewer and the object in which the fetishization becomes a form of marketing. In other words, lightsabers function as anthropological and psychosexual fetishes within the films, binding the narrative and the imaginative culture of the universe while simultaneously functioning as an object of desire for the viewer, who then seeks to possess the (admittedly imaginary) object. Lastly, we must note the changing nature and increasing presence of the use of the lightsaber from film to film. As fans grew more enamored of the lightsaber, its use (and screen time) increased with each subsequent film. Jedi love lightsabers. So do viewers.

Let us begin by defining fetish and fetishism. The words are overdetermined and overused in much critical writing, so I here return to the three simple original definitions and add a fourth for the purpose of understanding the role of the fetishization of lightsabers within both *Star Wars* and its fan community. The term "fetish," for which different linguistic origins have been given, most likely emerged out of West Africa as a pidgin term between the Portuguese and the indigenous peoples to describe powerful objects which could not be traded and thus (appropriately for this discussion), "emerged from imperialist discourses," as Amanda Fernbach notes (104). The notion of an object that is endowed with magical powers that serve as an obstacle to trade gives way to the three traditional notions of fetishism: anthropological/magical, psychosexual, as defined by Freud, and economic, as defined by Marx.

Anthropological fetishism, as coined by Charles de Brosses in *Du culte des dieux fetishes* (1760), refers to material objects that are perceived as being endowed with supernatural powers and worshipped or used as such. The object is familiar, but because of its endowment of supernatural qualities it is also estranged. The fetish can be prayed to or can have a variety of powers allowing it to affect material reality. The fetish can also be a magical tool that, in the hands of one who knows how to use it, gives the wielder tremendous power and abilities.

Freud, on the other hand, sees fetishes as the desire for something that the subject lacks; specifically, he defines the fetish as the substitute for the female penis. In his 1927 essay "Fetishism," Freud argues that fetishism (the use of a fetish object for sexual arousal and pleasure) is in response to castration anxiety produced by the "terrifying shock" of the "sight of the female genitals," which creates the fear that one might lose one's own genitals (201). For Freud, the fetish is "a token of triumph over the threat of castration and a safeguard against it" (200). It is a substitute for the penis, a protection against castration, and a source of pleasure. One might also see the fetish as a weapon against the father, who seeks to castrate the son in response to the son's own murderous oedipal drive. Given that women do not have castration anxiety, yet many do have fetishes, the definition of a psychosexual fetish has expanded since Freud to imply any desire for something lacked by the subject.

In Marxism, Marx appropriates the term to mean commodity: the fetish is a metaphor for the goods one buys and sells. What is fetishized is the exchange value rather than the actual object. According to Marx, objects that are the product of labor become divided into the "useful thing" they actually are and "the value" that they are ascribed as commodities (Tucker 321). One wishes to purchase an object for reasons beyond its use value; the reason may be the person or company that made the object, the prestige that the object brings to its owner, or because others have a similar object.

The meaning of fetish can thus refer to objects that are endowed with special powers, significance and meanings, an object that fills a lack in the subject that can also serve as a penis substitute, or a commodity that one wishes to purchase. Amanda Fernbach has also recently argued that fetishes and fetishism go beyond Freud's assertion of a response to castration anxiety and actually are a direct reversal of Freud's theory. She sees fetishism as a response to modern technology in which "the transformation of the body or self is paramount" (4). In other words, the fetish is both transformative and transgressing; one's use of the fetishized objects makes one fundamentally different from mainstream categories and can serve as a point of identification. One enjoys the services of a dominatrix, for example, not because one fears castration anxiety but because of the transformative nature of the role-playing involved. The fetish is empowering, transgressive of the realm of the everyday and mundane, and transforms the user, thus marking a return in a sense to the original meaning of the fetish. Thus, generally, fetishized objects are those that have acquired special meanings and values beyond their simple material worth or use and can transform the user, both repairing a lack within him or her and transforming him or her beyond the mundane borders of the self. In this essay, I seek to demonstrate that the lightsaber, as the material object at the center of the *Star Wars* films, not only embodies all of these definitions, but also in doing so, creates a narrative and material through line in the films as well as serving as an object of desire marketed to the viewer. The viewer becomes invested in the object, not only because the characters are invested in the object, but because the viewer wants the object for himself. I will also pay particular attention to the changing nature of the lightsaber from film to film and from trilogy to trilogy.

We see in both trilogies the characters' faith in objects, to the point of fetishization. Han tells Luke and Obi-Wan in *A New Hope*: "Hokey religions and ancient weapons are no match for a good blaster at your side." He expresses faith in his blaster. Later in the same film, he reassures them about the Millennium Falcon: "Don't worry—she'll hold together," adding a *sotto voce* prayer, "You hear me, baby, hold together." The prayer demonstrates the faith Han has in his ship: he anthropomorphizes it, attributes powers to it, and even prays to it. For Han, the Falcon is a magical fetish. It is also a sexual one. He is not a man without it. He fears the loss of the Falcon more than the loss of Leia.

The viewer fetishizes the ship as well. Audiences cheered when the Millennium Falcon briefly appeared in *Sith*, landing on the Senate Landing platform on Coruscant in the lower right hand corner of the screen. The Falcon is arguably better known than many of the secondary characters. The ship itself is so fetishized by the fans that it is evidence that individual objects are valued more that the characters. In *Jedi*, as he is leaving for the mission to destroy the shield generators, Han says, "I just got a funny feeling. Like I'm not going to see her again." This statement is the surviving part of an original plan to have the ship destroyed during the destruction of the second Death Star. The foreshadowing of the loss of the Falcon proved unnecessary, as John Baxter reports, "after poor reactions during preview screenings, probably more at the loss of the well-loved Falcon than Lando's underdrawn character, both were allowed to survive" (327). Lando Calrissian represents an acceptable loss, the Falcon would be an unbearable one. What is this if not fetishization on the part of fans? So beloved is the ship that it makes the aforementioned cameo in *Sith*. At the end of that same film, construction has begun on the Death Star, the space station that will destroy Alderaan in *A New Hope* and that will be infiltrated by the Falcon in order to rescue the Princess and subsequently be destroyed by Luke Skywalker with the assistance of the Falcon. These two ships, linked throughout *A New Hope*, are both referenced and joined together at the end of *Sith*.

When viewing the films, we read objects in the second trilogy in terms of the first, but as the order is reversed, we reread the first trilogy in terms of the second. In other words, we can read the films in the chronological order in which they were released (IV, V, VI, I, II, and III), or we can read them in narrative order (I, II, III, IV, V, VI), and each reading produces echoes in the other films. The objects of these six films move back and forth, so to speak, between the films, allowing the audience to understand the original trilogy in new ways even as they shape the second trilogy. In the case of the lightsaber, if one views the films in chronological order, from *New Hope* to *Sith*, there is a slow build of lightsabers, from three featured in a few scenes to dozens if not hundreds throughout the films. If one views the films in narrative order, from *Phantom* to *Jedi*, the audience sees the decline and rebirth of the lightsaber. In the prequel trilogy, lightsabers are common. By *A New Hope*, the technology to build them is lost and only three are known to exist. In *Jedi*, Luke Skywalker builds the first new lightsaber in a generation. I will now spend the rest of this essay in a more detailed study of the fetishization of lightsabers in general and one lightsaber, Anakin's then Luke's, in particular. This lightsaber, which is a material symbol of the link between Luke and his father, and between the world of the first trilogy and the world of the second trilogy, is one of the few surviving links between the two. Obi-Wan, the Emperor, and Anakin/Vader are the only human characters linking the two, but the objects of the film—the lightsabers, the ships, the droids, the speeders, the armor of the clone troops, etc.—are present in all six films.

"In the early drafts" of the script, Bouzereau reports, "the laser sword was a generic weapon, but eventually the sword became a unique weapon characteristic of a Jedi warrior" (24). When Anakin drops his lightsaber in *Clones*, Obi-Wan hands it back to him saying, "Next time try not to lose it. This weapon is your life." In this case, Obi-Wan not only means that the lightsaber will defend and protect Anakin, but that it is literally who he is: lightsabers define the Jedi (only Jedi may carry them), lightsabers serve as synecdoche for the Jedi, and the nature of the Jedi is determined by its color (only Sith use red lightsabers).

Lightsabers are the most fetishized objects in the series. Not only are they the most original (the viewer has seen ships and robots before, but this weapon was unique), they profoundly shape the narrative and influence events. The lightsaber was introduced in *A New Hope*, back when it was called *Star Wars*. Ben Kenobi hands Luke an object, which he then activates, demonstrating to audiences for the first time the weapon of the Jedi:

> BEN: Your father wanted you to have this when you were old enough.
> LUKE: What is it?
> BEN: Your father's lightsaber. This is the weapon of a Jedi Knight. Not as clumsy or as random as a blaster. An elegant weapon for a more civilized time. For over a thousand generations, the Jedi Knights were the guardians of peace and justice in the Old Republic. Before the dark times. Before the Empire.

The lightsaber, when introduced, is immediately linked to Luke's father. The lightsaber is the only thing of his father's (other than his name) that

Luke has. It is fetishized as the missing father (in the Freudian sense: Luke fills the lack of a father with both Ben Kenobi and with his father's lightsaber). Looking further at these lines, we might note that the characters of the prequel trilogy represent the last of the thousand generations. Luke is the titular Jedi who returns, the presumable beginning of a new series of generations of Jedi.[1] This speech also already links the fall of the Republic and start of Empire to the events of *A New Hope*.

It is also worth noting that the lightsaber is introduced fairly early in the film and then put away for awhile. It is not a *deus ex machina* that solves every problem. Instead, it is used sparingly. Luke only uses his for training and we see Obi-Wan use his twice: once in Mos Eisley and once on the Death Star. The mystery is preserved in the first film. That mystery, of course, serves only to make the lightsaber an object of wonder and desire. As an eight year old seeing the film for the first time, like many my age, I thought it was the greatest thing I had ever seen and I wanted one. As a viewer, I fetishized the lightsaber in the Freudian sense (it was a lack that I wanted to fill), in the Marxist sense (it was a commodity I valued and wanted to possess), in the anthropological sense (I ascribed to it all sorts of abilities and knew that if I had one I would know how to use it and I would use it well), and even in Fernbach's transformative/identity sense (I would be the kid with the lightsaber and it would transform me from geek to kid with a lightsaber, thereby ensuring that I would be the coolest kid in my neighborhood and quite possibly the universe!). In the absence of an actual lightsaber, a wiffle bat, broom handle, or yardstick could substitute. Visual fetish gives way to simulacra/substitute, but that served enough to address the issues raised by the fetishization of the lightsaber. The lightsaber of *A New Hope* thus becomes link to the past for Luke but object of desire for the viewer.

The prequel trilogy sets up an intertext with this quotation, shaping the role and understanding of the lightsaber. Obi-Wan continues to instruct Anakin in the ways of lightsaber fighting in *Clones*, echoing his earlier training of Luke. Seeing Yoda with the "younglings" and their remotes echoes the earlier training of Luke by Yoda and the scene on the Millennium Falcon in which Luke trains with a remote as well. Even this specific quotation is referenced in *Sith* when Obi-Wan shoots General Grievous with a blaster. The threat over, Obi-Wan drops the blaster, cursing, "So uncivilized." Though he can use a blaster with deadly accuracy, the Jedi's preferred weapon is the lightsaber, the more elegant weapon.

Given the linkage between *Star Wars* and the lightsaber, it is fascinating to note that only three lightsabers appear in only four scenes in the original film: Luke activates his father's lightsaber in Ben's house, Obi-Wan uses his in the Cantina scene, cutting off an arm of a threatening alien, Luke trains with his on the Millennium Falcon, and the duel between Vader and Kenobi features each with his own.

Empire decreases the number of sabers (only two), but increases the number of scenes to five (Luke uses his in the Wampa cave, Han uses Luke's with the Tauntaun, Luke uses his to plant a bomb in an ATAT walker on Hoth, Luke brings his into the Dark Side place on Dagobah, where he meets Vader with a lightsaber, and the final battle between Luke and Vader). The rest of the time, though, it is inelegant and uncivilized; Luke uses a blaster. Luke draws a blaster on Yoda, earning the famous line, "Away put your weapon, I mean you no harm." Luke runs around Bespin with a blaster as well. It is not until he faces Vader that the blaster is put away and the lightsaber comes out. Given the events of *Sith*, we should note that Luke is now fighting his father with his father's own lightsaber. The weapon Anakin dropped when Obi-Wan cut off three of his limbs is now in the hands of his son, who will try to kill him with it. The lightsaber which would have killed Obi-Wan in *Sith* is now used to attempt to kill Anakin, its previous owner in *Empire*. The sixth film in the series now creates echoes in the second. It is at least a little ironic that Vader cuts off Luke's hand, thereby losing the lightsaber that Anakin lost when Obi-Wan cut off his hand. Although Obi-Wan took the lightsaber after that duel, now it is lost forever. Although the original audience may have remembered that Luke is carrying his father's lightsaber, it is not until *Sith* that this scene will retroactively take on additional significance.

In *Jedi*, Luke has manufactured a new lightsaber, which is good because it receives a workout in this film. From the four scenes in the original, the use of lightsabers in the third film has extended greatly in terms of on-screen time. Though only used in six scenes, the extended battle between Luke and Vader occupies much of the last third of the film, in addition to its presence at the Sarlacc Pit battle, the speeder bike fight, the capture of Luke, and his meeting of the Emperor. The final fight is longer, more complex, and contains the final echo: Luke cuts off his father's hand, dropping his lightsaber. Luke then makes the fundamental choice to turn off his lightsaber, ending its use as a weapon now that his opponent is down. Again, the scene in *Sith* echoes this duel as well, not only from the swelling music, but also because of the difference in its ending.

George Lucas sees the transition of the fetishized lightsaber in a Freudian sense:

> In the first film Luke takes on the responsibility of his father; he is given his father's lightsaber. In the second film the father destroys that ... The new lightsaber that Luke built himself symbolizes that he has detached himself completely from his father and now is on his own [qtd. in Bouzereau 274–75].

Based on this statement, it is possible to see the lightsaber in a Freudian sense.[2] The child takes on a phallic symbol that is originally his father's. When his father destroys that symbol, he must make his own phallus and thus become his own man.

If one looks at this quotation more closely, however, Lucas defines the relationship between father and son through a single object. Beyond the psychosexual nature of the prop, we might note that the lightsaber *is* his father in *A New Hope*; it is both symbol of his father, the Jedi, as well as the only material thing he has of his father's. The lightsaber further defines the relationship between the two. By a lightsaber was Anakin made into Darth Vader; by a lightsaber was Luke trained and taught his own worth as a Jedi, even if he must lose a hand to learn the lesson; and by a lightsaber is Darth Vader saved from the Dark Side.

The new trilogy substantially raises the presence of the lightsaber, introducing two new types: Darth Maul's double-bladed model and Mace Windu's purple lightsaber. The use of the lightsaber is substantially transformed. In *Phantom Menace* we see the first extended use of lightsabers as weapons against something other than lightsabers. In the first trilogy, Ben may cut off an arm in Mos Eisley, Han may open up a Tauntaun, or Luke may cut through the underbelly of an ATAT walker to place a charge, but the use is quick, simple, and not against an armed opponent. Only on Jabba's sail barge do we see a lightsaber used against opponents armed with blasters, not lightsabers. This type of combat becomes the standard in the new trilogy, saving lightsaber duels for climactic moments. In the first major lightsaber scene in *Phantom*, Qui-Gon and Obi-Wan fight a series of droids on the Trade Federation ship, employing the lightsabers defensively to repel blaster fire and offensively to cut the droids to pieces. This type of fight (lightsaber versus other weapons) will be repeated several times: while rescuing the Queen on Naboo, while escaping the hanger, after returning to Naboo a second time, in the palace. Not until Darth Maul arrives on Tatooine does a lightsaber duel occur. Only one other lightsaber duel is shown in *Phantom*: the climactic battle between Qui-Gon, Obi-Wan, and Darth Maul.

This new conceptualization of the lightsaber as an all-purpose weapon is expanded in *Attack of the Clones* where its screen time is expanded exponentially and the number of scenes in which lightsabers are used is greatly increased. No fewer than ten scenes representing almost a third of screen time feature lightsabers: they are employed in Padmé's bedroom against the venomous animals sent to kill her; Anakin uses his on Zam Westell's ship; Obi-Wan uses his in the bar, echoing the original Cantina scene; and again against Jango Fett on Kamino; and we see him using his in his holotransmission from Geonosis. Anakin uses his against the Sand People and on the droid assembly line on Geonosis.

More important, however, are the first scenes of multiple lightsabers. Until now, the maximum number on a screen has been three (in *Phantom*) and, much more typically, one or two. Instead, in *Clones*, Obi-Wan visits Master Yoda's class, in which dozens of "younglings" are training with lightsabers. Dozens of weapons are visible on screen. Again, in the arena on Geonosis, the Jedi knights arrive to fight *en masse*, and again dozens of lightsabers are visible, including Mace Windu's famed purple one. Also, *Clones* marks the first time Master Yoda is shown using a lightsaber. In four films, we have seen him train others, but he himself is finally revealed as the "great warrior" Luke was looking for in *Empire*. Yoda battles Dooku, whom the audience has just seen defeat Obi-Wan and Anakin rather soundly, and wins, although Dooku escapes by threatening Yoda's young friends, forcing him to choose between saving them and arresting the Sith lord. Yet the series of lightsaber battles that come at this film's climax outdoes anything in the original trilogy.

Revenge of the Sith, as both final film and climactic episode, features more lightsaber action than any of the others and certainly more than the three films of the first trilogy combined. The entire first sequence sees repeated use of lightsabers against droids. Anakin also cuts a hole in the elevator using his. The sequence then features not one but two duels, first against Dooku, whose head is severed when Anakin uses two lightsabers, scissor-like, and then against Grievous and his bodyguards. Until this film, this sort of extended battle was reserved for the end of the film.

The next sequence involves the battle between Obi-Wan and Grievous on Utapau, in which Darth Maul's double bladed lightsaber is done one better by Grievous using four lightsabers, one in each of his four arms. Whereas in the opening, we saw three lightsabers in action, now we are shown five. The next sequence features six lightsabers. The attempted arrest of Palpatine features Mace Windu leading three other Jedi Masters, all armed, against Palpatine, who also has a lightsaber. After Palpatine defeats the other three, Mace defeats him, and Anakin arrives with his lightsaber. Mace is literally disarmed and the balance of power shifts.

The massacre at the Jedi Temple follows, coinciding with the execution of Order 66. A montage sequence shows the deaths of several Jedi (only some of whom fight defensively with their lightsabers; others are killed outright) and Anakin's fights with other Jedi at the Temple are hinted at, to be eventually shown as a hologram for Yoda and Obi-Wan. Immediately, Anakin is also shown using his lightsaber on Mustafar to eliminate the Separatists. The film then ends with a pair of climactic duels: Anakin versus Obi-Wan and Yoda versus Palpatine.

It is interesting to note that the fate of the galaxy rests upon two lightsaber duels. If Yoda and Obi-Wan win, then the Empire will be stopped. If Anakin and Palpatine win, the Empire will be created and the Jedi are destroyed forever. Palpatine wins his duel, but Obi-Wan defeats Anakin. In both cases, however, defeat is not complete. Anakin lives to be transformed into Darth Vader, Yoda lives to go into exile on Dagobah and wait for the Skywalker twins to become old enough to train.

It is at the moment of defeat that Anakin tells Obi-Wan he hates him. Obi-Wan is then clearly shown picking up Anakin's lightsaber, which he will hand to Luke at the beginning of *A New Hope*, which brings the series full-cycle. We might note two things, however. First, is that Anakin did not want his son to have his lightsaber when he was old enough; this is just part of the fiction Obi-Wan tells Luke to slowly bring him into the world of the Jedi and his destiny. Whereas "Darth Vader betrayed and murdered your father" can be seen as metaphorically true, in no way did Anakin want his son to get his hands on a lightsaber. The irony is that it is Luke's training with a lightsaber that eventually allows him to defeat Vader in *Jedi* and therefore save him. Vader then thanks Luke for saving him, all of which would not have been possible without his father's lightsaber. So in this sense, Vader might retroactively be glad Luke received and trained with the lightsaber, but he did not want him to have it in the sense Obi-Wan suggests. Second, is that when Obi-Wan turns off his lightsaber after his duel with Anakin, it is theoretically possible that that is the last use of a lightsaber in the galaxy until Luke turns his on at the beginning of *A New Hope*. Given that the proclivity has been to use lightsabers primarily against other lightsabers, that the Sith have other weapons at their disposal, and that Obi-Wan and Yoda, the last of the Jedi, are hiding in exile, it is not out of the impossible to assume that we have witnessed the last use of lightsabers until the beginning of the new trilogy, which would also explain Luke's ignorance. Anakin, growing up on Tatooine, knew what a lightsaber was. Luke did not. They have vanished from common knowledge by the time Luke becomes sentient.

In the Fernbach's sense, the lightsaber is also transformative for the Jedi and, arguably even more than the Force or their distinctive dress, the chief identifier of Jedi (to others) and source of Jedi identification (to themselves). In *Phantom*, young Anakin recognizes Qui-Gon as a Jedi. "I saw your laser sword. Only Jedis carry that kind of weapon," he tells him. "Perhaps I killed a Jedi and took it from him," a smiling Qui-Gon responds. "I don't think so. No one can kill a Jedi," concludes Anakin, also fetishizing the weapon (and the Jedi) by ascribing powers of immortality, invulnerability, and invincibility to its wielders.

Interestingly, the second trilogy proves Anakin wrong again and again: at the end of *Phantom*, Qui-Gon himself will be killed by Darth

Maul, other Jedi will be shot by blasters in the battle in the arena on Geonosis in *Clones*, and Anakin himself will kill hundreds of Jedi as the clone troopers kill the rest in *Sith*. The lightsaber seems to convey both invincibility and imperviousness to harm (witness Qui-Gon Jinn and Obi-Wan Kenobi in *Phantom* catching every single blaster bolt that comes their way, even turning them against their adversaries), but also is the major means by which a Jedi can be killed: Qui-Gon Jinn, Mace Windu, and even Obi-Wan Kenobi perish in lightsaber duels, and the sense of invincibility conveyed in the first trilogy and in the first half of *Phantom* is displayed to be unfounded in the end. The fetish, in a sense, fails.

Yet it is Anakin's lightsaber that both bookends the trilogy and forms the object around which the narrative unfolds. The lightsaber is present at many of the major events of four of the six films. The history of the first lightsaber the viewer ever sees is shown in *Clones* and *Sith*. The hunting down and killing of Jedi that Ben Kenobi tells Luke about in *A New Hope* is shown in *Sith*. By the time Obi-Wan picks the lightsaber up at the conclusion of *Sith*, it has acquired a good deal of dramatic weight. Other individual lightsabers begin to acquire dramatic weight between the films as well. The lightsaber that killed Jango Fett is used against the Chancellor, and swept out the window with Mace Windu. Never again, in narrative order, is a purple lightsaber seen. When this specific one was introduced, its very presence made its absence from the first trilogy noticeable. In re-viewing (and reviewing) the original trilogy, the presence of an absence of other lightsabers reminds us of how much the Jedi order and their material culture has vanished from this universe. It is also this lack of lightsabers at the end of *Sith* that will create the void at the beginning of *A New Hope*, and, subsequently, the continued desire in the viewer for one.

Turning, then, to the real world significance of the fetishization of these objects within the individual films and between the trilogies, the end result of this fetishization of material objects in the *Star Wars* universe is that everything in that world becomes a fetishized object: action figures, toy lightsabers, clothing, alarm clocks, food, sheets, cups, plates, etc. If it can be a material object, it can be *Star Wars*. One might ask what does Darth Vader have to do with Corn Flakes, Yoda with Fruit Roll Ups, or Qui-Gin Jinn with brushing one's teeth, but the question is irrelevant. Meaning is built around the linkage of the material object to the film, to the point where the objects are more valued than the artist. At Celebration III, the *Star Wars* convention that took place in April 2005 in Indianapolis, just before the opening of Episode III, for example, there was a seven hour long line for *Sith*-related toys, which was longer than the line to see George Lucas himself (Jensen 25).

In 1978, the year after the first film opened, Kenner sold 42,322,500 action figures (Jensen 25). That number is now in the billions. In May 2005 the hottest toy in the United States for age four and up was a twenty dollar lightsaber (Boucher E1). There is also one that changes colors and uses digital samples from the films for six times that amount. Before the opening of *Revenge of the Sith* there had been already over nine billion dollars in merchandise sales alone (Boucher E10). Many toys, such as the plastic lightsaber and the Darth Vader Mr. Potato Head, were clearly aimed at an age group that would not be able to see the film which had been rated PG-13. Brian Goldner, who oversees the United States line of toys for Hasbro, the makers of the action figures, notes, "Even if they can't go to the movie, they can be a part of it" by buying the toys (qtd. in Boucher E10). The experience of the film no longer has primacy; it is the surrounding one's self with the objects of the films that allows one to fully participate in the narrative and world of the films. One might note that action figures reduce performers and characters down from living beings and narrative concepts to an object which can be possessed and ultimately fetishized. By purchasing Han Solo or Darth Maul, one may possess and control them.

There are even books on objects. The Lucasfilm publishing empire has devoted numerous books to the objects of the *Star Wars* universe— *Visual Dictionaries*, *Incredible Cross Sections*, and guides to ships and droids have been published for each of the films. People who would never read the instruction book that came with an appliance they use in their kitchen every day devour the inner workings of a device that does not and cannot exist except in the imagination. What is that if not fetishization?

Objects are routinely ignored in non-genre films. No one seeks to have a replica of the bat used in *Field of Dreams* (1989) or the couch in *American Pie* (1999), but large amounts of money are spent on replicas from *Star Wars* and other, similar films, such as the *Star Trek* (1966–2005) series and the *Lord of the Rings* (2001–03) series. The difference in many cases is that the items fetishized in many of these films never existed. At least Aragorn carried a real sword. Worf used a real blade in his fights. Like phasers, lightsabers as seen in the films really only exist in computers. But since film is a commercial enterprise, as Andrew Sofer argues of the stage, I argue of film: "everything that appears ... is not only a theatrical sign but a commodity offered for the consumer's visual consumption" (17). One initially consumes the lightsaber on the screen as a spectator and can then run to the local toy store to purchase a simulacra of the real thing.

The lightsaber has become an important touchstone, both within the films and within our culture. They are parodied in films such as *Jay and Silent Bob Strike Back* (2001) and *Bill and Ted's Excellent Adventure*

(1989). They are made manifest in a variety of toys (at a variety of prices). Their sounds and images have become immediately recognizable to a worldwide audience. Yet, they also form a link between all six films. Like the droids, the ships and the other material objects of this universe, the lightsaber forms a fetishized object that continues to give meaning and pleasure long after the films are over. They fulfill a lack in the characters, even as they create a desire in the viewer. They serve as source of identification and identity. They are the ultimate commodity: a nonexistent object whose replicas sell for hundreds of dollars. This is not bad for something that defies the laws of physics and cannot and does not exist. And, in conclusion, if I am honest, I must admit that I still want one.

Notes

1. Although I argue in *The Empire Triumphant* that it is actually Anakin Skywalker that is referred to in the title of *Jedi*, along with the conceptual return of the order through Luke. Anakin turns Sith lord in *Sith*, and it is Luke's faith in him that causes him to reject the Emperor and return to the Jedi, so to speak. Thus, the return of the title does not merely refer to the Jedi order as embodied in Luke, but the recuperation of Anakin Skywalker. The two trilogies together form a greater narrative about the fall and redemption of Anakin Skywalker. See Kevin Wetmore's *The Empire Triumphant: Race, Religion and Rebellion in the Star Wars Films.*

2. A Freudian reading of the lightsaber itself is given in a special issue of the Dark Horse comic series *Star Wars Tales*, entitled *A Jedi's Weapon*. In the narrative, Obi-Wan and a teenaged Anakin are sent on a diplomatic mission to Kashir, "a world almost ready to join the Republic" (Gilroy, Garcia, Palmiotti 1). Obi-Wan tells Anakin that, "The Lightsaber is a Jedi's weapon. As a physical representation of who we are, it is especially important in this case" (Gilroy, Garcia, Palmiotti 1). The Kashir insist that all weapons hang down from the centre of the belt, directly over the groin, so that they are always visible (shaping the already-phallic lightsaber into an even more obvious substitute for the Jedi's manhood). Ashala, one of the King of Kashir's wives, steals Anakin's lightsaber and offers to return it for a price. "Passion is forbidden" to a Jedi, he tells her (Gilroy, Garcia, Palmiotti 8). She then reveals that she no longer has the lightsaber. It is then revealed that Obi-Wan stole it back from her and is protecting it for Anakin, who may have it back when he admits he lost it. The entire comic is both homoerotic and misogynistic. Women seek to steal the weapon of the Jedi. Jedi must hold onto their weapons and the older Jedi must watch out to ensure that the younger Jedi do not misuse their weapon or allow it to be taken by women. Only when a young man is able to protect and manage his own "weapon" will he truly be a Jedi. Freudian indeed.

Works Cited

Baxter, John. *Mythmaker: The Life and Work of George Lucas.* New York: Spike, 1999.

Boucher, Geoff. "Gone to the Dark Side." *Los Angeles Times*, 10 May 2005: E1, E10.

Bouzereau, Laurent. *Star Wars: The Annotated Screenplays.* New York: Del Rey, 1997.

Fernbach, Amanda. *Fantasies of Fetishism: From Decadence to the Post-Human.* New Brunswick: Rutgers University Press, 2002.

Freud, Sigmund. *Collected Papers,* volume 5. Ed. James Strachey. Trans. Joan Riviere. New York: Basic, 1959.

Gilroy, Henry, and Manuel Garcia. *Star Wars Tales: A Jedi's Weapon*. Milwaukie: Dark Horse Comics, 2002.

Jensen, Jeff. "What a Long Strange Trip It's Been." *Entertainment Weekly*, May 20, 2005: 22–30.

Malt, Johanna. *Obscure Objects of Desire: Surrealism, Fetishism and Politics*. Oxford: Oxford University Press, 2004.

Sofer, Andrew. *The Stage Life of Props*. Ann Arbor: University of Michigan Press, 2003.

Star Wars Episode I: The Phantom Menace. Dir. George Lucas. Screenplay by George Lucas. Twentieth Century Fox, 1999.

Star Wars Episode II: Attack of the Clones. Dir. George Lucas. Screenplay by George Lucas and Jonathan Hales. Twentieth Century Fox, 2002.

Star Wars Episode III: Revenge of the Sith. Dir. George Lucas. Screenplay by George Lucas. Twentieth Century Fox, 2005.

Star Wars Episode IV: A New Hope. 1977. Dir. George Lucas. Screenplay by George Lucas. Twentieth Century Fox. 1981.

Star Wars Episode V: The Empire Strikes Back. Dir. Irvin Kershner. Screenplay by Leigh Brackett and Lawrence Kasdan. Story by George Lucas. Twentieth Century Fox, 1980.

Star Wars Episode VI: Return of the Jedi. Dir. Richard Marquand. Screenplay by Lawrence Kasdan and George Lucas. Story by George Lucas. Twentieth Century Fox, 1983.

Tucker, Robert C., ed. *The Marx-Engels Reader*. 2nd ed. New York: W.W. Norton, 1978.

Wetmore, Kevin J., Jr. *The Empire Triumphant: Race, Religion and Rebellion in the Star Wars Films*. Jefferson: McFarland, 2005.

9

The Emperor's New Clones; or, Digitization and Walter Benjamin in the *Star Wars* Universe

Graham Lyons and Janice Morris

Star Wars *and Aura: A Prequel*

The 2004 DVD release of the *Star Wars* trilogy has renewed and reinvigorated the popular controversy over George Lucas's digital changes to the original films—the most contentious of which are those tied to issues of authenticity, directorial rights, and narrative integrity.[1] Already generative in the popular domain, this controversy occasions a new site of critical analysis that moves beyond the myth criticism that has come to characterize much of the scholarship surrounding the films. Indeed, with the release of the sixth and final film of the series, the time has come to engage with the specific implications of Lucas's digital project. Given the pioneering nature of the films,[2] the uniqueness of the *Star Wars* universe renders it a particularly apt site for dialogue[3] with Walter Benjamin's notion of "aura" and its relation to mechanical (digital) reproduction, since Benjamin is also concerned with uniqueness, both experientially and technologically. Tied to authenticity,[4] for Benjamin aura signals the uniqueness of a work of art—not a qualitative uniqueness embedded in the art object itself, but one activated by an interaction between the object and the subject. According to Benjamin, in his landmark essay, "The Work of Art in the Age of Mechanical Reproduction,"[5] technological reproducibility in general (and cinema in particular) destabilizes both the subject and the object and, by extension, "withers" the uniqueness of the interaction, that is the aura, between the two (221).

And this auratic decay, by refiguring the art experience, opens up space for social change, for what Benjamin famously terms "politicizing art" (242).[6] Like Benjamin, we too are interested in how auratic decay refigures the art experience, though in the Age of Digital (rather than Mechanical) Reproduction. However, our focus is aesthetic rather than political. We ask, what is the effect of digitization—a mode of technologization that adds yet another layer of reproducibility—upon the art experience? How does it (re)refigure the interaction between subject and object?

Although Lucas does not mention "aura" specifically, he has been responding to these questions for years. In a 2004 interview concerning the digital alteration of the *Star Wars* trilogy upon its inaugural DVD release, Lucas remarks,

> *Star Wars* was not meant, in the end, to be seen more than once in a movie theatre. It was designed to be a large, theatrical experience that, if you saw it once on a giant screen, would blow you away. But this was before there was such a thing as DVD [qtd. in Harris 34].

While Lucas seemingly recognizes and acknowledges the cinematic shift that has taken place with the onset of new media technologies, specifically digitization, he envisions digitization as the way to unproblematically recapture and fulfill an artist's original creative imaginings. As we will show, in the case of the *Star Wars* trilogy,[7] Lucas claims to be digitally editing the films to "correct" or "redeem" past renderings previously confined by the limits of time, money, and technology. And while these assertions appear to signal an artist's fulfillment of the trilogy's intended aura, in fact, the move from analog/celluloid to digital image takes the decomposition of aura (and the authenticity of the art object) to new extremes. Moreover, through (re)packaging and (re)editioning—supplementing the "original" films with a myriad of DVD extras and "Special Features"—Lucas's digital project also reconstructs and reorients the spectator's auratic experience, further problematizing notions of authenticity and permanence. Ironically, while Lucas envisions his digital project as somehow preserving the "authentic" art experience, he fails to recognize the extent to which digitization opens up and destabilizes the films and tampers with the unique interaction that is the aura.

Episode I: The "Phantom" Framework

Digitization has at least two edges—it at once empowers and destabilizes—and Walter Benjamin offers a lens through which we might reveal this duality. We aim not to position ourselves as Benjaminian apologists as we proceed through this analysis, and we acknowledge, at the outset, that Benjamin's artwork essay works toward a wider scope of application than our work here—and it opens out to wide-ranging critique as a result. His fifteen sections (as well as a "Preface" and "Epilogue") trace an historical trajectory for politics and art, continuously shot through with the progression of technology and a concomitant progression toward proletarian revolution. Benjamin optimistically predicts that the withering of aura, wrought through the inherent reproducibility of the art object, will combine with the mass exposure ("exhibition") afforded by new technologized forms of art (especially film) to wrest modern man from an alienated existence under capitalism and, especially, fascism (225–6). However, critics such as Noël Carroll find "attributions of a morally charged *telos* to technologically reproducible art [to be] metaphysically perplexing, a matter of allegorically reading into mass art one's fondest wishes" (145).[8] In a less revolutionary, and certainly less deterministic, vein, perhaps we could say that aesthetic reorientation in the face of mechanical reproducibility opens up possibilities for emancipation yet unseen along the historical trajectory Benjamin outlines. But we might be weakening the "force" of Benjamin's thesis.[9] Though, as some would claim, Benjamin's complex artwork essay seems to collapse into simple wish-fulfillment—an unalloyed progression towards emancipation—it also gains vitality through its optimistic, even hopeful, projections, and, important for our purposes, it nonetheless broaches a relevant vocabulary for reckoning with new forms of technologized art. We might be tempted to ask, is digitization a further step on Benjamin's *teleology,* a further emancipation? Though a vital question, we do not claim to present a fulsome answer to it. This intervention is the first step in a critical engagement with Benjaminian aura in *Star Wars,* a textual analysis of George Lucas's digital changes as a forceful "withering" of aura at the level of the art object, and an exploration of the implications of DVD extras for the art experience. The final effects, the emancipatory potential of such changes, are open to further engagement.

In the fourth section of an early draft of the artwork essay, Benjamin asks a question that will serve as the lever to our analysis: "What, then, is the aura?" ("Reproducibility" 104). His clearest answer is also his most perplexing—a metaphorized definition open to myriad interpretations:

> [Aura is] the *unique* phenomenon [*einmalige Erscheinung*] of a distance, however close it may be. If, while resting on a summer afternoon, you follow with your eyes a mountain range on the horizon or a branch which casts its shadow over you, you experience the aura of those mountains, of that branch [222–3].

There is much to discuss here. To begin, Benjamin's *"einmalige Erscheinung"* poses a difficult problem of translation. While Harry Zohn chooses "unique phenomenon" above, *erscheinung* might also be interpreted as "apparition" or "appearance." If we were to plot these varied *erscheinung* on an axis between subject and viewer, each translation would position the aura at a different point on that continuum. Nonetheless, what is important to us (and, we suggest, to Benjamin) is the experience *between* the subject and object, the in-betweenness of the experience—and how that "unique [*einmalige*]" in-betweenness is reoriented when either component shifts. As Peter Larsen argues, "The aura [for Benjamin] is not really 'of' the mountain range on the horizon or 'of' the branch nearby; it refers to a complex, contradictory *quality of experience* produced by a particular *constellation* between subject and object" (115). Read through Benjamin's metaphorical evocation (an "image" [223]) of the mountain and the branch, this "phenomenon of a distance" holds varying levels of auratic significance, depending on how one might qualify the experience. We are left with a perplexing paradox: how does distance overcome spatial nearness? What *"quality of experience"* figures as auratic, and what as "withering"? To restate, we choose to read Benjaminian aura as the unique interaction *between* the viewer and the art object, an experience or a phenomenon that cannot be attached to particular items or persons but rather in the distance created when the two interact. Far from engaging in semantic hair-splitting, the process of fixing a definition for "aura"—if in a necessarily provisional way—is an important one, not in order to arrive at iron-clad, contained definitions, but paradoxically, to show just how open and generative Benjamin's terminology can be. Most important, then, is the fundamentally metaphorical quality of Benjamin's essay, a largely poetic journey that multiplies possible interpretations and testifies to the productiveness of Benjamin's now seventy-year-old thesis. Benjamin's fifteen sections each broach intriguing and relevant aesthetic issues and observations, which might serve academe in very different ways depending on their deployment. This new notion of a paradoxical, but highly volatile, aura can be seen as the central thesis of Benjamin's essay, but we can find other intriguing complexities if we dig for them. Read this way, Benjamin's artwork essay creates an *ercheinung* of multiplicity, no matter how fixed we might try to make it.

Our approach is indebted to Larson and his forceful explication of Benjaminian aura in "Benjamin at the Movies: Aura, Gaze and History in the Artwork Essay." He succinctly rebuffs those who have misread Benjamin and his "poetic text," and he reminds us that Benjamin uses aura as

> a label; a textual focal point; a metaphor—or, to use Benjamin's own term, a "concept." But a special kind of concept, one that cannot be defined once and for all: Aura "grows" with and out of the context; its meaning is constantly being defined and redefined as new arguments, new examples and illustrations are added to the text [114].

Indeed, Benjamin's invocation of natural objects is not meant to deploy aura in or of the "mountain" or "branch," as some inherent quality, but rather as a metaphorical illustration of aura as a *series* of interrelated historical qualities (authority, presence, origination, permanence, and more important for our analysis, authenticity). Benjamin's metaphor implies that these qualities converge into a "phenomenon of a distance," into the aura—a term which, in this case, subsumes the various specificities of subject and/or object, which are important but not primary factors in creating the auratic effect. Unfortunately, this multifaceted notion of aura leaves us in a difficult place as film critics: we cannot register the significance of every interaction between every subject and every object. Thus, for the purposes of this study, we cast our interest primarily toward the art object (the original *Star Wars* trilogy, Lucas's digital changes, and the implications of DVD technology as a profoundly altering mode of circulation) and, by extrapolation, toward the viewer subject. As the art object shifts, so too, we contend, does the unique "distance" it creates as it is viewed. This approach positions us necessarily in an exclusionary role—as we focus upon one aspect (the art object) of a complex and shifting process of meaning production—but it serves as a vital opening stance from which we can leap into addressing larger implications and significances of Benjamin's thesis nearly seventy years later.

Read thusly, Benjamin's terminology and phrasing in the artwork essay can serve as a lever to open up *Star Wars* and the implications of digitization as another layer of reproducibility. We should note that we are not suggesting a *teleological* progression of technology—from art to reproduced art to digitally reproduced art, with a further withering of aura at each stage—but we are hoping to register the subtle auratic differences between analog and digital that might alter Benjamin's thesis, the core of which remains vital and productive.[10] Following from Benjamin's terminology, we aim to asses what *Star Wars*—framed as an auratic, one-time experience by Lucas himself—loses *and* gains in the transition, and what implications follow from this doubled movement. Lucas, for his part, marginalizes technology's role in aesthetics, asserting, "In the end, cinematography is not about technology; it's about art, it's about taste, it's about understanding your craft, it's about lighting and composition, and anyone who gets off on technological things is missing the point" (qtd. in Magid, "Exploring" 48–9). While Lucas might see his claim here as a way to let himself off the hook—presuming that artistic license takes precedence over technological form—he neglects to consider the intricate interrelationship between technology and representation. A mere assertion cannot separate them without consequences, as we shall see. Following from Heidegger's assertion that "technology is no mere means [but rather] a way of revealing," Jean-Pierre Geuens[11] contends that different means of production are not interchangeable [...], that new empowering devices do not simply provide a better, more efficient way of doing the same thing. On the contrary, each interjects a distinct filter, an engineered mediation that regulates the labor of those who use it [16].

In other words, following from Benjamin, artistic production—now inherently technologized—carries with it political and ethical implications far beyond the mere production of auratic effect. It is vital to register the significance of the "means of production" as an integral part of the work of art. If the longevity of Benjamin's artwork essay reinforces its critical value—if Benjamin's work is still vital, as we hope to show—we must remember its central principle: as the technology changes, so too does the status of art.

Episode II: "Fixing" Star Wars

In the documentary *Empire of Dreams: The Story of the Star Wars Trilogy*—a supplementary feature packaged with the DVD of the original trilogy on a disc of "Bonus Materials"—the narrator, after chronicling the intriguing and problem-ridden production of the original movies through the late 1970s and early 1980s, quickly moves the narrative forward to 1997:

> The digital changes that Lucas himself had ushered in would eventually lead him back full circle to *Star Wars*. In 1993, after helping create ILM's groundbreaking effects in Steven Spielberg's *Jurassic Park*, Lucas concluded that digital technology had finally caught up to his original vision. In 1997, he would revisit and perfect his galactic saga at last, with the *Star Wars* trilogy Special Edition [*Empire of Dreams*].

Unsurprisingly echoing Lucas's own sentiments, the documentary recalls the problems associated with the production of the original trilogy—primarily the lack of technology and money to fulfill Lucas's ostensibly boundless imagination—and suggests that digitization would provide the balm for the shortcomings of celluloid cinema. *Star Wars* would at last be "perfect." While we can dispense with the hyperbole of a Lucasfilm-sanctioned documentary, the notion that "digital technology had finally caught up to [Lucas's] original vision" situates *Star Wars* as a profound site for Benjaminian analysis. With the release of the Special Edition, Lucas's digital project comes sharply into focus. As he claims, his intent was to "correct"—that is, to "change [...] the things that [he] tried to do originally but [...] couldn't for whatever reason" (qtd. in Harris 34).

Lucas insists that editorial fudging was necessary given the budgetary and time constraints during the filming of the original trilogy. According to Lucas, digital technology allowed him to finish the films the way they were *meant* to be finished. Citing the original theatrical release of *Star Wars* as a painful rendering that represents only "25 percent of what [he] wanted it to be," Lucas maintains that, more than an issue of directorial 'force' or self-gratification, his desire is to deliver unto the audience a polished final product (qtd. in Harris 34). Nonetheless, at the same time, Lucas avers, "It has to do with the creative predilections of the director—what he wants and how strongly he feels about it. [...] The real issue is, who has the right to do that? I fall 100 percent on the side of the right of the artist to alter it" (qtd. in Harris 34). Lucas's "creative predilection" to have his work seen as he intended necessarily positions him in opposition to film purists who resist the idea of taking the film out of film, especially since he went beyond his own 1997 Special Edition and continued to make even more alterations with the 2004 DVD release—a move he insists is not simply a change of mind. Unlike a director's cut, which Lucas himself admits is often more palatable for film critics because it points to an untouched, permanent original (qtd. Harris 34), his changes ostensibly reflect his initial directorial intent, indeed the auratic intent, and thus represent a recapturing of a more "authentic" filmic rendering. Thus, we ask, what are these changes that have caused so much controversy in the popular realm? More importantly, what is the effect on the uniqueness of the work of art, on the interaction between the viewing subject and the cinematic object? For Lucas, digitization allows for artistic freedom while simultaneously attaching a degree of permanence and narrative authenticity by "fixing" it—a term that registers here as both "correction" *and* stabilization. However, what Lucas fails to recognize is that digital film, itself inherently iterable, thus arrives on the scene as always already ruptured; as a medium, its intrinsic value is *vested* in the reproducibility and mutability of its data. It is this paradoxical nature of digital film, a medium whose mode of production at once artistically empowers directorial intent *and* infinitely destabilizes the film-text through continuous alteration, which results in the refiguring of the filmic aura.

Digital changes (with the 1997 Special Edition and the 2004 DVD) to the original trilogy are best understood in terms of their relation to the original theatrical releases, and thus our analyses of the changes proceed chronologically. To begin, less contentious, but no less relevant, are those changes which deal with establishing shots—pan and long shots of landscapes, crowd scenes, and major set pieces. In *Star Wars*, as the Jawa sandcrawler carrying R2-D2 and C-3PO approaches the Lars Homestead, the bare, isolated dustbowl effect of the Tunisian desert is obvious.

With the Special Edition, the sandcrawler and surrounding Tatooine environs are rendered considerably more crisp, with added terrain features and vivid coloring. The DVD version builds on the Special Edition with digital enhancements that improve the shot's overall clarity even more. Similarly, exterior shots of Ben Kenobi's 1977 home reflect the kind of budgetary constraints that kept sets and locations modest: the frame shows a small stone hut, with a single entrance, on a sandy hill, but very little of the surroundings. By comparison, the Special Edition and DVD offer a much grander view, increasing the size and particularities of the Kenobi homestead—including a moisture vaporator next to a more elaborate stone structure—against a similarly more detailed background. In the case of the Mos Eisley Space Port, digital modifications deal more with issues of activity and movement appropriate to a bustling transport hub than major set pieces or backdrops. In addition to increasingly fine-tuned coloration and sharpened lines, the Special Edition and DVD versions of *Episode IV* include additional creatures (rontos and other space fauna).

While digitization widens the scope of the *Star Wars* universe, deepening the visual field and amplifying the relative desolation of remote spaces—the isolated Kenobi homestead, for example—with it comes an attendant dismantling of what Lucas himself terms a "used future" (*Force*). For Lucas, "used future" encapsulates his original design concept of a lived-in space and time: the material realities of rust, grease, and grime correlates to a textual reality that, in turn, connects to authority. To believe in this universe is to believe in its characters. However, while it might be argued that digitization allows Lucas to recapture his original auratic intention, it nonetheless undercuts the very heart of that aura and moves the viewer from a world of textual reality achieved through constancy, to one of simulatory reality marked by difference. As Benjamin reminds us,

> Film is the first art form whose artistic character is entirely determined by its reproducibility [...]. The finished film is the exact antithesis of a work created at a single stroke. It is assembled from a very large number of images and image sequences that offer an array of choices to the editor; these images, moreover, can be improved in any desired way in the process leading from the initial take to the final cut [...]. *The film is therefore the artwork most capable of improvement. And this capability is linked to its radical renunciation of eternal value* ["Reproducibility" 109].

Elsewhere, Benjamin is more specific about this "*capability*":

> [Film's] illusionary nature is that of the second degree, the result of cutting. That is to say, in the studio the mechanical equipment has penetrated so deeply into reality that its pure aspect freed from the

foreign substance of equipment is the result of a special procedure, namely, the shooting by the specially adjusted camera and the mounting of the shot together with other similar ones. The equipment-free aspect of reality here has become the height of artifice; the sight of immediate reality has become an orchid in the land of technology [233].

Clearly, Benjamin understands that film, by nature, is a changeable medium, and therefore never permanently fixed, never whole at "a single stroke." It might achieve a measure of believability—an acceptable "used future"—but it does so *through* a heightened level of artificiality and a necessary changeability. Digitization takes this realism through artifice, this "orchid" of technology, even further. Implicating the viewer in the process, critic Najmeh Khalili suggests,

While the indexical nature of a film image increases the believability of the photo-realistically captured scene, the *awareness* of a digitizing apparatus creates a distance between the screen and the spectator which he/she can fill according to his/her own individuality.

So while Lucas may achieve visual "correction," even improvement, at the level of the individual shot or frame, this does not equate to authoritative "*value*," its ritualistic functionality. According to Benjamin, the technological basis of these changes decomposes Lucas's authority over the intended look of his landscapes, no matter how crisp and detailed they might be. Put another way, Geuens observes,

The luxuriousness of the new images should not, however, blind us to the underlying disjunction at the core of [digital cinema] projects. To construct a coherent picture out of material gathered from radically different sources [...] involves a redeployment away from the traditional source of the medium—the world of everyday life [20].

This notion of "everyday life" echoes back to Benjamin's fundamental belief in "the desire of contemporary masses to bring things 'closer' spatially and humanly" (223). Indeed, while Lucas's digital "*improvement*[s]" (as Benjamin reminds above) to seemingly innocuous establishing shots may actualize *his* artistic intentions toward the "used" reality of the *Star Wars* universe, he fails to recognize the ever-present disconnection between an envisioned reality and the lived experience it attempts to represent. So, the once bleak, desolate landscapes of long ago and far, far away are now characterized by a digitally displaced world, which, while at times luminous, renounces Benjaminian "*eternal value*" and belies any hope for believability in a used future.

Perhaps the most contentious change in the history of the original trilogy concerns the face-off between Han Solo and the bounty hunter

Greedo. In the original 1977 theatrical release of *Star Wars*, Solo, cornered by Greedo in the Mos Eisley Cantina, shoots first and establishes his character as the calm, cool, but impassioned anti-hero. Stylistically, the scene is too darkly lit, and while viewers know from Greedo's reaction that he has been shot (he collapses onto the table in a cloud of white smoke), the actual shots are quite unclear: we hear two blaster shots, but do not know whose blaster is the source. For the Special Edition, Lucas digitally altered the scene so that Greedo actually shoots first (he misses, but we see the blaster shot), thus transforming Han Solo from an ice-cool space pirate to simply a lucky guy acting out of retaliation. The digital alterations result in some considerably awkward effects, including the bizarre angle of Greedo's blaster shot, which does not correspond to the angle of his actual blaster, as well as the robotic head bob of Han Solo as he dodges the blast. These performative irregularities recall Benjamin's observation about the disjointed performance required of an actor in the face of the "apparatus":

> The camera that presents the performance of the film actor to the public need not respect the performance as an integral whole. Guided by the cameraman, the camera continually changes its position with respect to the performance. The sequence of positional views which the editor composes from the material supplied him constitutes the completed film [228].

Here, Benjamin notices the transition of performative control—from an actor's holistic performance to an editor's constitution of disparate parts. Geuens observes that digitization amplifies this artistic command:

> all phases involving the making of a movie have now merged into one. Not only can one edit and create special effects while on location, one can also rewrite, restage, and reshoot—essentially think the film anew—while editing. The discrete operations have combined into one general interface where all facets of the story as well as of the moviemaking process are accessible and revisable at any time [22]

In the digital arena, we might think of Lucas' usual title (director) as a conflation of the roles of editor, cinematographer and cameraman, among others. Importantly, Lucas wields a great deal of control over each stage of the production process.[12] And, it might be argued, this increased control stems directly from the advances of digitization, which collapse all productive processes into one. Lucas can edit-on-the-fly, readjust, add, and subtract, as he sees fit. As director in the digital landscape, he functions, we might say, as a synecdoche for the multitude of professionals involved in the making of any film. In this sense, the actor's performance is even less of "an integral whole." With digitization, the actor is, at the outset, a composite, subject to change at the director's whim.[13] If we connect this digitized hybridity to aura, we find that Lucas's assertions of editorial control carry with them unintended, but visible, corollaries. Again, Benjamin outlines an aspect of this problematic:

> This situation might also be characterized as follows: for the first time—and this is the effect of the film—man [represented here by the actor] has to operate with his whole living person, yet forgoing its aura. For aura is tied to presence; there can be no replica of it. The aura which, on the stage, emanates from Macbeth, cannot be separated for the spectators from that of the actor. However, the singularity of the shot in the studio is that the camera is substituted for the public. Consequently, the aura that envelops the actor vanishes, and with it the aura of the figure he portrays [229].

Just as the actor's aura (his physical authenticity) disappears because his audience does not view him in the moment, so too does his performance lose traction in the theatre, by Benjamin's reckoning: "No sooner has [the spectator's] eye grasped a scene than it is already changed. It cannot be arrested" (238). The unique art experience presumed by the film as it is created loses force once it is exhibited. Thus, we have a doubled deflation of aura: the actor (cannot be present) and his performance on the finished film ("cannot be arrested"). If we are in the business of conflating roles—*and* if we are bequeathing added control to Lucas as the synecdochic director—Benjamin's assertion here undercuts Lucas's artistic aura as a "presen[t]" entity. In other words, through a conflation of the production process (the director is simultaneously editor, cameraman, cinematographer, actor, and so on), we can extend Benjamin's invocation of exhibition here to suggest that Han Solo's representation to public—filtered through Lucas's assertion of directorial control via digitization—is profoundly de-auraticized. So, even as Harrison Ford, his head bobbing inhumanly to avoid a digital blaster shot, "vanishes" as a "whole living person" and becomes a piece of equipment for Lucas to manipulate as needed, the auratic efficacy of the Han Solo/Greedo scene cannot be "fixed." Much as he may wish it, the aura cannot be harnessed by Lucas without transforming it in the process.

In spite (or ignorance) of these implications, the 2004 DVD release shattered many a film purist's dream when, despite widespread complaint, Lucas refused to reverse his digital changes to the Special Edition, choosing instead to clean up Ford's jarring head bob, tighten the overall timing, and sharpen the blaster shots. Lucas defends his digital decision, claiming, "In my mind [Greedo] shot first or at the same time. We like to think of [Han Solo] as a murderer because that's hip—I don't think that's a good thing for people. I mean, I don't see how you could redeem somebody who kills people in cold blood" (qtd. in Harris 34).[14] While Lucas appears to echo this own notion of "redemption" in his director's commentary that accompanies the 2004 DVD release, note the apparent contradiction: "In the course of the movie, Han Solo's character arc is that he goes from being a self-centered, selfish, cynical character to a caring, compassionate, try-to-make-this-a-better-place kind of character." We ask, does the arc of Solo's character—from self-serving grifter to thoughtful do-gooder—not require that he begin from a place of self-interested, flagrant disregard for human life that *presumes* the inclination toward cold-blooded murder? Is Lucas interested in narrative redemption or artistic license? Indeed, the Solo/Greedo face off requires a rethinking of what has traditionally been the preeminence once assigned to principle photography over post-production processes typically aimed at fine-tuning. While Lucas claims that the digital alterations reflect an outright "correction," so too does he contradictorily contend, "[W]hat's really important is the story, and the development of the characters" (qtd. in Harris 34–35). But here's the rub: ironically, it is Lucas's very desire to "fix" the films—to exact control spatially, temporally, and artistically—that reveals their qualitative openness. In the digital world, the performers (Harrison Ford as Solo, Paul Blake as Greedo) abdicate their performance to a conflated director/editor/cameraman who relies on an unstable and changeable medium to "fix" the scene, to wield control. This contradiction—fixity through difference—disrupts narrative arc and, more significantly, unexpectedly destabilizes power relations both behind and in front of the camera lens.

As with changes to existing scenes, the inclusion of previously deleted or completely new scenes is similarly problematic, especially as we consider the role of the aura. Again, the (dis)embodiment of the actor plays a central role. For the Special Edition release of *Star Wars Episode IV: A New Hope*, Lucas restored the scene in which Han Solo, after his confrontation with Greedo, encounters Jabba the Hutt. The scene was originally filmed with actor Declan Mulholland as Jabba. However, for whatever reason, the scene was not included in the original 1977 theatrical release of *Star Wars*. As a result, viewers were first introduced to Jabba via the full-scale puppet creature of *Return of the Jedi* (later *Star Wars Episode VI: Return of the Jedi*), not *Star Wars*. Narratively speaking, the very presence of this restored Special Edition scene is unnecessary, as viewers learn nothing more than they already know via the prior Han Solo/ Greedo altercation, not to mention the fact that its inclusion also disrupts what was Jabba's timely appearance in *Return of the Jedi* (one unique experience counteracts another). There are also characterization issues, as Special Edition Jabba is rendered considerably kinder and nicer than eventually revealed to be.[15] Stylistically, the Special Edition restoration required the creation of a slug-like "CGI Jabba" in order to cover up Mulholland, which results in a decidedly awkward exchange with Han Solo. Their relative movements are jarringly awkward, and there are instances where each occupies the personal space of the other—including a sequence where Solo steps on Jabba's tail, without reacting to Jabba's wide-eyed and groaning response. Furthermore, Special Edition CGI Jabba appears very little like the puppet used in the original theatrical release of *Return of the Jedi*, which, while somewhat improved digitally by the 2004 DVD release (although still clumsily out of place), nonetheless disrupts narrative continuity and the unique viewing experience, especially for those who saw chronologically all three films prior to the Special Edition or DVD release. Solo's final line to Jabba in the restored scene—"you're a wonderful human being"—jarringly reminds us that digital compositing of Han and Jabba lays bare what can only be described as the alienation of the actor from the filmmaking process. Mulholland, the "human being" in this scenario, is forcefully removed in favor of an unfortunate CGI replacement. In a featurette on the "Bonus Materials" disc included with the 2004 DVD release, Lucas recognizes that, with traditional filmmaking techniques, taking an idea from conception to reality is not possible without the final inclusion of the actor, for it is the actor who, in breathing life into dialogue, costumes, makeup, sets, and lighting, ultimately brings the design concept into being (*Characters*). However, as Lucas fails to acknowledge, in the case of digital film, an actor's movement, once the product of a continuous interaction with, and engagement of, living bodies, unique looks, or behaviors, now lacks the context and continuity fundamental to acting— especially live acting. Benjamin would remind us that the performance ultimately becomes one addressed to no one, with gestures and expressions having no immediate relevance, that is, no fixed aura. Again we see that the digital film practices on display in the Special Edition and DVD Han Solo/Jabba exchange forever disrupt the romantic notion that performance in general, or characterization specifically, originates with the identifiable, sentient being of the actor.

Further, returning to our framework, Benjamin likens the "cameraman"—a role we can give to Lucas as the "artist" in question—to a surgeon (in contrast to the painter, an authoritative and distancing "magician"):

> The surgeon represents the polar opposite of the magician. The magician heals a sick person by the laying on of hands; the surgeon cuts into the patient's body. The magician maintains the natural distance between the patient and himself; though he reduces it very slightly by the laying on of hands, he greatly increases it by virtue of his authority. The surgeon does exactly the reverse; he greatly diminishes the

distance between himself and the patient by penetrating into the patient's body, and increases it but little by the caution with which his hand moves among the organs. In short, in contrast to the magician—who is still hidden in the medical practitioner—the surgeon at the decisive moment abstains from facing the patient man to man; rather, it is through the operation that he penetrates into him [233].

If Declan Mulholland experiences the "caution" of Lucas's surgeon's hands—as Lucas excises Mulholland's body in favor of a CGI slug—he also suffers from the facelessness of digitization, which affords Lucas the ability to insert Mulholland's scene in the film, but without Mulholland's actual presence. He exists only as an invisible interlocutor for Ford. Mulholland as Jabba both *is* and *is not* present; Lucas uses the "operation" of digitization to "penetrate into him" without "facing" him (in both senses of the word). As such, the potential for a personal authenticity—and, by association, an aura—is "effaced" by Lucas's plastic surgery.

The notion of an identifiable presence located in the physicality of the actor is perhaps forever destabilized when considering the insertion of completely different actors that occurs in the case of digital changes to the original theatrical releases of *The Empire Strikes Back* and *Return of the Jedi*. In the original theatrical *Empire*, the Emperor resembles an old, shrouded woman. The 2004 DVD *Empire* finds the old woman replaced with actor Ian McDiarmid, who had portrayed the Emperor in 1983's *Return of the Jedi* and has continued to do so in the more recent prequel trilogy. Similarly, while the original theatrical release of *Return of the Jedi* presents Anakin Skywalker's "Force Ghost" as portrayed by actor Sebastian Shaw, the 2004 DVD reveals a newly inserted Hayden Christensen, who portrays the young Anakin in the prequel trilogy's *Episodes II* and *III*. The premise of the scene—the affirmation of Luke Skywalker by the ghostly images of his father and his Jedi mentors—relies on an understanding and acceptance of all that has come before that, in turn, is predicated on a certain consistency and context. Notwithstanding the fact that the fatherly characterization of Anakin is completely lost with the insertion of Christensen, this particular digital alteration defies the logic of chronology, given that Christensen was merely two years old at the time of *Return of the Jedi*. It would seem that, in this case, Lucas's at-times contradictory stance toward his own edits—that is, preserving at once the intended, "correct" shot *and* the narrative integrity of the story—completely collapses. While one might appreciate the apparent attempt at some kind of cinematic consistency, Lucas's convenient duality explains nothing in the case of this insertion, since it can be explained neither as a "correction" (Christensen was clearly not the intended actor in 1983), nor narratively integral (the swap has the necessary effect of re-inscribing Luke's personal journey away from a father/son narrative arc to one that seems inexplicable, or at least unexplained, since Luke never met his father at the age Christensen represents). Moreover, if we accept that the loss of actorly control in the Solo/Greedo showdown and Mulholland's disembodiment in the Solo/Jabba scene wither the performative aura, we might say that Christensen's insertion here comprises the ultimate assertion both of directorial control and of auratic decay. The double move of aura returns again, as Lucas's digital project moves the filmmaker, the film, and the film viewer from the experiential, from a particular time and space, to the experimental, further and further from the origination of the actors, the original vision, indeed the authenticity that reasserts aura. In light of this problematic, Lucas might do well to heed the advice of Princess Leia, who, in *A New Hope*, tells Grand Moff Tarkin, "The more you tighten your grip, the more systems will slip through your fingers." In this way, digitization—a "technological monstrosity" on par, perhaps, with the Death Star—tightens the reigns on Lucas's vision, just as the "slip" of iterability refigures it.

Episode III: Revenge of the Work of Art in the Age of Digital Reproduction, or Concluding Thoughts

The auratic implications of Lucas's digital project multiply and compound when viewed across the entire series. Let us revisit Lucas's claim that "*Star Wars* was not meant, in the end, to be seen more than once in a movie theatre. It was designed to be a large theatrical experience that, if you saw it once on a giant screen, would blow you away" (qtd. in Harris 34). Lucas invokes the primacy of an auratic experience between viewer and film that even he admits can be found only once and, thus, never replicated. The marketing campaign for the theatrical release of the Special Edition, twenty years after the release of *Star Wars*, recalls this "experience" through a tantalizing negative: a television advertisement proclaims, "For an entire generation people have experienced Star Wars the only way it's been possible: on the TV screen. But if you've only seen it this way, you haven't seen it at all" (*Empire of Dreams*). As the announcer invokes the auratic experience—being "blown away"—an X-Wing fighter emerges out of a miniature television screen, and the frame fills suddenly with the sights and sounds of the digitally "enhanced" *Star Wars*. Far from a recapturing of original intent, then, the television ad reasserts aura and authenticity, an imaginative ride "far, far away" yet present to the moment of 1997 (when you finally see the movies the way they are supposed to be seen). In this sense, it might be argued that filmmakers, as purveyors of nothing more than the illusion of movement, of character, of story, are doing nothing new in moving toward digitization and that viewers themselves are misguidedly committed to the idea of a fixed original located in a nostalgic past marked by the strange confluence of rebel filmmakers and breathless fans. Alternatively, we might say that the viewer oscillates between a dialectic of past and present, between a desire for the original 1977 version (free from the contaminations wrought by digitization), and a desire for a new auratic experience provided by Lucas and his ILM compatriots. But we would also suggest that Lucas holds the reins on this potentially relative auratic experience. It is noteworthy that, when asked about a rumored new trilogy—*Episodes VII*, *VIII*, and *IX*—Lucas responds pointedly, "I'm not going to do it. [...] And I don't want anybody else to do it, so I've locked it up so nobody can ever do it" (qtd. in Harris 36). Granted, Lucas's rights to his own art necessarily mean that any and all changes are at his discretion, according to his "creative predilections." But it is this particularly myopic view toward the work of art as that which can be somehow "fixed" correctively and "locked" temporally that also de-auraticizes that same process. The actor is disembodied, excised by the surgical camera, just as the inherent changeability—and the CGI slickness—of the landscape undercuts the authenticity of the realism Lucas sought at the outset. Narrativity and believability become tenuous threads cut by the power and the danger of digitization.

If *Star Wars* Special Edition represents the liminal space in the transition from analog to digital, from the celluloid original trilogy to the fully digitized prequel trilogy, so too does it highlight the inherent problematics—the new abilities and new worries—that continue the decomposition of Benjaminian aura into the next decades. Recalling that for Benjamin aura signifies a unique artistic "phenomenon" activated by the interaction between subject and object, we contend that digitization destabilizes any "fixed" aura because, like mechanical reproduction in Benjamin's time, it is inherently reproducible. In this technological "withering," digitization *is* in fact another step along Benjamin's teleology. However, as Lucas "tighten[s] [his] grip" on his auratic vision, he does deploy digitization to mould the art object—the film-text—to his current wishes. While we might (and do) critique the inconsistency of these changes, in relation to his statements of intention, most relevant for our analysis here is the power struggle caught up in Lucas's corrections. If, as Benjamin suggests, the actor must forgo his holistic aura in the face of the apparatus, his performance is further undercut by Lucas's "digital-backlot" of composite images and edit-on-the-fly digital recording tools (Magid, "Master" 26). The apparatus functions *as* the point of production, rather than as an intermediary between actor and spectator. As a result of digitization, then, further layers of intermediation—not least,

Lucas as the director synechdoche—disconnect the art object from its original context, its authenticity, and, vitally, the auratic effect derived from this present origination. According to Lucas, *Star Wars*, circa 1977, was intended to "blow you away" in the theatre; if the ad campaign is any guide, the Special Edition was intended to do the same twenty years later. As we have attempted to demonstrate, in a number of ways, the aura of one experience does not, indeed cannot, stand-in for the other. Hayden Christensen cannot simply replace Sebastian Shaw without consequences. And neither, we suggest, can the 1997 Special Edition nor the 2004 DVD—digitally enhanced and directorally "fixed"—replace *Star Wars*, in spite of George Lucas's protestations.

"Bonus Materials"—An Epilogue: Exhibition, Ritual, and the "Unique Phenomenon" of DVD

The implications of DVD (digital video disc) produce more fruitful contradictions that we might work through. Let's begin with Benjamin, who claims that

> the contemporary decay of aura [...] rests on two circumstances. Namely, the desire of contemporary masses to bring things 'closer' spatially and humanly, which is just as ardent as their bent toward overcoming the uniqueness of every reality by accepting its reproduction. Every day the urge grows stronger to get hold of an object at very close range by way of its likeness, its reproduction. [...] The adjustment of reality to the masses and of the masses to reality is a process of unlimited scope, as much for thinking as for perception [223].

The proliferation of DVDs into Western homes suggests that this "urge [...] to get hold of an object at very close range" has yet to flag in this new century. As a result, mass reproduction and home theatres have opened up access to cinema in unprecedented ways, with the attendant effect of "overcoming the uniqueness of every reality." Thus, Lucas's "used future" suffers another blow, as the suspension of credibility bumps up against a repeatable viewing experience. In other words, upon repeated viewings made possible by DVD, we may begin to notice the chinks in the filmic armor, the gaps and mistakes we were not meant to see; this is an issue to which we will return. For his part, Benjamin suggests that "exhibition" lies at the heart of this phenomenon:

> With the different methods of technical reproduction of a work of art, its fitness for exhibition increased to such an extent that the quantitative shift between its two poles ["cult value" vs. "exhibition

value" (224)] turned into a qualitative transformation of its nature.
[...] [B]y the absolute emphasis on its exhibition value the work of
art become a creation with entirely new functions, among which the
one we are conscious of, the artistic function, later may be recognized as incidental [225].

So, beyond the repetition afforded by DVD distribution, heightened
"exhibition value" also alters the very "nature" of art—disconnecting it
from the ritualized reception characteristic of auratic art forms. What
Benjamin notices in relation to theatre showings moves even further along
the continuum when we consider DVD, which reconstructs "the artistic function" as an "incidental" aspect of the larger context of filmic consumption. More important, we might assume, is the reception of the
"masses," who "get hold" of the film and incorporate it in a myriad of
ways. DVD exhibition, then, subsumes, at least to some extent, the
authenticity (and thereby the aura) attached to the artistic process and
to the creation of the film at the moment and site of production by the
hand of the authoritative director/cameraman/cinematographer. Moreover, as Benjamin tells us,

> Above all, [technical reproduction] enables the original to meet the
> beholder halfway, be it in the form of a photograph or a phonograph
> record. The cathedral leaves its locale to be received in the studio of
> a lover of art; the choral production, performed in an auditorium or
> in open air, resounds in the drawing room [221].

The spectator gains partial control over the authority of the object, as it
is lifted from its original context and moved elsewhere (the studio, the
drawing room, the den, the back of a minivan, and so on). Benjamin
implies that technology, DVD in this case, equalizes consumption and
individualizes the art experience, with powerful results:

> The representation of human beings by means of an apparatus has
> made possible a highly productive use of the human being's self-
> alienation. [...] While he stands before the apparatus, [the actor]
> knows that in the end he is confronting the masses. It is they who
> will control him. Those who are not visible, not present while he exe-
> cutes his performance, are precisely the ones who will control it.
> This invisibility heightens the authority of their control ["Repro-
> ducibility" 113].

If Hayden Christensen's performance as Anakin's "force ghost" at the
close of *Jedi* might some day be played on a cell phone, for example, the
aura of that original performance "withers" quite profoundly—both
through intermediation (the director, the apparatus, the inherent changeability of film) and, more relevant here, through mass consumption. DVD

delivers unto the audience heretofore unseen levels of "control" over the auratic experience itself. Consumers choose when, where, and how to view the movies. Once again, digitization, via the "exhibition value" of DVD, carries with it concomitant destabilizations to the very control it affords.

DVD Extras, or, How to Become "Somewhat of an Expert" on Star Wars

Again less particular to *Star Wars* (but no less relevant to its auratic status) is the addition of DVD extras that supplement the film proper. The 2004 DVD release of the original trilogy features a separate "Bonus Materials" disc that includes a number of featurettes—*The Force Is with Them: The Legacy of Star Wars*, *The Birth of the Lightsaber*, *The Characters of Star Wars*, and *Star Wars: Episode III Behind-the-Scenes Preview—The Return of Darth Vader*—an extensive "Production Photo Gallery," and, perhaps most significantly, the lengthy making-of documentary, *Empire of Dreams*. Each of these projects provides supplementary background information on the process of production that led, inexorably, to the auratic object(s), the films themselves. At first blush, we might suggest that these behind-the-scenes documentaries and archival records reinvest the original films with an increased level of authenticity and presence, since they remind the viewer of the original context of production, the place and time in which the art object was constructed. Indeed, the documentaries and featurettes narrativize the production of the original movies and project an image of Lucas as a maverick independent filmmaker—pitted against the corporatism of the major studios—overcoming nearly impossible odds to make an unimaginably successful final product (to rave reviews and enthusiastic audience response). If, as Benjamin suggests, reproducibility destabilizes historical testimony—and undercuts "the authority of the object" (221)—we might read these narratives as an attempt to reinvest *Star Wars* with an authority lost by the vagaries of time and technology, lost by the temporal and ontological movement away from origination necessitated by mechanical reproduction. Through DVD extras, it might seem that we are returned to the site of production, to the authentic art moment which will, in turn, evoke a unique, auratic experience in us. But Benjamin also asserts that authenticity dwells within the auratic object, as the "essence of all that is transmissible from its beginning, ranging from its substantive duration to its testimony to the history which it has experienced" (221). The "Bonus Materials" included in the DVD release of *Star Wars*, on the other hand, function as a *supplement* to the auratic art object, an unstable inside/outside perspective that both informs *and* unseats the auratic authority of the films.[16] In other words, the art object itself is unchanged in the process, but our *perception* of the originals cannot *but* alter as we view the "Bonus Materials." As such, we ask, can the *Star Wars* films invest aura *without* the revelations in the supplementary materials? More vitally, perhaps, do the "Bonus Materials" call for an aesthetic status equivalent to the films themselves? Are they not *also* art objects that create, to a greater or lesser extent, "the unique phenomenon of a distance"? Critics Deborah Parker and Mark Parker, though less specifically concerned with aura, give us part of the answer, focusing on an altered viewing experience:

> [I]n the most rudimentary, physical sense, the DVD version [of a film] is a reconstruction [because it has been "changed physically by the process of digitization"]. Even more transformative, however, is the new relation between film and audience offered by the DVD. The effect of the film is now, at least potentially, intensely mediated by "supplementary materials," which include extensive commentary by directors and writers, the reminiscence of actors, the technical remarks of cameramen and set designers , and the critical remarks of scholars. The DVD edition is essentially a reorientation of the film, often carried out by a variety of agents, and subject to a wide variety of choices made by the eventual viewers. Consciously or not, the DVD constitutes a new edition, and it should be seen in these terms [14].

As with the "exhibition value" attached to DVD distribution, the "Bonus Materials" give the audience a great deal of power over the relative aura produced by the films. This "reconstruction" of traditional film, just as it reinvests aura through authenticity, disconnects the object from its original context. We can witness the *making-of* before we watch the film itself. Will *Star Wars* still "blow you away" if you know how it was made, what problems Lucas and his cohorts encountered?

In part, then, DVD extras pivot on the relation between knowledge, critique, and access. Benjamin highlights this relationship in the consumption of films when he asserts, "It is inherent in the technique of film as well as that of sports that everybody who witnesses its accomplishments is somewhat of an expert" ("Mechanical Reproduction" 231). In a similar vein, Benjamin compares the real-time filming of a scene in a studio to the performance of that same scene on the stage, positing an irreconcilable difference between the two at the moment of performance: "In the theater one is well aware of the place from which the play cannot immediately be detected as illusionary. There is no such place for the movie scene that is being shot" ("Mechanical Reproduction" 233). Central to both assertions is the role of knowledge. If one becomes "somewhat of an expert" on CGI and digital filmmaking—as a result of the supplementary documentaries, featurettes, and commentary audio tracks—the potential for "illusion," for the creation of "distance" through filmic techniques, loses force. As a result of this all-access digital back-lot, where all aspects of film production are items for public consumption, Khalili claims,

> The computer-aided cineastes of today also do not seek to hide the elaborate scientific and technological tricks of their trade from the spectators; on the contrary, the very devices of image making and effect generation are now a source of entertainment in their own right.

There is, one might admit, a level of pleasure gained (and status afforded) from those revealing documentaries that chronicle the inner workings of cinema. There might even be something ritualistic about watching films *and* watching the internal mechanism that brought the art object to fruition. Aura might be recast in this model as a process caught up in revelation and fulfillment, rather than tradition and cult. But we also suggest that DVD extras in general, and the "Bonus Materials" released with the 2004 DVD version of *Star Wars*, refigure the nature of audience reception and explode any possibility of nostalgically recapturing the auratic experience of a near or distant past, precisely *because* that past is captured by film. Thanks to digitization, mediation—indeed, Benjamin's *teleology*—goes one step further, and the supplement cannot (and does not) replace the original.[17]

Notes

1. For details and discussion in the popular media regarding the controversy around Lucas's digital changes, see Ian Austen's "A Galaxy Far, Far Away is Becoming Fully Digital"; Benjamin Bergery's "Digital Cinema By George" and "Framing the future"; Jane Black's "Hollywood's Digital Love/Hate Story"; Richard Corliss's "The Star Treatment"; Lina Lofaro, and Carolina A. Miranda; Gloria Goodale's "Is That All Folks? The End ... of Film as We Know It—Enter Digital"; Tobey Grumet's "Digital Celluloid"; Dave Kehr's "When a Cyberstar Is Born"; Debra Klein's "You Should Be in Pixels"; Shawn Levy's "Send in the Clones"; Bill Machrone's "Film's Dead. Are Actors Next?"; Ron Magid's "Brave New Worlds," "Master of His Universe," and "Exploring a New Universe"; Rob Sabin's "Taking Film Out of Films"; Gavin Smith's "Genius of the System" and "Digital Dawn"; Gregory Solman's "Fancy Math"; James Sterngold's "Digital Studios: It's the Economy Stupid"; Kara Swisher's "As Net Boom Wanes, Lucas Is New Digital Force"; Roy B. White's "*Star Wars*: Attack of the Digital Clones"; and Anna Wilde Mathews's "Cinema's Digital Divide."

2. Our characterization of *Star Wars* as "pioneering" is based a number of trajectories the series charts: (1) its status as a 1970s torchbearer for a new brand of filmmaking invested in special effects and spectacle; (2) its traversal across almost three decades of filmmaking and film technology; (3) its unprecedented cinematic achievements and blockbuster success sustained across a series of six films; and (4) its promise as a technological revisioning for a new millennium.

3. We want register "dialogue" here as an acknowledgment of the fact that, while our analysis depends primarily on a reading of the *Star Wars* universe through Benjamin, in fact this analysis is at times a dialectical relation. *Star Wars* might also illuminate and/or evaluate Benjamin's ideas. We suggest that this illumination, rather than a dispute over Benjamin's thesis, is a way to revitalize it as an essay that has much to offer seven decades after its original publication.

4. Benjamin characterizes the "authenticity of a thing" as "the essence of all that is transmissible from its beginning, ranging from its substantive duration to its testimony to the history which it has experienced" (221). In other words, for Benjamin, authenticity ties to the art object in its productive context and in its material existence in time and space; the authentic art object contains or implies the marks of its own production and history.

5. Unless otherwise noted, "The Work of Art in the Age of Mechanical Reproduction" (hereafter called "artwork essay"), translated by Harry Zohn, is the primary source for Benjaminian notions of aura and reproducibility (both here and elsewhere). Belknap Press's recent publication of Benjamin's *Selected Writings* (2002) perhaps provides a more authoritative translation of the artwork essay (as well as several versions of it)—but it does not carry with it the historical precedent of the Zohn translation, which has been the "way in" to Benjamin for English-speaking scholars for at least four decades.

6. It is significant to note the antinomies at play in this process—"politicizing art" as a communist response to a fascist aestheticization of politics. Najmeh Khalili and Jean-Pierre Geuens, among others, have begun to register the political implications of this antinomy in the age of digital reproduction—most particularly connecting the tendencies of fascism in the 1930s to corporatism in the 2000s.

7. In this context, "*Stars Wars* trilogy" refers to *Episodes IV, V,* and *VI* (also referred to as the "original trilogy"). While we recognize that these three films dialogue with *Episodes I, II,* and *III* (the "prequel trilogy"), especially in relation to digitization, this paper will focus primarily on the original trilogy and its 2004 DVD release.

8. Benjamin's artwork essay, as a seminal text in both media and film theory, has elicited much critique since its publication. We cite Carroll here as a recent representation of the most oft-mentioned counterargument to Benjamin's thesis—a critique at the level of method: historical materialism as limited and unsatisfactory. Benjamin's Frankfurt school colleague Theodor Adorno is perhaps the most famous opponent of Benjamin's artwork essay on this count.

9. Benjamin's (in)famous formulation at the close of the artwork essay can also be read as an ambivalent response to technologized art, since it lends itself very easily to what he saw as the fascist aestheticization of politics. We read Benjamin's essay as carefully optimistic about the potentialities of film and new media as emancipatory aesthetic forms.

10. Like Benjamin, our analysis aims to be more qualitative than quantitative, and thus, it is not our intent to delve into a scientific analysis of the differences between analog waves and digital data.

11. We do not claim to unproblematically trumpet Geuens perspective, lucid though it is. Clearly, Lucas's digital project has enlivened critics over the last few years, inciting biting commentary, like Geuens's in the following case regarding the interpenetration of the simulated and the real: "Lucas's drive to lord over everyone and everything in his images, to make them conform to his wishes and to milk every bit of surplus value out of them, is reminiscent of a similar labor performed by the less savory characters of the Marquis de Sade, who also made mincemeat of their victims' bodies, seeing in them but human matter to be played with as long as pleasure was ultimately attained" (23). While we admit much discomfort in his polemical analogies—Lucas as the Marquis de Sade and, at another point, as the "Butcher of Prague" (23)—Geuens' assessment of Lucas's drive for control over his images mirrors our own analysis: Lucas seeks to "fix" the *Star Wars* films, to protect them from the variegations of technology (and of the human) that might destabilize them.

12. This redistribution of control has the potential to alter the production process at the level of the film set, reconfiguring the distribution of labor. As Stephen Prince argues, in the early stages of cinema, "[n]either directing nor cinematography extended much into postproduction, and the images they created were essentially completed, as images if not as edited scenes, at the end of the production stage. By contrast, the advent of digital grading in contemporary film suggests that we now need to think of cinematography, and even

directing, as *image-capture* processes. In special-effects-intensive movies, like *Spider-Man* or the *Star Wars* films, directing is merely a means for grabbing live action elements needed for compositing with computer-generated images" (30). Or, as Lucas claims, digitization "gives the director, the cinematographer, and the art director a lot more freedom to design the look of a movie, and to rethink the movie during the process of making it" (qtd. in Magid, "Master" 27). In this way, postproduction takes on a significance unheard of in Benjamin's time (though, as we have seen, he presciently foregrounded its importance even in his 1936 essay). Read through an allegory of industry—an image that is constantly invoked, both by theorists (Geuens, Prince, Khalili) and by those involved in the process (recall what the "I" in ILM signifies)—we might propose that digitization is a post–Fordist reconception of film production, a corporatist model suitable to late capitalism because it invests great power in the upper management (Lucas, *Star Wars* executive producer Rick McCallum, Steven Spielberg) and outsources acting and cinematography to CGI artists and the like. Again, the political implications of this transition are open to further investigation.

13. To be clear, we point out that Geuens and Prince are speaking specifically of the wholly digital process Lucas used in the filming of the prequel trilogy, which allowed for this conflation of cinematic powers at the point of production—the actual film set. To push this further, the Benjaminian implications of this more recent situation, which disembodies and disempowers the actor even further than we might presume for the original trilogy, further withers the aura of presence and authenticity. At what point is the authentic point of production (the actor's performance) subsumed into the merged function Lucas inhabits as the at-once director/editor/cameraman/ cinematographer? The answer, outside of our scope here, holds implications both for Lucas's presumed artistic intent (which is itself changeable in this instance) and for digitization as an art form further emancipated from the test of authenticity and, by extension, aura. To bridge these issues with the focus of our thesis here, we might think of the 1997 Special Edition as a generative representation of the liminal stage in the transition between analog celluloid (of 1977, 1980, and 1983) and digital (of 1999 and beyond). Thus, we might consider authenticity and aura to be in transit as well.

14. Lucas's statements here take on a further significance in relation to the narrative arc established by *Star Wars: Episode III—Revenge of the Sith*, when Anakin Skywalker (as he becomes Darth Vader) kills a defenseless group of younglings in the Jedi Temple on Coruscant. If *Episodes IV, V,* and *VI* serve to illustrate the redemption of Anakin Skywalker—culminating in the climax of *Jedi,* when a battered Darth Vader kills the Emperor and saves his son—how might we accept these murders (of children, no less) as he turns to the dark side? Indeed, how "could you redeem somebody who kills people in cold blood"? As soon as Lucas "corrects" one problem, digitization—and the statements he makes to justify it—creates new ones. And, again, artistic intent loses traction with each statement.

15. In the scene, Jabba lets Solo go with a warning and a negotiated 15 percent surcharge on money owed. "Vile Gangster Jabba the Hutt" becomes bank manager Jabba the CGI slug.

16. We are thinking here, in particular, of Jacques Derrida's notion of the supplement as an undecidable term (like différance, iterability, or the trace) that both breeches and broaches the possibility of wholeness or plenitude.

17. We also acknowledge the supplementary nature of our own "Featurettes" in the present chapter. While a fulsome analysis of the DVD extras in the *Star Wars Trilogy* is beyond our scope here, one can certainly acknowledge the common Benjaminian concerns in both Lucas's digital changes and in the remediation and re-editioning (via DVD) of his films. Again, digitization is our central trope here.

Works Cited

Austen, Ian. "A Galaxy Far, Far Away Is Becoming Fully Digital." *New York Times* 149:51399 (May 2000): G8.

Benjamin, Walter. "The Work of Art in the Age of Its Technological Reproducibility." 1936. Trans. Edmund Jephcott. *Walter Benjamin: Selected Writings, Volume 3,1935–1938.* Ed. Howard Eiland and Michael W. Jennings. Cambridge: Belknap Press of Harvard University Press, 2002. 101–33.

_____. "The Work of Art in the Age of Mechanical Reproduction." 1936. Trans. Harry Zohn. *Illuminations: Essays and Reflections.* Ed. Hannah Arendt. New York: Schocken, 1969. 217–251.

Bergery, Benjamin. "Digital Cinema, by George." *American Cinematographer* 82:9 (Sep 2001): 66–75.

_____. "Framing the Future." *American Cinematographer* 82:9 (Sep 2001): 76–83.

Black, Jane. "Hollywood's Digital Love/Hate Story." *Business Week Online* (Dec 2002): N.PAG.

Carroll, Noël. *A Philosophy of Mass Art.* New York: Clarendon, 1998.

The Characters of Star Wars. DVD Featurette. Dirs. Edith Becker and Kevin Burns. Prod. Gary Leva. Leva FilmWorks, Inc. Twentieth Century Fox Home Entertainment, 2004.

Corliss, Richard, Lina Lofaro, and Carolina A. Miranda. "The Star Treatment." *Time* 164:11 (Sep 2004): 80–81.

Empire of Dreams: The Story of the Star Wars *Trilogy.* DVD Documentary. Dirs. Edith Becker and Kevin Burns. Lucasfilm Ltd. Twentieth Century Fox Home Entertainment, 2004.

The Force Is with Them: The Legacy of Star Wars. DVD Featurette. Dirs. Edith Becker and Kevin Burns. Prod. Gary Leva. Leva FilmWorks, Inc. Twentieth Century Fox Home Entertainment, 2004.

Geuens, Jean-Pierre. "The Digital World Picture." *Film Quarterly* 55:4 (2002): 16–27.

Goodale, Gloria. "At the Movies, Digital 'Revolution' Gets Mixed Reviews." *Christian Science Monitor* 91:145 (Jun 1999): 2.

_____. "Is That All Folks? The End ... of Film as We Know It—Enter Digital." *Christian Science Monitor* 91:93 (Apr 1999): 13.

Grumet, Tobey. "Digital Celluloid." *Popular Mechanics* 176:11 (Nov 1999): 36–37.

Harris, Mark. "Dear Mr. Fantasy." *Entertainment Weekly* 785 (Sep 2004): 33–36.

Kehr, Dave. "When a Cyberstar Is Born." *New York Times* 151:51941 (Nov 2001): B1.

Khalili, Najmeh. "The Work of Cinema in the Age of Digital (Re)production." *Offscreen.* 7:10 (Oct 2003) <http://www.horschamp.qc.ca/new_offscreen/new_media.html>.

Klein, Debra. "You Should Be in Pixels." *Newsweek* 137:14 (Apr 2001): 65–66.

Larson, Peter. "Benjamin at the Movies: Aura, Gaze, and History in the Artwork Essay." *Orbis Litterarum.* 48 (1993): 109–34.

Levy, Shawn. "Send in the Clones." *Sight and Sound* 12:7 (July 2002): 20–22.

Machrone, Bill. "Film's Dead. Are Actors Next?" *PC Magazine* 18:15 (Sep 1999): 85.

Magid, Ron. "Brave New Worlds." *American Cinematographer* 83:9 (Sep 2002): 50–59.

_____. "Exploring a New Universe." *American Cinematographer* 83:9 (Sep 2002): 40–49.

_____. "Master of His Universe." *American Cinematographer* 80:9 (Sep 1999): 26–35.

Parker, Deborah, and Mark Parker. "Directors and DVD Commentary: The Specifics of Intention." *The Journal of Aesthetics and Art Criticism* 62:1 (Winter 2004): 13–22.

Prince, Stephen. "The Emergence of Filmic Artifacts: Cinema and Cinematography in the Digital Era." *Film Quarterly.* 57:3 (Spring 2004): 24–33.

Sabin, Rob. "Taking Film Out of Films." *New York Times* 148:51636 (Sep 1999): B12.

Smith, Gavin. "Digital Dawn." *Film Comment* 38:4 (Jul/Aug 2002): 2.

_____. "The Genius of the System." *Film Comment* 38:4 (Jul/Aug 2002): 31–32.

Solman, Gregory. "Fancy Math." *Film Comment* 38:4 (Jul/Aug 2002): 22–26.

Star Wars. Dir. George Lucas. Screenplay by George Lucas. Twentieth Century Fox. 1977.

Star Wars Episode I: The Phantom Menace. Dir. George Lucas. Screenplay by George Lucas. Twentieth Century Fox, 1999.

Star Wars Episode II: Attack of the Clones. Dir. George Lucas. Screenplay by George Lucas and Jonathan Hales. Twentieth Century Fox, 2002.

Star Wars Episode III: Revenge of the Sith. Dir. George Lucas. Screenplay by George Lucas. Twentieth Century Fox, 2005.

Star Wars Episode IV: A New Hope. 1977. Dir. George Lucas. Screenplay by George Lucas. Twentieth Century Fox. 1981.

Star Wars Episode IV: A New Hope. 1977. Dir. George Lucas. Screenplay by George Lucas. Twentieth Century Fox. Special Edition. 1997.

Star Wars Episode IV: A New Hope. 1977. Dir. George Lucas. Screenplay by George Lucas. Twentieth Century Fox. DVD Special Edition. 2004.

Star Wars Episode V: The Empire Strikes Back. Dir. Irvin Kershner. Screenplay by Leigh Brackett and Lawrence Kasdan. Story by George Lucas. Twentieth Century Fox, 1980.

Star Wars Episode V: The Empire Strikes Back. 1980. Dir. Irvin Kershner. Screenplay by Leigh Brackett and Lawrence Kasdan. Story by George Lucas. Twentieth Century Fox, Special Edition 1997.

Star Wars Episode V: The Empire Strikes Back. 1980. Dir. Irvin Kershner. Screenplay by Leigh Brackett and Lawrence Kasdan. Story by George Lucas. Twentieth Century Fox, DVD Special Edition 2004.

Star Wars Episode VI: Return of the Jedi. Dir. Richard Marquand. Screenplay by Lawrence Kasdan and George Lucas. Story by George Lucas. Twentieth Century Fox, 1983.

Star Wars Episode VI: Return of the Jedi. 1983. Dir. Richard Marquand. Screenplay by Lawrence Kasdan and George Lucas. Story by George Lucas. Twentieth Century Fox, Special Edition. 1997.

Star Wars Episode VI: Return of the Jedi. 1983. Dir. Richard Marquand. Screenplay by Lawrence Kasdan and George Lucas. Story by George Lucas. Twentieth Century Fox, DVD Special Edition. 2004.

Sterngold, James. "Digital Studios: It's the Economy, Stupid." *New York Times* 145:50286 (Dec 1995): 53.

Swisher, Kara. "As Net Boom Wanes, Lucas Is New Digital Force." *Wall Street Journal— Eastern Edition* 237:15 (Jan 2001): B1.

White, Roy B. "*Star Wars*: Attack of the Digital Clones." *Time* 159:21 (May 2002): 21.

Wilde Matthews, Anna. "Cinema's Digital Divide." *Wall Street Journal—Eastern Edition* 28 239:61 (Mar 2002): B1.

Contributors

Christopher Deis is a doctoral student in the Political Science Department at the University of Chicago, where his research focuses on black politics, popular culture, and critical whiteness theory. His dissertation, and what will be his first book, *Who We Be: Hip Hop Music, Black Politics, and Public Opinion*, explores the intersections between hip hop music and black politics and how this overlap challenges our conceptions of social movement emergence and the boundaries of what is considered to constitute "the political." His articles include "Thinking About Whiteness and American Politics," which appeared in *Readings in American Political Issues* (2004), as well as "Wrestling with Race: The Rock, The WWE and the Marketing of Racial Ambiguity?" which will appear in the forthcoming volume, *Somebody Ring the Damn Bell! Professional Wrestling and Sports Entertainment*.

Diana Dominguez earned her Ph.D. in medieval Irish literature (with a feminist focus) from Texas Tech University. She is currently an assistant professor of English at the University of Texas–Brownsville/Texas Southmost College. Her research interests include gender portrayal issues in medieval literature, popular culture, and children's/YA literature, with a specific focus on the warrior woman figure in ancient and medieval literature and current popular culture. She has presented both scholarly and creative work at numerous academic conferences and has published scholarly work on gender and popular culture, several scholarly book reviews, and several short stories, creative non-fiction essays, and non-fiction feature (non-scholarly) articles.

John Lyden is professor and chair of the Religion Department at Dana College in Blair, Nebraska. He received his B.A. in philosophy from Wesleyan University, his M.A. in theology from Yale University, and his Ph.D. in theology from the University of Chicago. He is the author of *Film as Religion: Myths, Morals, and Rituals* (NYU Press, 2003) and the editor of *Enduring Issues in Religion* (Greenhaven Press, 1995). He has also published numerous articles on such topics as interreligious dialogue and religion and film. He has been an avid *Star Wars* fan since the original film opened in 1977. He lives in Omaha with his wife and three children.

Graham Lyons is pursuing a doctorate in literature at Simon Fraser University in Burnaby, British Columbia. While his research interests are expansive—including Romantic authorship, critical and media theory, film and television, and contemporary poetics—his dissertation critiques the revolutionary poststructuralist "linguistic turn" by charting the trajectory of life writing in the twentieth century and by linking the aesthetic strategies of Anglo-American Modernist autobiographies to French poststructuralist autobiographies.

Janice Morris is a Ph.D candidate in the Department of English at the University of British Columbia. A current SSHRC CGS Doctoral Scholarship holder, Janice's research interests include graphic novels, film and media studies, and critical approaches to trauma. Janice's doctoral dissertation will focus on historicizing and theorizing "Holocomics"—graphic novels and the representation of the Holocaust.

Dan North is a lecturer in film and visual culture within the School of English at the University of Exeter, UK. He is interested primarily in film technology and the aesthetics of special effects and illusionism in film, from pre-cinematic magic theatre and optical toys to contemporary digital animation. He is currently writing a book on this subject for Wallflower Press, entitled *Performing Illusions*, and is also editing a collection of essays on unfinished British films for Cambridge Scholars Press.

Carl Silvio received his Ph.D. in literature from West Virginia University in 2001. He is an assistant professor in the English/Philosophy Department of Monroe Community College, specializing in American Literature, argumentative writing, science fiction, and technology in literature. His research interests include science fiction, anime, and the art of comic book narration. His work has appeared in *Science Fiction Studies*, *College Literature*, and *Studies in Popular Culture*.

Tony M. Vinci is an instructor in the English/Philosophy Department of Monroe Community College, where he specializes in children's and popular literature. His scholarship focuses primarily on the expression of Romantic philosophy in contemporary horror and fantasy narratives. He has recently completed his first novel for young adults, *Stars of Illyria*.

Kevin J. Wetmore, Jr., is the author of *The Empire Triumphant: Race, Religion and Rebellion in the* Star Wars *Films* (McFarland, 2005), as well as books about youth culture, Shakespeare, African adaptations of Greek tragedy, and modern Japanese theatre. He is also the author of articles on Japanese cinema for *Education about Asia* and *In Godzilla's Footsteps*. He teaches theatre at Loyola Marymount University and lives in Los Angeles, where he is also an actor, director, and stage combat choreographer.

Veronica A. Wilson received her Ph.D. in U.S. and women's history from Rutgers University in 2002. She is currently an assistant professor of history at the University of Pittsburgh at Johnstown, where she teaches U.S. history, the history of women and gender, and the study of cold war popular culture. Her dissertation, "Red Masquerades: Gender and Political Subversion during the Cold War, 1945–1963," analyzes intersecting issues of gender, espionage, and Cold War politics and popular culture. She is currently revising her dissertation for publication.

Works Cited

Ahlstrom, Sidney E. *A Religious History of the American People*. New Haven: Yale University Press, 1972.

Ahrens, Frank. "Final *Star Wars* Caps Moneymaking Empire." *The Washington Post* 14 May, 2005. 31 Jul. 2005. <http://www.washingtonpost.com/wp-dyn/content/article/2005/05/13/AR2005051301512_pf.html>.

Aisenberg, Nadya. *Ordinary Heroines: Transforming the Male Myth*. New York: Continuum, 1994.

Allen, Henry. "Planet Rock: *Star Wars* and Hip Hop." *A Galaxy Not So Far Away*. Ed. Glenn Kenny. New York: Henry Holt, 2002. 153–9.

Althusser, Louis. "Ideology and Ideological State Apparatuses." *Lenin and Philosophy and Other Essays*. Trans. Ben Brewster. London: New Left, 1972. 123–73.

Anderson, Kevin J. *Tales of the Jedi: The Fall of the Sith Empire*. Milwaukie: Dark Horse Comics, 1998.

_____. *Tales of the Jedi: The Golden Age of the Sith*. Milwaukie: Dark Horse Comics, 1997.

_____. *Tales of the Jedi: The Sith War*. Milwaukie: Dark Horse Comics, 1996.

_____, and Daniel Wallace. *Star Wars: The Essential Chronology*. New York: Del Rey, 2000.

Angelhonest (pseudonym). "Padmé's Death in Episode 3." Online Posting. 2 June 2005. *Star Wars: Message Boards: Episode III*. 10 Aug. 2005 <http://forums.starwars.com/thread.jspa?threadID=211073>.

Auerbach, Nina. *The Woman and the Demon: The Life of a Victorian Myth*. Cambridge: Harvard University Press, 1982.

Austen, Ian. "A Galaxy Far, Far Away Is Becoming Fully Digital." *New York Times* 149:51399 (May 2000): G8.

Baldwin, Chuck. "Darth Vader and G.W. Bush: A Common Vision of Empire." *The Humanist* July/August 2005: 4–5.

Baum, L. Frank. *The Wonderful Wizard of Oz*. New York: Dover, 1960.

Baxter, John. *Mythmaker: The Life and Work of George Lucas*. New York: Spike, 1999.

Bell, Daniel. *The Coming of Post-Industrial Society*. New York: Basic, 1973.

Benjamin, Walter. "The Work of Art in the Age of Its Technological Reproducibility." 1936. Trans. Edmund Jephcott. *Walter Benjamin: Selected Writings, Volume 3, 1935–1938*. Ed. Howard Eiland and Michael W. Jennings. Cambridge, MA: Belknap Press of Harvard University Press, 2002. 101–33.

_____. "The Work of Art in the Age of Mechanical Reproduction." 1936. Trans.

Harry Zohn. *Illuminations: Essays and Reflections.* Ed. Hannah Arendt. New York: Schocken, 1969. 217–251.

Berardinelli, James. "Review of *Star Wars Episode 1: The Phantom Menace.*" *Reelviews* May 1999. 01 Sep. 2005. <http://movie-reviews.colossus.net/movies/s/sw99.html>.

Bergery, Benjamin. "Digital Cinema, by George." *American Cinematographer* 82:9 (Sep 2001): 66–75.

_____. "Framing the Future." *American Cinematographer* 82:9 (Sep 2001): 76–83.

Bernardi, David. *Star Trek and History: Race-ing Toward a White Future.* New Brunswick: Rutgers University Press, 1998.

Biskind, Peter. *Easy Riders, Raging Bulls: How the Sex-Drugs-and-Rock 'n' Roll Generation Saved Hollywood.* New York: Simon and Schuster, 1999.

Bissell, Tom. "Pale Starship, Pale Rider: The Ambiguous Appeal of Boba Fett." *A Galaxy Not So Far Away.* Ed. Glenn Kenny. New York: Henry Holt, 2002. 10–40.

Black, Jane. "Hollywood's Digital Love/Hate Story." *Business Week Online* (Dec 2002): N.PAG.

Boucher, Geoff. "Gone to the Dark Side." *Los Angeles Times* 10 May 2005: E1, E10.

Bouzereau, Laurent. *Star Wars: The Annotated Screenplays.* New York: Del Rey, 1997.

Boyer, Paul S. *When Time Shall Be No More: Prophecy Belief in Modern American Culture.* Cambridge: Harvard University Press, 1992.

Brokoph-Mauch, Gudrun. "Salome and Ophelia: The Portrayal of Women in Art and Literature at the Turn of the Century." *The Turn of the Century: Modernism and Modernity in Literature and the Arts: International Conference Papers.* Eds. Christian Berg, Frank Duriuex, and Geert Maria Jan Lernout. Walter De Gruyter, 1995.

Brooker, William. "Internet Fandom and the Continuing Narratives of Star Wars, *Blade Runner* and *Alien.*" *Alien Zone II: The Spaces of Science-Fiction Cinema.* Ed. Annette Kuhn. London: Verso, 2000. 50–72.

_____. "Readings of Racism: Interpretation, Stereotyping, and *The Phantom Menace.*" *Continuum: Journal of Media and Cultural Studies* 15.1 (2001): 15–32.

_____. *Using the Force: Creativity, Community and Star Wars Fans.* New York: Continuum, 2002.

Brophy, Philip. "Clone Tones: Philip Brophy Sounds Off on *Star Wars.*" *Film Comment* 38.4 (2002): 28.

Brosnan, John. *Movie Magic: The Story of Special Effects in the Cinema.* London: MacDonald & Jane's, 1974.

Brown, Lyn Mikel, and Carol Gilligan. *Meeting at the Crossroads: Women's Psychology and Girls' Development.* New York: Ballantine, 1992.

Bush, Vanessa. "A Thin Line Between Love & Hate: Dating Violence Strikes One in Every Five Teenage Girls. Could a Young Woman You Know Be at Risk?—The War on Girls." *Essence* Nov. 2002. 10 Apr. 2004. <http://www.findarticles.com/p/articles/mi_m1264/is_7_33/ai_94384286/print>.

Butler, Judith. *Bodies That Matter: On the Discursive Limits of "Sex."* New York: Routledge, 1992.

Byars, Jackie. *All That Hollywood Allows: Re-reading Gender in 1950s Melodrama.* Chapel Hill: University of North Carolina Press, 1991.

Cagle, Jess. "So What's the Deal with Leia's Hair?" *Time Online Edition* 29 Apr. 2002. 9 Oct. 2004 <http://www.time.com/time/covers/1101020429/qa.html>.

Campbell, Joseph. *The Hero with a Thousand Faces*. 2nd ed. Princeton: Princeton University Press, 1968.

_____, and Bill Moyers. *The Power of Myth*. New York: Doubleday, 1988.

Campea, John. "*Star Wars Special Edition* vs. *Star Wars* 2004: A Shot by Shot Comparison of Lucas' Alterations." *The MovieBlog.com* 2 Aug. 2005. <http://www.themovie blog.com/archives/2004/08/star_wars_special_edition_vs_star_wars_2004_still_shot_comparisons_of_lucas_alterations.html>.

Carroll, Noël. *A Philosophy of Mass Art*. New York: Clarendon, 1998.

Carson, Tom. "Jedi Uber Alles." *A Galaxy Not So Far Away: Writers and Artists on Twenty-Five Years of* Star Wars. Ed. Genn Kenny. New York: Henry Holt, 2002. 160–71.

Cassel, David. "*Star Wars* Lovers Call for Jar Jar's Head." *Salon* 28 May 1999. 12 May, 2005. <http://archive.salon.com/tech/log/1999/05/28/jar_jar/>.

Cassirer, Ernst. *The Myth of the State*. New Haven: Yale University Press, 1946.

Cavagna, Carlo. "Review of *Star Wars Episode 1: The Phantom Menace*." *About-Film* Jun. 1999. 1 Sep. 2005. <http://www.aboutfilm.com/movies/s/starwars1b.htm>.

Center for Disease Control (CDC). "Intimate Partner Violence: Fact Sheet." *National Center for Injury Prevention and Control*. 30 Nov. 2004. 5 Sept. 2005 <http://www.cdc.gov/ncipc/factsheets/ipvfacts.htm>.

The Characters of Star Wars. Dirs. Edith Becker and Kevin Burns. Prod. Gary Leva. Leva FilmWorks, Inc. DVD Featurette. Twentieth Century Fox Home Entertainment, 2004.

Condit, C. "The Rhetorical Limits of Polysemy." *Critical Studies in Mass Communication* 6 (1989): 103–122.

Corliss, Richard, and Jess Cagle. "Dark Victory." *Time Magazine* 29 Apr. 2002: 56–68.

Corliss, Richard, Lina Lofaro, and Carolina A. Miranda. "The Star Treatment." *Time* 164:11 (Sep 2004): 80–81.

Craig, Alastair. "Petition to George Lucas." *Support Jar Jar Binks*. 31 Jul. 2005. <http://www.petitiononline.com/jjbf5436/petition.html>.

The Death to Jar Jar Binks Web Page. 15 May, 2005. <http://www.mindspring.com/~ernestm/jarjar/deathtojarjar.html>.

Decker, Kevin S. "By Any Means Necessary: Tyranny, Democracy, Republic, and Empire." *Star Wars and Philosophy*. Eds. Kevin S. Decker and Jason T. Eberl. Chicago: Open Court, 2005. 168–180.

_____, and Jason T. Eberl, eds. *Star Wars and Philosophy*. Chicago: Open Court, 2005.

Deis, Christopher. "Talking About Whiteness and American Politics." *Readings in American Political Issues*. Eds. Franklin D. Jones and Michael O. Adams. Iowa: Kendall Hunt, 2004. 35–46.

De Lisle, Tim. "Space Invaders." *Guardian Unlimited* 6 May 2005. 1 Sep. 2005. <http://www.guardian.co.uk/arts/fridayreview/story/0,1476958,00.html>.

DeviatedPrevert (pseudonym). "Padmé's Death." Online Posting. 28 June 2005. *Empire Online Film Forums: Star Wars*. 10 Aug. 2005 <http://ubb.empireonline.co.uk/showflat.php?Cat=&Number=1144418&page=&view=&sb=5&o=&fpart=1&vc=1>.

Dijkstra, Bram. *Idols of Perversity: Fantasies of Feminine Evil in Fin-de-Siècle Culture*. New York: Oxford University Press, 1986.

Doane, Mary Ann. *Femmes Fatales: Feminism, Film theory, Psychoanalysis*. New York: Routledge, 1991.

Duncan, Jody. "Q & A: George Lucas." *Cinefex* 102 (2005): 57–64.

Ebert, Roger. "Review of *Star Wars Episode I: The Phantom Menace*." *Chicago Sun Times* 17 May 1999. 1 Sep. 2005. <http://rogerebert.suntimes.com/apps/pbcs/.dll/article?AID=/19990517/REVIEWS/905170301/1023>.

"80 Billion Tons of Jar Jar Merchandise Now 70 Percent Off." *The Onion.com* 4 Aug. 1999. 31 Aug. 2005.

Ellis, Kathleen. "New World, Old Habits: Patriarchal Ideology in *Star Wars: A New Hope*." *Australian Screen Education* 30: 135–138.

Empire of Dreams: The Story of the Star Wars Trilogy. Dirs. Edith Becker and Kevin Burns. DVD Documentary. Lucasfilm Ltd. Twentieth Century Fox Home Entertainment, 2004.

Fader, Shanti. "'A Certain Point of View:' Lying Jedi, Honest Sith, and the Viewers Who Love Them." *Star Wars and Philosophy*. Eds. Kevin S. Decker and Jason T. Eberl. Chicago: Open Court, 2005. 192–204.

Feagin, Joe. *Racist America: Roots, Current Realities, and Future Reparations*. New York: Routledge, 2000.

Fernbach, Amanda. *Fantasies of Fetishism: From Decadence to the Post-Human*. New Brunswick: Rutgers University Press, 2002.

Fiske, John. *Understanding Popular Culture*. New York: Routledge, 1992.

The Force Is with Them: The Legacy of Star Wars. Dirs. Edith Becker and Kevin Burns. Prod. Gary Leva. Leva FilmWorks, Inc. DVD Featurette. Twentieth Century Fox Home Entertainment, 2004.

Freud, Sigmund. *Collected Papers,* volume 5. Ed. James Strachey. Trans. Joan Riviere. New York: Basic, 1959.

Frith, Simon. *Performing Rites: On the Value of Music*. Cambridge: Harvard University Press, 1996.

_____. ed. *Popular Music: Critical Concepts in Media and Cultural Studies*. New York: Routledge, 2004.

Fritscher, Jack. *Popular Witchcraft: Straight from the Witch's Mouth*. Madison: University of Wisconsin Press, 2004.

Fukuyama, Francis. *The End of History and the Last Man*. New York: Macmillan, 1992.

"The Galactic Empire and *Star Wars*: Xenophobic Racism and the Empire." *Wikipedia.com*. 5 Oct. 2005. <http://en.wikipedia.org/wiki/Galactic_Empire_%28Star_Wars%29#The_ Empire_and_xenophobic_racism>.

Galipeau, Steven A. *The Journey of Luke Skywalker: An Analysis of Modern Myth and Symbol*. Chicago: Open Court, 2001.

Gavin, Edward. "The Cult of Darth Vader." *Rolling Stone* 2 Jun. 2005: 42–46.

Geuens, Jean-Pierre. "The Digital World Picture." *Film Quarterly* 55:4 (2002): 16–27.

Gilligan, Carol. *In a Different Voice: Psychological Theory and Women's Development*. 1982. Cambridge: Harvard University Press, 1993.

Gilroy, Henry, and Manuel Garcia. *Star Wars Tales: A Jedi's Weapon*. Milwaukie: Dark Horse Comics, 2002.

Goldberg, David Theodore. *The Racial State*. Cambridge: Blackwell, 2002.

Goldman, Robert, Stephen Papson, and Noah Kersey. *Landscapes of Capital*. 14 Feb. 2005. <http://it.stlawu.edu/~global/>.

Golumbia, David. "Black and White World: Race, Ideology, and Utopia in *Triton* and *Star Trek*." *Cultural Critique* 32 (Winter 1995–1996): 75–95.

Goodale, Gloria. "At the Movies, Digital 'Revolution' Gets Mixed Reviews." *Christian Science Monitor* 91:145 (Jun 1999): 2.

_____. "Is That All Folks? The End ... of Film as We Know It—Enter Digital." *Christian Science Monitor* 91:93 (Apr 1999): 13.

Gordon, Andrew. "*Star Wars*: A Myth for Our Time." *Literature and Film Quarterly* 6 (1978): 314–26.

_____. "*Star Wars*: A Myth for Our Time." *Screening the Sacred: Religion, Myth, and Ideology in Popular American Film.* Eds. Joel W. Martin and Conrad E. Ostwalt, Jr. Boulder: Westview Press, 1995. 73–82.

Grewell, Greg. "Colonizing the Universe: Science Fictions Then, Now, and in the (Imagined) Future." *Rocky Mountain Review of Language and Literature* 55.2 (2001): 25–47.

Grocery Store Wars. Dir. Louis Fox. FreeRangeStudios.com 1 Sep. 2005. <http://www.storewars.org/flash/index.html>.

Grumet, Tobey. "Digital Celluloid." *Popular Mechanics* 176:11 (Nov 1999): 36–37.

Gurian, Michael, and Kathy Stevens. *The Minds of Boys: Saving Our Sons from Falling Behind in School and Life.* San Francisco: Jossey-Bass, 2005.

Halbfinger, David. "*Star Wars* Is Quickly Politicized." *The New York Times* 19 May 2005: Arts and Culture, Final.

Hall, Jason, et al. *Greedo Shoots First.* 5 Aug. 2005. <http://willow.club.fr/Greedo_Comic/Greedo_Comic_01.htm>.

Han Shoots First.org. 26 Aug. 2005. <http://www.hanshootsfirst.org/>.

Hansen, Todd. "A Big Dumb Movie About Space Wizards: Struggling to Cope with *The Phantom Menace.*" *A Galaxy Not So Far Away: Writers and Artists on Twenty-Five Years of* Star Wars. Ed. Glenn Kenny. New York: Henry Holt, 2002. 172–202.

Hanson, Michael J., and Max X. Kay. *Star Wars: The New Myth.* Xlibris Corporation, 2002.

Hardt, Michael, and Antonio Negri. *Empire.* Cambridge: Harvard University Press, 2001.

Harries, Dan, ed. *The New Media Book.* London: British Film Institute, 2002.

Harris, Mark. "Dear Mr. Fantasy." *Entertainment Weekly* 785 (Sep 2004): 33–36.

Harvey, David. *The Condition of Postmodernity.* Cambridge: Blackwell, 1989.

Hatton, Lois. "*Star Wars* Heroes Slay Stereotypes." *USA Today* 1 July 2005: 13a. *Academic Search Premier.* EBSCOhost. Oliveira Memorial Lib., Brownsville, TX. 10 Aug. 2005 <http://pathfinder.utb.edu:2048/login?url=http://search.epnet.com/login.aspx?direct=true&db=aph&an=J0E161651458505>.

Hebdidge, Dick. *Subculture: The Meaning of Style.* London: Methuen, 1979.

Henderson, Mary. *Star Wars and the Magic of Myth.* New York: Bantam, 1997.

Herbert, Frank. *Dune.* 1965. New York: Ace, 1990.

Hills, Matt. "*Star Wars* in Fandom, Film Theory, and the Museum: The Cultural Status of the Cult Blockbuster." *Movie Blockbusters.* Ed. Julian Stringer. London: Routledge, 2003. 178–189.

Hobermann, J. "All Droid Up. *Phantom Menace*: Star Bores." *The Village Voice* 19 May 1999. 1 Sep/ 2005. <http://www.villagevoice.com/film/9920,hoberman,5854,20.html>.

Hodges, Michael H. "Critics Say 'Clones' Has Racial Stereotypes." *Detroit News* 18 May 2002: Entertainment Section.

hooks, bell. *Reel to Real: Race, Sex, and Class at the Movies.* New York: Routledge, 1996.

Inness, Sherrie A. "'It's a Girl Thing': Tough Female Action Figures in the Toy Store." *Action Chicks: New Images of Tough Women in Popular Culture.* Ed. Sherrie A. Inness. New York: Palgrave Macmillan, 2004. 75–94.

Irigaray, Luce. "The Power of Discourse and the Subordination of the Feminine." *This Sex Which Is Not One*. Trans. Catherine Porter. Ithaca: Cornell University Press, 1985. 68–85.

Jameson, Fredric. *Postmodernism or, the Cultural Logic of Late Capitalism*. Durham: Duke University Press, 1991.

"Jar Jar, E.T., and Draco Made Our List of Worst CG Characters." *Entertainment Weekly*. 18 May, 2005. <http://www.bbc.co.uk/films/2001/08/28/kim_newman_8_article.shtml>.

Jenkins, Garry. *Empire Building: The Remarkable Life Story of* Star Wars. Secaucus: Citadel, 1999.

Jensen, Jeff. "What a Long Strange Trip It's Been." *Entertainment Weekly*, May 20, 2005: 22–30.

JerryJenkins.com. 2005. 28 Aug. 2005. < http://www.jerryjenkins.com/>.

Jeter, H. W. *The Mandalorian Armor: Star Wars: The Bounty Hunter Wars, Book 1*. New York: Bantam, 1998.

jobloffski (pseudonym). "Padmé's Death." Online Posting. 28 June 2005. *Empire Online Film Forums: Star Wars*. 10 Aug. 2005 <http://ubb.empireonline.co.uk/showflat.php?Cat=&Number=1144418&page=&view=&sb=5&o=&fpart=1&vc=1>.

Jones, Sarah Gwenllian. "Phantom Menace: Killer Fans, Consumer Activism and Digital Filmmakers." *Underground U. S. A.: Filmmaking beyond the Hollywood Canon*. Eds. Xavier Mendik & Stephen J. Schneider. London: Wallflower, 2002: 169–179.

Joyrich, Lynne. "Feminist Enterprise? *Star Trek: The Next Generation* and the Occupation of Femininity." *Cinema Journal* 35.2 (Winter 1996): 61–84.

Kahn, James. *The Star Wars Trilogy: Special Tenth Anniversary Omnibus Edition*. New York: Del Rey, 1987.

Kaplan, E. Ann., ed. *Women in Film Noir*. London: British Film Institute, 1980.

Kaufman, Roger. "High Camp in a Galaxy Far Away." *Gay and Lesbian Review-Worldwide* 9.5: 33–5.

Kehr, Dave. "When a Cyberstar Is Born." *New York Times* 151:51941 (Nov 2001): B1.

Kenny, Glenn, ed. *A Galaxy Not So Far Away: Writers and Artists on Twenty-Five Years of* Star Wars. New York: Henry Holt, 2002.

Khalili, Najmeh. "The Work of Cinema in the Age of Digital (Re)production." *Offscreen*. 7:10 (Oct 2003) <http://www.horschamp.qc.ca/new_offscreen/new_media.html>.

Kim, Sue. "Beyond Black and White: Race and Postmodernism in *The Lord of The Rings* Films." *Modern Fiction Studies* 50.4 (Winter 2004): 875–907.

Kincheloe, Joe, L., et al., eds. *White Reign: Deploying Whiteness in America*. New York: St. Martin's, 1998.

Klein, Debra. "You Should Be in Pixels." *Newsweek* 137:14 (Apr 2001): 65–66.

Kleinfeld, Judith S. "The Myth That Schools Shortchange Girls: Social Science in the Service of Deception." *The Women's Freedom Network*. May 1998. 15 Oct. 2005. <http://www.womensfreedom.org//wp2.PDF>.

Klevan, Andrew. *Film Performance: From Achievement to Appreciation*. London: Wallflower, 2005.

Klinger, Barbara. "Digressions at the Cinema: Reception and Mass Culture." *Cinema Journal* 28.4 (1989): 3–19.

Kondracke, Morton. "Tales from Dark Side Don't Live Up to Hype." *Chicago-Sun Times 5* June 2005: Editorial.

Kramer, Heinrich, and Jacob Sprenger. *Malleus Maleficarum: Hammer of the Witches*. 1486. Trans. Montague Summers. London: Hogarth, 1928.

Krämer, Peter. "'It's Aimed at Kids—The Kid in Everybody': George Lucas, *Star Wars* and Children's Entertainment." *Scope: An Online Journal of Film Studies* 20 Nov. 2001. 1 Sep. 2005. <http://www.nottingham.ac.uk/film/journal/articles/its-aimed-at-kids.htm>.

Kuiper, Koenraad. "*Star Wars*: An Imperial Myth." *Journal of Popular Culture* 21 (Spring 1988): 77–86.

Lancashire, Anne. "*Attack of the Clones* and the Politics of *Star Wars*." *Dalhousie Review* 82 (Summer 2002): 235–253.

_____. "*The Phantom Menace*: Repetition, Variation, Integration." *Film Criticism* 24.3 (2000): 23.

Larson, Peter. "Benjamin at the Movies: Aura, Gaze, and History in the Artwork Essay." *Orbis Litterarum*. 48 (1993): 109–34.

lazypadawan (pseudonym). "The Perils of Padmé: The Short Life and Fast Times of a Tragic Heroine." *Saga Journal* 1.8 (Aug. 2005). 15 Aug. 2005 <http://www.sagajournal.com/lptheperilsofpadme.html>.

_____. "Princess Leia and the Woman Warrior." *Saga Journal* 1.4 (Apr. 2005). 15 Aug. 2005 <http://www.sagajournal.com/lpwomanwarrior.html>.

Lefebvre, Henri. *The Production of Space*. Trans. Donald Nicholson-Smith. New York: Blackwell, 1991.

Leo, John. "Fu Manchu on Naboo." *U.S. New and World Report* 12 Jul. 1999: 14.

Lev, Peter. "Whose Future? Star Wars, Alien, and Blade Runner." *Literature/Film Quarterly*, 26.1 (1998): 30–37.

Levy, Shawn. "Send in the Clones." *Sight and Sound* 12:7 (July 2002): 20–22.

Libreri, Kim. "12 Predictions on the Future of VFX." *VFXWorld* 7 Dec. 2004. 12 Sep. 2005. <http://vfxworld.com/?sa =adv&code=57c5ed8a&atype= articles&id=2319&page=1>.

Lipsitz, George. *The Possessive Investment in Whiteness: How White People Profit from Identity Politics*. Philadelphia: Temple University Press, 1998.

"List of Changes in the *Star Wars* Re-Releases." *Wikipedia*. 2 Aug. 2005. <http://en.wikipedia.org/wiki/List_of_changes_in_Star_Wars_re-releases>.

"List of Highest-Grossing Films." *Answers.com*. <http://www.answers.com> 8 Aug, 2005.

Lister, Martin, et al. *New Media: A Critical Introduction*. London: Routledge, 2003.

Lohse, Eduard. *The New Testament Environment*. Trans. John E. Steely. Nashville: Abingdon, 1976.

"Lucas on Star Wars, Filmmaking and His New DVD." *FOXNews.com* 19 Sep.2004. 14Sep. 2004. <http://www.foxnews.com/story/0,2933,132871,00.html>.

Luceno, James. *Dark Lord: The Rise of Darth Vader*. New York: Del Rey, 2005.

Luther, Martin. "The Bondage of the Will." *Martin Luther: Selections from His Writings*. Ed. John Dillenberger. New York: Anchor, 1961. 166–203.

Lyden, John. "The Apocalyptic Cosmology of *Star Wars*." *Journal of Religion and Film* 4:1 (April 2000). <www.unomaha.edu/~wwwjrf/LydenStWars.htm>.

_____. *Film as Religion: Myths, Morals, and Rituals*. New York: New York University Press, 2003.

_____. "To Commend or to Critique? The Question of Religion and Film Studies." *Journal of Religion and Film* 2:1 (April 1998). <www.unomaha.edu/~wwwjrf/tocommend.htm>.

Machrone, Bill. "Film's Dead. Are Actors Next?" *PC Magazine* 18:15 (Sep 1999): 85.

Mackay, Daniel. "*Star Wars*: The Magic of the Anti-Myth." *Foundation* 76 (1999): 63–75.

Magid, Ron. "Brave New Worlds." *American Cinematographer* 83:9 (Sep 2002): 50–59.

———. "Edit-Suite Filmmaking." *American Cinematographer* 80.9 (Dec 1999): 118–124.

———. "Exploring a New Universe." *American Cinematographer* 83:9 (Sep 2002): 40–49.

———. "Master of His Universe." *American Cinematographer* 80:9 (Sep 1999): 26–35.

Malt, Johanna. *Obscure Objects of Desire: Surrealism, Fetishism and Politics.* Oxford: Oxford University Press, 2004.

Mandel, Ernest. *Late Capitalism.* Trans. Joris De Bres. London: New Left, 1975.

Manovich, Lev. *The Language of New Media.* Cambridge: MIT Press, 2001.

Marcan, Darko, et al. *Star Wars: Jedi vs. Sith.* Milwaukie: Dark Horse Comics, 2002.

Marx, Karl, and Ernest Mandel. *Capital: A Critique of Political Economy. Volume One.* Trans. Ben Fowkes. New York: Vintage, 1977.

The Matrix Revolutions. Dir. Andy Wachowski and Larry Wachowski. 2003. DVD. Warner Home Video. 2004.

Metz, Christian. "History/Discourse: Note on Two Voyeurisms." *Edinburgh 76 Magazine* (1976): 21–25.

Meyer, David S. "Star Wars, *Star Wars* and American Political Culture." *The Journal of Popular Culture* 26.2 (1992): 99–115.

Miller, Martin, and Robert Sprich. "The Appeal of *Star Wars.*" *American Imago* 38.2 (Summer 1981): 203–220.

Mills, Charles W. *The Racial Contract.* Ithaca: Cornell University Press, 1997.

Mishel, Lawerence, Jared Bernstein, and John Schmitt. *The State of Working America, 1989–99.* Ithaca: Cornell University Press, 1999.

Mitchell, Elvis. "Works Every Time." *A Galaxy Not So Far Away.* Ed. Glenn Kenny. New York: Henry Holt, 2002. 77–85.

Mitchell, Sally. *The Fallen Angel: Chastity, Class, and Women's Reading, 1835–1880.* Bowling Green: Bowling Green University Press, 1981.

Mulvey, Laura. "Visual Pleasure and Narrative Cinema." *The Critical Tradition: Classic Texts and Contemporary Trends.* 2nd ed. Ed. David H. Richter. Boston: Bedford, 1998. 1444–1453.

Murray, Jill. *But I Love Him: Protecting Your Daughter from Controlling, Abusive Dating Relationships.* New York: Regan, 2001.

Nakayama, T. "Show/Down Time: 'Race,' Gender, Sexuality, and Popular Culture." *Critical Studies in Mass Communication* 11 (1994): 162–179.

The National Association for the Extermination of the Gungan Race. 5 Aug. 2005. <http://www.angelfire.com/ca3/jarjarburn/>.

New Oxford Annotated Bible with the Apocrypha, Revised Standard Version. Eds. Herbert G. May and Bruce M. Metzger. New York: Oxford University Press, 1977.

Newman, Kim. "Review of *Star Wars Episode IV: A New Hope.*" *Sight and Sound* 7.4 (1997): 50–51.

———. "Why *Star Wars* Is Rubbish." *BBC.* 4 Aug. 2005. <http://www.bbc.co.uk/films/2001/08/28/kim_newman_8_article.shtml>.

Nishime, Leilani. "The Mulatto Cyborg: Imagining a Multiracial Future." *Cinema Journal* 44.2 (Winter 2005): 34–49.

North, Dan. "Virtual Actors, Spectacle and Special Effects: Kung Fu Meets 'All That CGI Bullshit.'" *The Matrix Trilogy: Cyberpunk Reloaded.* Ed. Stacy Gillis. London: Wallflower, 2005: 48–61.

Oliver, Melvin L., and Thomas M. Shapiro. *Black Wealth/White Wealth: A New Perspective on Racial Inequality.* New York: Routledge, 1995.

Omi, Michael, and Howard Winant. *Racial Formation in the United States: From the 1960s to the 1990s.* New York: Routledge, 1994.

Ott, Brian L., and Eric Aoki. "Counter Imagination as Interpretive Practice: Futuristic Fantasy and The Fifth Element." *Women's Studies in Communication* 27.2 (Summer 2004): 149–176.

Parker, Deborah, and Mark Parker. "Directors and DVD Commentary: The Specifics of Intention." *The Journal of Aesthetics and Art Criticism* 62:1 (Winter 2004): 13–22.

Pearson, Carol, and Katherine Pope. *The Female Hero in American and British Literature.* New York: R.R. Bowker, 1981.

Pierson, Michele. *Special Effects: Still in Search of Wonder.* New York: Columbia University Press, 2002.

Pipher, Mary. *Reviving Ophelia: Saving the Selves of Adolescent Girls.* New York: Ballantine, 1994.

Pollack, Dale. *Skywalking: The Life and Films of George Lucas.* New York: Da Capo, 1999.

Prince, Stephen. "The Emergence of Filmic Artifacts: Cinema and Cinematography in the Digital Era." *Film Quarterly.* 57:3 (Spring 2004): 24–33.

Rector, Brett. "Queen Mother of the Galaxy." *Star Wars Insider #82* Jul./Aug. 2005: 63.

Rickitt, Richard. *Special Effects: The History and Technique.* London: Virgin, 2000.

Roberts, John W. *From Trickster to Badman: The Black folk Hero in Slavery and Freedom.* Philadelphia: University of Pennsylvania Press, 1989.

Rossing, Barbara. *The Rapture Exposed: The Message of Hope in the Book of Revelation.* Boulder: Westview, 2004.

Rowe-Finkbeiner, Kristin. *The F-Word: Feminism in Jeopardy: Women, Politics, and the Future.* Emeryville: Seal, 2004.

Rubey, Dan. "*Star Wars* 'Not So Long Ago, Not So Far Away'" *Jump Cut.* Ed. Peter Steven. New York: Praeger, 1985. 83–105.

_____. "*Star Wars*: Not So Long Ago, Not So Far Away." *Jump Cut* 41 (1996): 2–12+.

Russell, Jeffrey B. *A History of Witchcraft: Sorcerers, Heretics, and Pagans.* New York: Thames and Hudson, 1980.

Ryan, Michael, and Douglas Kellner. *Camera Politica: The Politics and Ideology of Contemporary Hollywood Film.* Bloomington: Indiana University Press, 1988.

Sabin, Rob. "Taking Film Out of Films." *New York Times* 148:51636 (Sep 1999): B12.

Sanders, Andrew. *A Deed Without a Name: The Witch in Society and History.* Oxford: Berg, 1995.

Schechner, Richard. *Performance Theory.* London: Routledge, 2003.

Seiler, Andy. "Something to Offend Everyone: Minority Groups Say Hit Films Fill Screens with Stereotypes." *USA Today* 28 Jun. 1999: Life section, final edition.

Senge, Peter M. *The Fifth Discipline: The Art and Practice of the Learning Organization.* New York: Doubleday, 1990.

Sharpe, William, and Leonard Wallock, eds. *Visions of the Modern City: Essays in History, Art, and Literature.* Baltimore: Johns Hopkins University Press, 1987.

Shiel, Mark, and Tony Fitzmaurice, eds. *Screening the City.* London: Verso, 2003.

Showalter, Elaine. *The Female Malady: Women, Madness, and English Culture, 1830–1980.* New York: Pantheon, 1985.

Shuck, Glenn. *Marks of the Beast: The Left Behind Novels and the Search for Evangelical Identity.* New York: New York University Press, 2005.

Slavicsek, Bill, Steve Miller, and Owen K.C. Stephens. "Aliens and the New Order: An Excerpt from *The Rebellion Era Sourcebook.*" *Wizards of the Coast.* 5 Oct. 2005. <http://www.wizards.com/starwars/article.asp?x=sw20010823c_rebellion&c=rpg>.

Slavicsek, Bill, and J.D. Wiker. *The Dark Side Sourcebook:* Star Wars *Roleplaying Game.* Renton: Wizards of the Coast, 2001.

Smith, Gavin. "Digital Dawn." *Film Comment* 38:4 (Jul/Aug 2002): 2.

_____. "The Genius of the System." *Film Comment* 38:4 (Jul/Aug 2002): 31–32.

Smith, Thomas G. *Industrial Light and Magic: The Art of Special Effects.* London: Columbus, 1985.

Sofer, Andrew. *The Stage Life of Props.* Ann Arbor: University of Michigan Press, 2003.

Solman, Gregory. "Fancy Math." *Film Comment* 38.4 (2002): 22–26.

Sommers, Christina Hoff. *The War Against Boys: How Misguided Feminism Is Harming Our Young Men.* New York: Simon and Schuster, 2000.

Sophocles. "Oedipus the King." *The Three Theban Plays: Antigone, Oedipus the King, Oedipus at Colonus.* Trans. Robert Fagles. New York: Penguin, 1982. 155–252.

Sragow, Michael. "The Biggest Indie Film Ever Made." *Salon* 20 May 1999. 1 Sep. 2005. <http://www.salon.com/ent/col/srag/1999/05/20/mccallum/index.html>.

Staples, Brent. "Shuffling Through the Stars." *The New York Times* 20 Jun. 1999, late edition-final.

"Star-Crossed: Partisans Imagine Politics Among the Jedi Knights." *Pittsburgh Post-Gazette* (Pennsylvania) 21May 2005: Editorial, Sooner edition.

Star Wars. Dir. George Lucas. Screenplay by George Lucas. Twentieth Century Fox. 1977.

"The *Star Wars* Databank-'The Empire.'" *Star Wars.com* 5 Oct. 2005. <http://www.starwars.com/databank/organization/theempire/?id=eu>.

Star Wars Episode I: The Phantom Menace. Dir. George Lucas. Screenplay by George Lucas. Twentieth Century Fox, 1999.

Star Wars Episode II: Attack of the Clones. Dir. George Lucas. Screenplay by George Lucas and Jonathan Hales. Twentieth Century Fox, 2002.

Star Wars Episode III: Revenge of the Sith. Dir. George Lucas. Screenplay by George Lucas. Twentieth Century Fox, 2005.

Star Wars Episode IV: A New Hope. 1977. Dir. George Lucas. Screenplay by George Lucas. Twentieth Century Fox. 1981.

Star Wars Episode IV: A New Hope. 1977. Dir. George Lucas. Screenplay by George Lucas. Twentieth Century Fox. Special Edition. 1997.

Star Wars Episode IV: A New Hope. 1977. Dir. George Lucas. Screenplay by George Lucas. Twentieth Century Fox. DVD Special Edition. 2004.

Star Wars Episode V: The Empire Strikes Back. Dir. Irvin Kershner. Screenplay by Leigh Brackett and Lawrence Kasdan. Story by George Lucas. Twentieth Century Fox, 1980.

Star Wars Episode V: The Empire Strikes Back. 1980. Dir. Irvin Kershner. Screenplay by Leigh Brackett and Lawrence Kasdan. Story by George Lucas. Twentieth Century Fox, Special Edition 1997.

Star Wars Episode V: The Empire Strikes Back. 1980. Dir. Irvin Kershner. Screenplay by Leigh Brackett and Lawrence Kasdan. Story by George Lucas. Twentieth Century Fox, DVD Special Edition 2004.

Star Wars Episode VI: Return of the Jedi. Dir. Richard Marquand. Screenplay by Lawrence Kasdan and George Lucas. Story by George Lucas. Twentieth Century Fox, 1983.

Star Wars Episode VI: Return of the Jedi. 1983. Dir. Richard Marquand. Screenplay by Lawrence Kasdan and George Lucas. Story by George Lucas. Twentieth Century Fox, Special Edition. 1997.

Star Wars Episode VI: Return of the Jedi. 1983. Dir. Richard Marquand. Screenplay by Lawrence Kasdan and George Lucas. Story by George Lucas. Twentieth Century Fox, DVD Special Edition. 2004.

Starwarsfan77–05 (pseudonym). "Padmé's Death in Episode 3." Online Posting. 26 May 2005. *Star Wars: Message Boards: Episode III.* 10 Aug. 2005 <http://forums.starwars.com/thread.jspa?threadID=211073>.

_____. "Summary of Why Leia Remembers Padmé, and Some of Our Thoughts on Padmé's Death—What SHOULD Have Happened." Online Posting. 28 June 2005. *Star Wars: Blogs.*10 Aug. 2005 <http://blogs.starwars.com/starwarsfan77–05/1>.

Steiner, L. "Oppositional Decoding as an Act of Resistance." *Critical Studies in Mass Communication* 5 (1988): 1–15.

Sterngold, James. "Digital Studios: It's the Economy, Stupid." *New York Times* 145:50286 (Dec 1995): 53.

Stover, Mathew. *Revenge of the Sith.* New York: Lucas, 2005.

Street, John. *Politics and Popular Culture.* Philadelphia: Temple University Press, 1997.

Strinati, Dominic. *An Introduction to Some Theories of Popular Culture.* New York: Routledge, 1995.

Stroup, John, and Glenn Shuck. *Escape into the Future.* Waco: Baylor University Press, 2007 (forthcoming).

SuperShadow.com. 2005. 28 Aug. 2005 <http://www.supershadow.com/starwars/jedi_sith.html>.

Swisher, Kara. "As Net Boom Wanes, Lucas Is New Digital Force." *Wall Street Journal–Eastern Edition* 237:15 (Jan 2001): B1.

Tabbi, Joseph. *Postmodern Sublime: Technology and American Writing from Mailer to Cyberpunk.* Ithaca: Cornell University Press, 1995.

Tavris, Carol. *Mismeasure of a Woman.* New York: Simon and Schuster, 1992.

Terminator 2: Judgement Day. Dir. James Cameron. 1991. DVD. Artisan, 1997.

Thorpe, Jessica D. "Black and White and Strained All Over." *The Buffalo News* 5 Nov. 2000: Entertainment section.

Torgovnick, Marianna. *Gone Primitive: Savage Intellects, Modern Lives.* Chicago: University of Chicago Press, 1990.

Tucker, Robert C., ed. *The Marx-Engels Reader.* 2nd ed. New York: W.W. Norton, 1978.

Turan, Kenneth. "Review of *Star Wars Episode 1: The Phantom Menace.*" *Los Angeles Times* 18 May 1999. 20 Aug. 2005. <http://www.calendarlive.com/movies/reviews/clmovie990517–1,0,6661504.story>.

Vaz, Mark Cotta, and Patricia Rose Duignan. *Industrial Light and Magic: Into the Digital Realm.* London: Virgin, 1996.

Veitch, Tom, et al. *Tales of the Jedi: Dark Lords of the Sith*. Milwaukie: Dark Horse
    Comics, 1995.
Waller, Marguerite. "Poetic Influence in Hollywood: *Rebel Without a Cause* and
    Star Wars." *Diacritics* 10 (Autumn 1980): 57–66.
"Ways Jar Jar Binks Should Die." *Freaky Frea's Crazy Cosmos*. 19 May, 2005.
    <http://members.tripod.com/Freaky_Freya/diejarjar.html>.
Wetmore, Kevin J., Jr. *The Empire Triumphant: Race, Religion and Rebellion in the*
    Star Wars *Films*. Jefferson: McFarland 2005.
_____. "The Tao of *Star Wars*, or, Cultural Appropriation in a Galaxy Far, Far
    Away." *Studies in Popular Culture* (2000): 91-eoa.
White, Roy B. "*Star Wars*: Attack of the Digital Clones." *Time* 159:21 (May
    2002): 21.
Wilde Matthews, Anna. "Cinema's Digital Divide." *Wall Street Journal—Eastern
    Edition* 28 239:61 (Mar 2002): B1.
Willemen, Paul. "Of Mice and Men: Reflections on Digital Imagery." *292: Essays
    in Visual Culture* 1.1 (1999): 5–20.
Williams, Joe. "George Lucas Senses a Dark Side Rising in the United States."
    St. Louis Post-Dispatch (Missouri) 18 May 2005: Everyday, Late Edition.
Williams, Patricia J. "Diary of a Mad Law Professor: Racial Ventriloquism."
    Nation 5 July, 1999: 9.
Williams, Raymond. *The Country and the City*. New York: Oxford University
    Press, 1973.
Wilson, John. "The Twentieth Annual Razzies." *Razzies.com* 18 May, 2005.
    <http://razzies.com/asp/content/XcNewsPlus.asp?cmd=view&articleid=71>.
Wood, Robin. *Hollywood from Vietnam to Regan*. New York: Columbia Univer-
    sity Press, 1986.
Wright, Will. "The Empire Bites the Dust." *Social Text* 6 (Autumn 1982): 120–5.
Wurtzel, Elizabeth. *Bitch: In Praise of Difficult Women*. New York: Doubleday,
    1998.
Wyatt, David. "*Star Wars* and the Productions of Time." *Virginia Quarterly
    Review* 58.4 (1982): 600–15.
Žižek, Slavoj. *The Sublime Object of Ideology*. London: Verso, 1989.

Index